SHOW ME HOW

TO **PREACH**
EVANGELISTIC
SERMONS

Other Books by R. Larry Moyer

21 Things God Never Said
31 Days to Contagious Living
31 Days to Living as a New Believer
31 Days to Walking with God in the Workplace
31 Days with the Master Fisherman
Free and Clear
Growing in the Family
Show Me How to Answer Tough Questions
Show Me How to Illustrate Evangelistic Sermons
Show Me How to Share the Gospel
Show Me How to Share the Gospel in the Workplace (forthcoming)
Welcome to the Family

R. Larry Moyer is the founder and CEO of EvanTell, Inc., an evangelistic training ministry in Dallas Texas. EvanTell empowers ministry organizations and churches to train and equip their members and staff to share the gospel in the context and cultures they serve. For more information go to www.evantell.org.

R. Larry Moyer

SHOW
ME
HOW
S·E·R·I·E·S

SHOW ME HOW

TO **PREACH** EVANGELISTIC SERMONS

Kregel
Academic & Professional

Show Me How to Preach Evangelistic Sermons

© 2012 by R. Larry Moyer

Published by Kregel Publications, a division of Kregel, Inc., P.O. Box 2607, Grand Rapids, MI 49501.

Library of Congress Cataloging-in-Publication Data
Moyer, R. Larry (Richard Larry), 1947-
    Show me how to preach evangelistic sermons / R. Larry Moyer.
        p. cm.
    Includes bibliographical references (p. 241).
    1. Preaching. 2. Evangelistic work. I. Title.
        BV4211.3.M68 2010
        251'.3—dc22

                                                            2010027966

ISBN 978-0-8254-3880-6

Printed in the United States of America
12 13 14 15 16 / 5 4 3 2 1

Dedicated to
Dr. Haddon W. Robinson

*Thanks for teaching me the importance of being a
communicator, not just a speaker.
I am forever grateful.*

Contents

PART I
Looking at Our Opportunity

Chapter 1

Clear Message—Struggling Tongue (My Story)

SURELY THIS TIME WOULD be different. Ken was my friend. He lived within a mile of my house. Surely he wouldn't ridicule me.

I inched up to the table where Ken and some guys in my high school class sat around waiting for the first period bell to sound. In our conversation, I tried to say the word "swimming." "Sw" sounds were tough for me, and it came out sounding like "wimming." When the snickers started, Ken said, "Go ahead, Larry, say that again. Hey guys, listen to how funny he talks." His words hurt deeply. The laughter hurt more. Trapped! Again! I walked away embarrassed. Not mad; just hurt. The mockery was sometimes overwhelming.

One thing was certain—I hated school. Getting on the school bus each morning and stepping onto the school grounds felt like (forgive my frankness) hell on earth. Classmates waited for me to use words with "th" and "sw" sounds, which were difficult for me to pronounce. (Count how many times you use the word "the" in a conversation to get an idea of how overwhelming the ridicule became.) I tried to escape by hiding between parked cars or by seeking solitude in the bushes. Rainy days were the worst. On those days, I just had to let my classmates "enjoy" themselves at my expense.

The highlight of my day was getting off the bus and walking down the lane to our farm. The dairy farm was like heaven to me. Dairy cows didn't laugh at me, nor did my family. Home was my refuge.

By now you've figured out that I was born with a severe speech impediment. I inherited this impediment from my dad. My tongue did not know where to place itself for certain sounds. "The" was my hardest word. I could say "fa," "sa," "ta." I just couldn't say "the." My parents didn't seem concerned. On the dairy farm, the emphasis was on working, not talking. I had a strong work ethic and a high energy level; for me, talking was the hardest work of all.

One time in third grade I had to stand up and speak. All eyes were focused on me. The giggles began before I even spoke a word. I lasted thirty seconds before I froze up. I couldn't get another word out. I just stood there. The teacher had mercy on me. "Go ahead and sit down, Larry," she said. I sat down defeated, humiliated, and frustrated. Being laughed at by the whole class was far worse than the individual teasing I endured regularly.

Even before I trusted Christ, I told people I wanted to be a preacher. I had no idea why. Raised in a small, boring, liberal church, I thought a preacher was someone who got up and talked for thirty minutes each Sunday, then sat around for the rest of the week. I assumed that any major physical activity would shatter his "holiness." Seriously! I knew that was not the kind of person I wanted to be. I had too much energy. So I resolved to stop telling people that I wanted to be a preacher. But the next time I was asked, "What are you going to be when you grow up?" I blurted out once again, "I'm going to be a preacher."

When I was a pre-teen, I went to my family doctor for the treatment of a simple cold. As he knelt down and put his icy stethoscope on my chest, he asked, "Well, what are you going to be when you grow up?" I answered, "I'm going to be a speaker." (Somehow I thought "speaker" wouldn't hit him as hard as "preacher".) His next words pierced like a knife. "Well, you can give that up." I hoped that was all he would say. But then, as though to twist the dagger, he continued without a pause, "You could never speak with your problem."

His harsh words reverberated in my mind like a gong. If I couldn't be a preacher, what else was there? I walked down the steps of the doctor's office feeling as though I was walking into a grave—my future had collapsed.

God, however, had only started His work.

Each year in November, Dad rewarded us for our hard work all year on the dairy farm by giving us time off from chores to go hunting. So I would head to the woods every day after school and all day Saturday. A sense of wonder saturated me as I gazed upon prancing deer, skittish squirrels, the curvature of tree trunks and their bark, rows of neatly plowed soil, rolling green hills, and scattered ponds. Even the sound of the ground as it crunched beneath my feet intrigued me. This was Lancaster County, Pennsylvania—"garden spot of the world." I decided there had to be a Creator. But why did He make it, then leave it? How could a person know Him, touch Him, feel Him? Why did nature seem so full and yet I felt so empty?

These questions led me to study the Bible. At first I found it boring—even confusing. Christ's words, "He who believes in Me out of his heart will flow rivers of living water," didn't make sense. I asked my mother what she thought it meant. She explained, "It probably refers to having babies." That answer didn't fit. The text said "he."

My Bible study technique was also very poor. I would close my eyes, let the Bible fall open, then point to a verse. Still, God was in control, and slowly I began to put things together. Jesus Christ was the only way to heaven. One night, as I approached my early teens, I knelt by my bed. My words were simple. "God, the best I know how, I'm trusting Christ as my only way to heaven." That night, the storm within me began to calm. As far as I know, it was that night that I crossed from darkness into light.

God did more than give me His gift of eternal life that night. He galvanized the direction of my life by setting me on a mission—an all-consuming one. I had to be an evangelist. To stand before people—fifty or fifty thousand—and tell them how they could know they were going to heaven would be like heaven itself. This would be the first of many "supernatural touches."

The next supernatural touch came while I was sitting in high school literature class. I sat by the window so I could see the outdoors. Impressed with God, but disheartened with life, I put my head between my hands as my eyes filled with tears. I didn't want my peers to see I was crying. My mind was on the inescapable, repeated ridicule due to the speech impediment I couldn't overcome. Embarrassment kept me defeated. I whispered simple words to God: "God, if you will heal me of this impediment, I'll always use my voice for you."

I can't explain what happened next. How do you explain the supernatural? Suddenly I had a control of my tongue I had never had before. Words came easier. Some sounds didn't seem as difficult. The teasing and jeers from others began to subside.

Upon graduating from high school, I attended Philadelphia College of Bible (now Philadelphia Biblical University). To God's glory, in my fourth year I was able to make a speech and was elected student body president. For graduate studies, I went to Dallas Theological Seminary. In 1973, again to God's glory, my classmates voted me one of the four best preachers in the fourth-year class.

After that fourth year's sermon, I walked into the office of Dr. Haddon Robinson, a man who had greatly influenced my life and had become my mentor. I could tell something was on his mind by the way he stared at me. "God has given you such a gift," he remarked. "I just wish you knew where to place your tongue for certain sounds." His words startled and puzzled me.

"What did you just say?" I asked.

"You don't know where to place your tongue for certain sounds," he explained. "People who do it right don't know how to tell you to do it. They just do it right."

Holding back my tears, I said, "Dr. Robinson, I've never had anyone tell me that. I've been told I'm lazy when I speak."

He interrupted me with a chuckle, "You're the last guy I'd call lazy." Throughout my seminary years he had observed my ambition and energy level.

Dr. Robinson referred me to Beverly Warren, a speech therapist and committed believer. I had graduated from seminary and started my full-time evangelistic ministry. My excitement was almost uncontrollable as I began to live out my God-given passion. I was on the road every other week proclaiming the gospel, night after night, in week-long crusades. Every week I was not traveling during 1973–1974, I had an appointment with Beverly. Five dollars a week is all she would accept for her coaching.

My first appointment with Beverly was memorable. She asked, "How did you get to where you are? God has obviously done something. You don't get where you are on your own." My mind flashed back to that moment in high school when I told God, "If you will heal me of this impediment, I'll always use my voice for you." I told her my story. Her excitement and expertise convinced me that she could take me the rest of the way. The sounds and syllables she gave me week-by-week brought me to a point where at last she said, "You're there. I don't know what more to tell you."

Does that mean I speak perfectly? No. But in regard to that, nearly identical comments of Beverly and Dr. Robinson have greatly ministered to me: "Whatever people notice will help you, not hurt you," they said. Dr. Robinson went further with his thoughts, "Non-Christians do not identify with losers. They identify with losers who have made it." I knew that he wasn't calling me a loser because he continued, "Non-Christians are not drawn to someone who has struggles and doesn't try. But they are drawn to someone who has struggled and made it."

I still ache to be able to speak without slurring a syllable. There are times I get teary-eyed even now when I listen to those who can. I'm passionate about speaking, especially to and about unbelievers. I'm a perfectionist. But years ago on my knees I made an agreement with God, "If You want to be glorified through my weakness, instead of allowing me to have perfect speech, that's okay." Paul wrote, "And He said to me, 'My grace is sufficient for you, for My strength is made perfect in weakness.' Therefore most gladly I will rather boast in my infirmities, that the power of Christ may rest upon me" (2 Cor. 12:9). My passion is not just to speak; it is to clearly present the message of the gospel.

I once went to Tennessee to speak. A believer who brought his friend to hear me asked him afterwards, "What do you think?" The man replied, "It is the strangest thing I've ever seen. He can't speak clearly and he's the clearest speaker I ever heard."

Doesn't God have a sense of humor? He took someone who physically needed His help each time he spoke (and still does), and gave him a passion spiritually to clearly present the plan of salvation.

I've surrendered this book to God to that end—that you too might not just preach the gospel, but that you might clearly preach it. So clearly, in fact, that there is no question in your listeners' minds about how to receive eternal life.

I'm still learning, but I want to share what I've learned through speaking in more than one thousand outreaches. I want to tell you what I wish someone had told me more than forty years ago. My prayer is that this book will help you, long after I'm gone, to speak in such a way that you are not only understood, but that you cannot be misunderstood.

I've told my loved ones, "When I'm gone, don't waste that valuable space on my tombstone with my name and years of existence. Just write in letters that encompass the tombstone: 'Be Clear! Be Clear! Be Clear!'"

Chapter 2

Evangelistic Speaking—
You Can Do It!

A SEVEN-YEAR-OLD BOY ASKED his pastor, "Do you know why they call that place where you preach a pulpit?" The pastor replied, "Well, son, I'm not sure of the background of that name." The boy replied, "I know. It's the place where you PULL people out of their PIT."[1]

That's a good description of effective communication—you pull people from a pit. That pit is called eternal separation from God, and it's a pit that all without Christ eventually face. One way God pulls people from such a pit is through an evangelistic message.

Church leaders who rarely speak to an audience of non-Christians feel very comfortable before their own people but may lack confidence before an audience of unbelievers.

I assure you, you can speak effectively to unbelievers. I can show you how to take your speaking skills and use them effectively before a non-Christian audience. There are several sound biblical reasons why church leaders need to speak evangelistically.

God encourages them to do so.

Timothy was apparently a gifted pastor-teacher. As such, he was commanded, "Preach the word! Be ready in season and out of season. Convince, rebuke, exhort, with all longsuffering and teaching" (2 Tim. 4:2). Paul then admonished him to "be watchful in all things, endure afflictions, do the work of an evangelist, fulfill your ministry" (v. 5), indicating that every vocational Christian worker must in some way be engaged in evangelism.

An evangelistic message is one of the many ways church leaders can fulfill that command. Through a message carefully prepared from Scripture and targeted toward non-Christians, we present the gospel to unbelievers.

It is a wise use of time and energy.

Our time, energy, and resources are not our own. They are God's. We are the managers; He is the owner.

Paul says to Timothy, "Command those who are rich in this present age not to be haughty, nor to trust in uncertain riches but in the living God, who gives us richly all things to enjoy" (1 Tim. 6:17). Note the words, "who gives us richly all things to enjoy." Our wealth is His; He owns it. It's simply ours to manage. The same can be said of our time and energy. Colossians 4:5 speaks of "redeeming the time," which means we should see our time as something He owns and we manage. We should grasp every opportunity to use that time in reaching non-Christians.

If you had thirty minutes to tell others how to get to heaven, would you rather tell one person or fifty? Witnessing to one person, even if it takes two hours, is important. But if God should provide you with the opportunity to use thirty minutes to tell a large group how to get to heaven instead, wouldn't that be a wiser use of time, energy, and resources?

It is helpful in reaching non-Christian church attendees.

One of the biggest mistakes a church leader can make is to assume that all who regularly attend church are saved. The gospel is so simple that many miss it. They may know the language but not the Lord. Like Nicodemus, they may be religious but not saved (see John 3). They are in need of Christ's admonition, "You must be born again" (v. 7). Church leaders cannot assume that everyone in the audience, even those who have been there repeatedly, and perhaps even are involved in the church, have clearly understood and believed.

Some time ago I spoke to a man who worked for one of the largest technology firms in the Dallas area. When he learned I was in ministry, he demonstrated an interest in spiritual things. He told me that he and his girlfriend were attending one of the most prominent Bible churches in the area. I asked, "When did you become a Christian?" His answer was nebulous. When I asked, "If you were to stand before God and He were to ask you why He should let you into heaven, what would you tell Him?" He answered, "I don't think He would ask that question." I asked him why. He replied, "Because He knows me and knows what a good person I've been." I continued, "Well, let me put it another way. What do you think you'd have to do to get to heaven?" He answered, "Well, you know, live a good life, keep the commandments, that sort of thing." At this point I had the opportunity to explain what I have been privileged to explain to many others. I went through the gospel using EvanTell's *Bad News/Good News* approach. Thirty minutes later, he trusted Christ alone as his only way to heaven.

I'm convinced that there are many people just like him sitting in solid Bible-teaching churches every Sunday. For whatever reason, they have missed the message of God's free grace. An evangelistic message, spoken with the assumption that everyone listening is an unbeliever, may be what God uses to bring regular church attendees face to face with their lost condition.

It is essential for saved church members.

While an evangelistic message helps non-Christians in church, it also helps believers. No church or Christian is immune to what was experienced by the churches of Galatia when many strayed from the gospel. Paul warns, "I marvel that you are turning away so soon from Him who called you in the grace of Christ, to a different gospel" (Gal. 1:6). Due to the influence of false teachers, some began to move from a gospel of grace to a gospel of grace plus works. Paul explains that such a gospel is no gospel at all. It's not another gospel of the same kind, but instead a gospel of a different kind and a perversion of the true gospel. He continues, "There are some who trouble you and want to pervert the gospel of Christ" (v. 7). This can happen within any assembly. An evangelistic message, as long as it makes the gospel *clear*, warns people not to add anything to the gospel of grace.

It allows you to be an example.

An evangelism professor once stated, "The degree to which the pastor is evangelistic will be reflected in the church. If he is lukewarm, the church will very likely be as well. If he is intensely evangelistic, the church will reflect the warmth and concern of the pastor for the lost."[2] Evangelist Luis Palau has said, "You breed according to your kind. If you spend your life talking about it but not doing it, you will breed those who spend their lives talking about it but not doing it."[3] I've told church leaders, "Your church is more likely to do what you do than what you say."

An evangelistic message delivered with clarity, passion, and simplicity demonstrates to the people a concern for unbelievers. This leads people, through example, into greater depths evangelistically. In a very specific way we are fulfilling the exhortation to be "examples to the flock" (1 Pet. 5:3). Through an evangelistic message that brings non-Christians to Christ, we are not merely saying, "Do as I say," but more importantly, "Do as I do."

It enhances your speaking.

Speaking to non-Christians will make you a better speaker to anyone. If you can speak in such a way that non-Christians sit up and listen, your communication skills to believers will be enhanced as well. Many church leaders have said to me, "What you teach in evangelistic speaking makes you a better speaker to anyone anywhere."

Conclusion

Nothing is more important than bringing people face to face with the message of the cross and empty tomb. When you do so, God uses you to populate heaven. You PULL people out of the PIT they would eventually face—the pit of everlasting separation from God.

As we travel down the highway of evangelistic speaking, I advocate an approach called expository evangelistic speaking. This type of speaking rests on the authority of Scripture. Non-Christians leave knowing not simply what you said, but where in the Bible God said it first. It's His voice through His Word that they have heard.

REFLECTING...

1. What are five benefits of church leaders delivering an evangelistic message?

2. What is one of the biggest mistakes church leaders can make when they examine their church audience?

3. How does an evangelistic message help church members who are saved?

4. In what way do you serve as an example in giving an evangelistic message?

5. How does speaking to non-Christians enhance your speaking to anyone?

Chapter 3

What Exactly Is Expository Evangelistic Preaching?

SAY THE WORD "PREACHING," and people know what you mean, even though their concepts may vary. One might think of an austere minister, making a rather cold declaration from behind an intimidating pulpit. Someone else might think of a preacher who didn't stand behind a pulpit but who ranted and raved across the platform. Still others may think of someone who spoke warmly and gently, in a conversational tone, to the people. Our understanding of the word "preaching" may be defined as much *by the person who did it* as by what he did.

Fast forward in your thinking to expository preaching. The emphasis goes more to *what* the speaker did than who did it. The preacher is still preaching, but "exposition" defines how he does it. Most people agree it has something to do with the biblical text. However, they are not always in agreement as to what makes a person an expositor. Questions arise:

- Is a message that refers to a biblical text an expository message?
- Does the speaker have to go verse by verse to be an expositor?
- If a speaker draws principles from a text, although those principles address a different subject than the text, is he still an expositor?
- If a speaker says "the Bible says" even though he has no particular text he speaks from, is that exposition?

Let's first define expository preaching and then we'll define expository evangelistic preaching.

What is expository preaching?

In my opinion, no one has better defined expository speaking than Dr.

Haddon Robinson, who says it is "the communication of a biblical concept, derived from and transmitted through a historical, grammatical, literary study of a passage in its context, which the Holy Spirit first applies to the personality and experience of the preacher, then through him to his hearers."[1]

Several ideas are inherent in that definition.

The message comes from a particular text.

Instead of preparing a message and then finding a text that will fit it, the speaker starts with a particular text. Everything he says is governed by what the text says. An expositor has no idea what to tell an audience until he first finds out what the text is saying. The message does not dictate the text we choose. Instead, the text chosen dictates the message given.

We ought not read a text and then leap from it into our own thoughts and ideas. Instead, we should read the text and then leap into it. People should leave the church service knowing what we said and where in the Bible God said it. If the text is Romans 3:10–18, man's sinful condition before God, we must clearly explain Romans 3:10–18. If the text is one verse such as 2 Corinthians 5:21 explaining how God let the One without sin die for sinners, we must clearly explain 2 Corinthians 5:21. The message comes from the text.

In *Preaching to a Shifting Culture*, the following comment is made:

> If expository preaching—which is biblical preaching—is the most relevant message we can offer to our hearers, then what do we mean by expository preaching? In the broadest sense, it is preaching that draws its substance from the Scriptures. Actually, true exposition is more of an attitude than a method. It is the honest answer to the questions, "Do I subject my thought to the Scripture, or do I subject the Scripture to my thought?"[2]

The message is also developed in context.

David Allen has well said, "There is no good preaching apart from good interpretation."[3] Before the speaker can determine what the text is saying to the people of our day, he must first determine what it is saying to the people of that day. What is done with any historical document must be done with the Bible. What exactly did the framers of our Constitution mean when they said, "One nation under God"? Similarly, what exactly did the words of Scripture mean in the day it was written?

That's one reason we must put ourselves in the historical and geographical setting of the text when we study. Mentally, we must stand on that dusty road in a pair of sandals, see the crowd, and hear the Master's beckoning voice, "I am the bread of life. He who comes to Me shall never hunger, and he who believes in Me shall never thirst" (John 6:35). Christ spoke to real people living in His time. Understanding what the Scripture meant to people living then helps us understand what the Scripture means to people living now. The message must be developed in context. When we say, "This is what the Lord is saying," that is an awesome claim. We better make sure we are right.

This means that sentences must be studied in relationship to one another. We cannot take a sentence out of its passage and expect to correctly determine its meaning. I often use the following example. Suppose I made three statements:

1. I stayed in Mike's house.
2. Mike had a fire in his fireplace.
3. It reminded me of hell.

If you repeated only my first and third statements, you would think that I stayed in Mike's house and it reminded me of hell. Of course, that is not what I said. Likewise, if we do not look at a passage of Scripture in the context of what precedes and follows it, we may make a conclusion quite different from the truth.

A friend of mine sent me this illustration that a project leader had sent to the human resources department at his company:

Line 1: Bob Smith, my assistant programmer, can always be found
Line 2: hard at work in his cubicle. Bob works independently, without
Line 3: wasting company time talking to colleagues. Bob never
Line 4: thinks twice about assisting fellow employees, and he always
Line 5: finishes given assignments on time. Often, Bob takes extended
Line 6: measures to complete his work, sometimes skipping coffee
Line 7: breaks. Bob is an individual who has absolutely no
Line 8: vanity in spite of his high accomplishments and profound
Line 9: knowledge in his field. I firmly believe that Bob can be
Line 10: classified as a high-caliber employee, the type who cannot be
Line 11: dispensed with. Consequently, I duly recommend that Bob be
Line 12: promoted to executive management, and a proposal will be
Line 13: executed as soon as possible.

Shortly thereafter, the department received the following memo from the project leader:

"Sorry, but that idiot was reading over my shoulder while I wrote the report sent to you earlier today. Kindly read only the odd numbered lines for my assessment."[4]

By skipping every other line, a completely different meaning emerges. The same can be true in dealing with the biblical text. If the speaker does not read carefully and skips sentences, the meaning can be misunderstood. Expository speaking looks carefully at what precedes and follows each sentence.

The message must be made relevant to the people of today.

Regardless of how much the message is developed in its historical context, it means little if it is not placed in the context of the present day. The speaker must make the text relevant so people can understand how it fits their lives right now. The Anglican preacher John Stott observes, "The characteristic fault of evangelicals is to be biblical but not contemporary. The characteristic fault of liberals is to be contemporary but not biblical. Few of us even begin to manage to be both simultaneously."[5]

A Christian once took an unbelieving friend to hear an evangelist. The evangelist spoke on the topic of man as a sinner before God. From the text he explained how each person has broken God's laws and has chosen to live as a rebellious, self-seeking person. He also explained what man does to avoid God and prevent his thoughts from turning to Him. After several moments the non-Christian turned to her friend. With a look of conviction on her face, she asked, "Did you tell him about me?"

The message must be relevant to the people of today. According to Dr. Peter Teague, president of Lancaster Bible College,

> A minister who loves his people will do everything he can to make the power of the biblical witness clearly relevant to the experience of the congregation. He will work desperately to be clear and interesting. Too much is a stake for him and his hearers. It borders on sin to bore his people with the Bible.[6]

Expository speaking explains the text, in its context, making it relevant to people today. Such speaking is desperately needed before an audience of non-Christians. John Stott, in *Between Two Worlds*, says this about the need for such speaking:

> We should be praying that God will raise up a new generation of Christian communicators who are determined to bridge the chasm; to relate God's unchanging Word to our ever changing world; who refuse to sacrifice truth to relevance or relevance to truth; but who resolve instead in equal measure to be faithful to Scripture and pertinent to today.[7]

Notice something else. In his earlier definition of expository speaking, Dr. Robinson adds the words "which the Holy Spirit first applies to the personality and experience of the preacher, then through him to his hearers."

If the message doesn't first affect the preacher, it won't affect the audience. The message is also transmitted through the speaker's personality. I've often heard preachers pray, "Hide me behind the cross" as they prepare to speak. Although they mean well, that's not what God does. He does not hide us from the people. He presents us to the people. Using our unique personality and way of saying things, He speaks to the audience. God does not speak apart from our personality and experiences. Rather, He speaks through them.

So what is expository *evangelistic* preaching?

As previously defined, expository preaching is a message that comes from a particular text that is developed in context and made relevant to the listener. Three additional components make it evangelistic.

It is directed to a specific audience.

Our message is not directed to the saved, but to the unsaved. Therefore, we should speak as though there are no believers in the audience. We don't ask, "Could a Christian identify with what I'm saying?" We ask, "Could an unbeliever identify?" An expository message should be so focused toward non-Christians that they know they are the ones being addressed. An expository evangelistic message is not prepared for believers and then given to a non-Christian audience. It is prepared for non-Christians and given to non-Christians. Usually, not everyone in the audience is lost. But if 80 percent of the audience is saved and 20 percent are non-Christians, we are speaking to that 20 percent.

It has a specific purpose.

Since our message is directed to non-Christians, its purpose is very specific—to present the gospel. We are not speaking about how to manage money or raise children. At times, such topics may be bridges to the gospel, depending on how we formulate our message, but they are not our purpose. We are speaking to non-Christians about how they can know they are going to heaven. We craft what we will say so that an unbeliever will understand, follow, and be led to the cross of Christ. That's why it is imperative that the gospel be made clear. Non-Christians must not leave thinking that they have merited heaven through a life of good behavior. Instead, because the gospel has been made clear, unbelievers know it is only through Christ's death and resurrection that they can be accepted by God. The message of eternal life, as a gift purchased through Christ's blood, must be made clear.

As the message is given, non-Christians must know that they are sinners, understand that Christ died for them and arose, and that they must trust in Christ alone to save them. As will be noted later, no text contains all three of those truths, unless we choose a rather lengthy passage, which is not advisable. One text may speak of one's condition and not mention the cross and resurrection. Another may speak of Christ's sacrifice on the cross without referring to our position as sinners. Still another may stress that eternal life is a gift apart from works without explaining why. So the speaker has to bring into the message at the proper point whatever the text does not address. That could be done with the use of a few sentences or a few paragraphs, depending on what the text doesn't explain. A few sample expositional evangelistic messages later in this book illustrate how this can be done. Inserting these elements into the message does not mean the speaker failed to be an expositor. Our purpose is to explain the gospel, so the speaker brings to the text the elements of the message of salvation not contained within the Scripture he is using.

It may give less attention to the text.

Note the word "less." I am not saying that it gives no attention to the text. The audience must leave knowing that you explained a particular text in such a way that God spoke through you to them. It was His word they heard, not yours. If you ignore the text, you may be an evangelistic speaker, but certainly not an expository evangelistic speaker.

The reason you may give less attention to the text in an expository evangelistic message is that the text may not be in front of your audience. You may be speaking in a secular setting, or even in some foreign countries, where audience members do not have a copy of the Bible. If they are without the Scriptures in front of them, to go too deeply would possibly lose them.

Other times, expository evangelistic messages may give less attention to the text because non-Christians are not attuned to go as deeply as we'd like to go. Once, as I spoke from the opening verses of Ephesians 2, I came to the verses which read, "and raised us up together, and made us sit together in the heavenly places in Christ Jesus, that in the ages to come He might show the exceeding riches of His grace in His kindness toward us in Christ Jesus" (vv. 6–7). Having carefully explained all the verses prior to those, I said, "The simplest way I know to bundle together what those verses are saying is, 'God has made it possible for us to have an exalted position with Christ.'" Afterward, a believer said to me, "I couldn't wait to see how you were going to deal with those two verses without getting bogged down in them and losing the audience. Those two verses would require more time to fully explain them. I like the simple way you stated them."

That began a discussion of the frustration I felt when I prepared the message. Since I was speaking to non-Christians, I knew I could not go as deeply as I would if I were speaking to believers. All you have to do is lose a non-Christian audience (as it becomes obvious they're no longer listening), and you quickly learn where to summarize for the sake of the unbeliever.

Conclusion

Suppose there are two people sitting in an evangelistic service. One is Jesus Christ and the other is an unbeliever. As I conclude the evangelistic message, I ask each one to respond. If I have done the job God called me to do, Christ should be able to say, "That's my Word!" The sinner should say, "That's me!" If those comments are made, I have preached an expository evangelistic message.

REFLECTING...

1. In your own words, define expository evangelistic preaching.

2. What three things characterize expository preaching?

3. What additional three things characterize expository *evangelistic* preaching?

4. Why must a passage of the Bible be preached in its proper context?

5. What is the specific audience and purpose of an expository evangelistic message?

Chapter 4

Why Is There So Little Expository Evangelistic Speaking?

THE SPEAKER'S PASSION WAS obvious. Urgency gripped him. His words were unmistakable. He understood the brevity of life. He knew that those whose eyes were fixed on him today might not be alive tomorrow. The time to come to Christ was *now*. Boldly he proclaimed, "Please come to Christ. Don't ignore what He did for you on the cross. He loves you, and He wants you with Him forever, not separated from Him for eternity. Tomorrow might be too late to accept His sacrifice for your sins. God has been speaking to you. He knows it. and so do you. Come to Christ— tonight!" His message was not the exposition of a particular passage of Scripture. But his message was clear: "Come to Christ now!"

Evangelicals are convinced that man's first need is to come to Christ. The consequences of sin are eternal. Unless people come to Christ, they will be separated from God forever. For that reason, we are compelled to preach evangelistically. Many have watched Billy Graham crusades on television. Believers observe their pastors giving evangelistic messages from the pulpit. Lay people have experienced evangelistic speaking on short-term mission trips. However, *expository* evangelistic speaking is not well known. I'm referring to a situation in which the speaker takes a passage of Scripture, clearly explains *that* passage to a non-Christian audience, and invites them to trust Christ.

Whom do you consider an expository evangelist? How many times have you heard a pastor or lay person give an expository evangelistic message directed solely to non-Christians? How many times have you heard a speaker who caused you to say, "He's not just an evangelist, he's an expositor"? The answer to these questions reveals the rarity of expository evangelistic speaking. For the most part, expositors have not been evangelists, and evangelists have not been expositors.

Why has there been so little expository evangelistic speaking?

There is little expository speaking—period.

When we talk about expository speaking, we are talking about the kind of speaking in which the speaker selects *a particular text* of Scripture. He explains it in the context of the day in which it was written. He then applies it to the day in which the listener is living. This kind of preaching is not the norm; it's the exception. "Springboard preaching" is far more common. That is, the speaker reads the text and then springboards from it to say anything he cares to say. It has been said that some people use the text like the national anthem at a football game. It gets things started, but then it's never heard from again.

A friend of mine named Joy was in her early twenties when a young man asked her for a date. After she politely declined, he insisted that God had told him that he was to go out with her. When she inquired as to how God revealed that to him, since He had clearly not revealed it to her, he told her that his Bible fell open to Isaiah 55:12a, "For you shall go out with joy." He was serious. As comical as that sounds, that is the way Scripture is many times handled from the pulpit, often by well-meaning people. The Scripture is used as a springboard, never to be heard from again. Or a word is taken out of context and given a meaning it was never intended to have.

There are expositors. But unfortunately, they are the exception. If expository speakers are few, and becoming fewer, it stands to reason that expository *evangelistic* speakers are fewer still.

Evangelists, for the most part, have not been expositors.

Some professional evangelists are known for reading a text of Scripture and then leaping from there to talk about anything on their minds. I once heard an evangelist read Luke 19:1–10, the story of Zaccheus, and then speak on the second coming of Christ. Evangelists have used everything from emotional experience and personal opinion or catchy clichés as their "Bible" instead of unfolding a particular text.

The absence of expository evangelistic speaking has caused some evangelists to lose respect within biblical circles. Bible teachers and theologians often view such evangelists as having a high regard for unbelievers but a low regard for Scripture.

Evangelists are people-oriented. They can weep at the thought of a person spending eternity in hell. They may lie awake thinking of multitudes they want to see come to Christ in a single outreach. A friend going through difficulty might move them to lend a helping hand—a helping hand that might bring that friend to the Savior. They are delighted when they visit a neighbor and discover that he is having a party—a house full of people to evangelize, not just one.

This people orientation often affects their speaking. They tend to organize their message around people rather than the text. Instead of explaining to people a portion of Scripture, they explain why people feel lonely, struggle with self-image, are plagued by guilt, or are prone to lusting and lying.

An expositor must relate to people. If he doesn't, his words will have no meaning. The people he relates to, though, are the people to whom the text relates. If he speaks on Luke 18: 9–14, the parable of the Pharisee and the tax collector, he'll explain how self-righteousness can keep us from seeing our need of Christ. When it comes to our salvation, being steeped in religion can be a hindrance, not a help. If he speaks on Luke 19:1–10, the story of Zaccheus, he'll explain that God loves sinners. We may be as wicked as a crooked tax collector, but God loves us. The expositor identifies with the people the text identifies with because his message is organized around the text.

A student came to me years ago who was considering our internship program. I explained that I'm committed to expository speaking in evangelism. The longer we talked, the more frustrated he became. He asked, "So suppose you are speaking some night on a particular text, and a person walked in who is a drug addict, what would you do?" I said, "I'd continue what I set out to do—explain the text I'd chosen for that night." He disagreed. "I would change my topic and speak on the dangers of addiction," he said. Evangelists often are so people-oriented that they organize their material around people, not the text. That's why they often develop a message and then find a text that seems to fit what they are saying. The problem is, often it doesn't fit, and they therefore impose upon the text a meaning that it does not have. Expository evangelistic speaking starts with the text and develops the message around that text. Like the motor of a car, it's the text that drives everything.

Speakers often lack a commitment to discipline and study.

Effective speaking requires communication, and clear communication is hard work. The same is true of expository evangelistic speaking. It does not come easily.

Too often, those in the preaching profession are noted for their lack of discipline and study. This is a sad commentary on the preaching profession. Sometimes it is a a sad commentary on speakers, period.

One pastor told me that those within his ministerial fellowship were asked how much time they spent on message preparation. The answer was fifteen minutes. Stephen Gregory comments, "When time is tight, a preacher can be tempted to use a biblical text as a springboard to whatever random thoughts he wants to communicate."[1] Don Sunukjian goes into greater detail when he says,

> We will find ourselves tempted to anything but the hard study required—we'll schedule meetings, arrange counseling appointments, tackle administrative tasks, clean our fingernails, find a sermon on the Internet, or settle for some superficial approach to our passage—anything to avoid the sheer labor required. For a man, preaching is probably as close as he will ever come to giving birth.[2]

Those in business have confessed to being frustrated with those in ministry. Business professionals are used to setting one-year and five-year goals, working long hours, engaging in hard work and careful research in areas such as product development and marketing. They are noted for their discipline and hard work. These professionals wonder why preachers cannot apply to their own profession the same principles of hard work and study that they've applied in their businesses.

This lack of time given to study is sometimes attributed to the pressures of counseling and the many other tasks involved with ministry. These are excuses, not viable explanations. We spend time doing what is important to us. If the study of the text in preparation for a message is important—and it is—then we must move other things out of our schedule.

Lack of discipline and study is not justifiable biblically, either. Paul encouraged Timothy, "Be diligent to present yourself approved to God, a worker who does not need to be ashamed, rightly dividing the word of truth" (2 Tim. 2:15). A worker is one who knows what it means to labor long and hard. Translated "labor," it's the same word used in Matthew 20:1: "For the kingdom of heaven is like a landowner who went out early in the morning to hire laborers for his vineyard."

The word "laborers" in that text refers to those who are willing to give themselves to steady, hard work. The same hard work is demanded of any speaker who unfolds the Word to the understanding of the people.

Paul writes, "I discipline my body and bring it into subjection, lest, when I have preached to others, I myself should become disqualified" (1 Cor. 9:27). His reference is most likely to the Isthmian games, named for the isthmus on which Corinth stood. Those contests were a time of great national and religious celebration. Contestants had to give satisfactory proof that for ten months they had undergone the necessary training.

For thirty days before the contests, all candidates attended exercises in the gymnasium. Upon completion of all requirements, they could compete before the multitudes. Although Paul was making application to the Christian life in general, what he said applies to speaking in particular. Strenuous effort and discipline were essential in athletic competition. They are essential in developing the skills of speaking to which an expositor is called. Unfortunately, the preaching profession and again, speakers in general, sometimes lack such discipline.

The nature of exposition frustrates some evangelistic speakers.

The final reason for a lack of expository preaching is also the reason that causes some to wonder if *expository* evangelistic speaking is possible. As expository evangelistic speakers, we have to tell unbelievers three things:

1. We are sinners;
2. Christ died for us and rose again;
3. We must trust Christ.

These three statements could be summarized as sin, substitution, and faith. No passage of Scripture, unless we choose a very large passage, will include all three of these truths.

If we choose John 3:16 as our text, it speaks to the issue of substitution: "For God so loved the world that He gave His only begotten Son." It speaks to the issue of faith: "that whoever believes in Him should not perish but have everlasting life." It does not mention that I'm a sinner.

Consider Romans 5:6–8: "For when we were still without strength, in due time Christ died for the ungodly. For scarcely for a righteous man will one die; yet perhaps for a good man someone would even dare to die. But God demonstrates His own love toward us, in that while we were still sinners, Christ died for us." It tells me that I'm a sinner. It tells me of Christ's substitution. It tells me that "Christ died for the ungodly" and that "while we were still sinners, Christ died for us." But it does not speak to the issue of faith.

Again, very few passages, if any, contain all three issues of sin, substitution, and faith. Some have assumed, therefore, that one cannot be both an expositor *and* an evangelistic speaker. This is not accurate, because whichever of the three subjects—sin, substitution, or faith—is not contained in the passage can be brought out in the course of developing the expositional message. For example, if speaking from John 3:16, we can explain our position before God as sinners by explaining the phrase, "that He gave His only begotten Son." Why did that Son die? To do for us what we could not do for ourselves—pay for our sin. How could a speaker bring out faith in explaining Romans 5:6–8? After explaining sin and substitution, we can

33

pose the question, "What must we now do?" The Bible's answer is "believe." All three elements—sin, substitution, and faith—may not be in a particular text, but we can still present an expository evangelistic message.

Conclusion

Think about how a message is normally crafted. Examine how evangelists think. Consider the hard and tedious work involved. Look at the frustration an expository evangelistic speaker faces. It is not difficult to see why there has been so little expository evangelistic speaking. However, explanations ought not become excuses. Just because something has not been done is no reason for not doing it. The need and time for expository evangelistic speaking is now.

REFLECTING...

1. Give four reasons why there is little expository evangelistic speaking.

2. Why have evangelists, for the most part, not been expositors?

3. What two things do speakers often lack a commitment to?

4. What frustrates some evangelistic speakers when attempting to give an *expository* evangelistic message?

5. What are the three things every evangelistic speaker must tell an audience?

Chapter 5

Why Is Expository Evangelistic Preaching Needed and What Are Its Benefits?

A PREACHER WAS FOND of speaking on baptism. Every text he selected was on baptism. The church elders grew weary and decided to solve the problem by suggesting his text. So they asked him to speak from Revelation 9:1–12, a text that does not even mention water. The next Sunday, the preacher read Revelation 9:1–12, and began his message, "Do you realize this is one of the few texts in the Bible that does not mention baptism? Speaking of baptism, let me say this . . ."

An evangelistic speaker who handles Scripture carefully does not take a text and leap from it. Instead, he takes a text and leaps into it. He does not preach a word. He preaches *the* Word. The Bible is at the center, not in the background, of his message. An unbeliever listening to him speak hears not only what the speaker said but also finds out where in the Bible God said it first. Tullian Tchividjian makes this helpful comment,

> [P]reachers need to be careful that people leave a sermon not so much with grand impressions of human personality, but with grand impressions of divine personality. That's where expository preaching helps, because you are explaining what God is saying. You are pointing away from yourself to what God is saying, but you obviously communicate through your personality.[1]

Why is a careful handling of Scripture so essential and needed?

To understand why careful handling of Scripture is essential, we must understand Romans 10:17: "So then faith comes by hearing, and hearing by the Word of God." God uses His Word to show unbelievers their need and to bring them to Christ. Our words are not divinely inspired; His Word is.

Hebrews 4:12 tells us *how* powerful God's Word is: "For the Word of God is living and powerful, and sharper than any two-edged sword, piercing even to the division of soul and spirit, and of joints and marrow, and is a discerner of the thoughts and intents of the heart." The Word of God has penetrating power greater than a double-edged sword. It probes the inmost recesses of our spiritual being, even to the division of soul and spirit. It distinguishes the natural from the spiritual—even when these elements are as closely connected as the joints and marrow of our body. God's Word exposes the natural and spiritual motivations of the heart.

The writer of Hebrews addresses believers. According to one commentator,

> The inner life of a Christian is often a strange mixture of motivations both genuinely spiritual and completely human. It takes a supernaturally discerning agent such as the Word of God to sort these out and to expose what is of the flesh. The readers might think they were contemplating certain steps out of purely spiritual motivation when, as God's Word could show them, they were acting unfaithfully as did Israel of old.[2]

The Word is active, not passive. God's book is alive. It is powerful. So when it works in the life of a non-Christian, what does it do? What does Romans 10:17 mean when it says, "faith comes by hearing, and hearing by the Word of God"?

The Holy Spirit convicts. "And when He has come, He will convict the world of sin, and of righteousness, and of judgment: of sin, because they do not believe in Me; of righteousness, because I go to My Father and you see Me no more; of judgment, because the ruler of this world is judged" (John 16:8–11).

The verb *elencho* (convict) appears seventeen times in the New Testament with various shades of meaning: to bring to light, expose, set forth, convince someone, point something out, reprove, correct, punish, or discipline. It has the idea of putting the truth before a person in such a way that it must be recognized as truth.

Westcott, in his commentary on the Gospel of John, makes a helpful observation:

> The idea of "conviction" is complex. It involves the conceptions of authoritative examination, of unquestionable proof, of decisive

judgment, of punitive power. Whatever the final issue may be, he who "convicts" another places the truth of the case in dispute in a clear light before him, so that it must be seen and acknowledged as truth. He who then rejects the conclusion which this exposition involves, rejects it with his eyes open and at his peril. Truth seen as truth carries with it condemnation to all who refuse to welcome it.[3]

What truth does God want to impart to a non-Christian? He convicts the world of three truths. As mentioned in John 16:8, they are sin, righteousness, and judgment.

"Of sin, because they do not believe in Me" (John 16:9). We think of ourselves as somewhat moral, upright people; not as bad as some people, better than most. Scripture portrays us as lost, rebellious at heart, deserving eternal hell. The Holy Spirit uses the Word to show us that we are what God calls us—sinners. Unless we see ourselves as God sees us, we will never see our need of Christ. Charles Spurgeon is reported to have said, "Before you can get people saved, you have to get them lost." Only when we see ourselves as sinners can we see that faith in Christ, and His sin payment, is the answer to our sin problem. In light of our condition, and His remedy, the ultimate sin is that of not believing in Christ: "He who believes in Him is not condemned; but he who does not believe is condemned already, because he has not believed in the name of the only begotten Son of God" (John 3:18).

"Of righteousness, because I go to My Father and you see Me no more" (John 16:10). Without a standard, sin cannot be fully understood. Merrill Tenney said, "There can be no transgression where there is no law, no darkness where there is no light, no sin where there is no holiness."[4] God does not use the preacher or the pope as His standard of righteousness; He uses His Son. By His life, death, resurrection, and ascension, Jesus proved He was the perfect Son of God (see Rom. 1:4). Measured by that standard, we see ourselves for who we are and Christ for who He is—the Son of God who became our substitute. Had He not been 100 percent perfect, He could not have made the payment for our sin.

"Of judgment, because the ruler of this world is judged" (John 16:11). "Judged" means that Satan was condemned and remains condemned. Through the cross, God met victory; Satan met defeat. As Jesus predicted His death on a cross, He said, "Now is the judgment of this world; now the ruler of this world will be cast out" (John 12:31). This judgment guarantees that all who are of Satan's world will also be condemned. The Holy Spirit convicts of the reality of this judgment—death and eternal separation from God.

It's the Word God uses to convict. That's why expository evangelistic speaking is needed. If a passage of Scripture is ripped out of its original context and taken to mean something the writer of Scripture never intended it to mean, it is no longer the Word of God. At that point, we have preached our words, not God's Word.

When I was in seminary, I heard an evangelist speak at a local church on 1 Samuel 20:3: "there is but a step between me and death." With fervor and dogmatism he shouted, "God is saying to you that there is one step between you and death. Come to Christ. Come to Christ tonight." It's true that there is one step between us and death. In fact, as many have observed, there is only one heartbeat between us and the grave. However, that is not what *that* verse is saying. In context, the passage does not speak about the need to come to anyone but instead to escape someone. Jonathan's father, Saul, was trying to kill David. David explained to Jonathan, "There is but a step between me and death." The passage has nothing to do with our relationship to Christ. It was strictly about David's relationship with Saul. The evangelist didn't speak God's Word. He spoke his own words.

Can God use such speaking to bring people to Christ? He certainly can and has. He can work through us or in spite of us. But since it is His Word that He uses to change people's eternal destinies, let's use what He promises to use—His Word handled and explained in its proper context.

What are the additional benefits of expository evangelistic speaking?

Hard work was essential on the dairy farm I was raised on in Lancaster County, Pennsylvania. Without it, there would be no crops. Planting the corn, then cultivating and harvesting it were necessary. No crops meant no food for the dairy cows. No dairy cows meant no milk. No milk meant no income.

Hard work was also beneficial. When I wrestled in high school, muscles built through strenuous farm labor gave me an advantage over my opponents. When I went to college, long days of classes and long nights of study didn't seem unusual. When I began my ministry, I knew constant plodding and hard work would have its rewards. Things which are necessary often have additional benefits.

That's true of expository evangelistic speaking. Not only is it necessary, it's also beneficial.

It gives the clear authority of the Bible to your message.

You are speaking His Word. He said it. You repeated it. He's the author. You're the communicator. Any argument the unbeliever has is with God, not you.

Suppose you speak on Ephesians 2:8–9: "For by grace you have been saved through faith, and that not of yourselves; it is the gift of God, not of works, lest anyone should boast." Someone who takes pride in his church attendance and moral life might wish to argue that a good life merits eternal life. But his disagreement is with God, not you. You didn't say that a person is not saved by works. Through expository evangelistic speaking, you explained that *God* said a person is not saved by works. Anyone who objects to your message is disputing God and His Word.

It gives your speaking content beyond the emotion.

Evangelism involves information and invitation. Non-Christians need to hear and understand that Christ died for their sins and arose. They must then be invited to trust in Christ alone to save them. Expository evangelistic speaking does just that; it gives listeners information. A text is unfolded. It then invites the people to respond to that information.

Evangelistic speaking has often been characterized by emotion devoid of information. I know of one evangelist who kept a notebook of moving stories before him, turning page after page until he found the one that moved his audience to tears. It appeared his goal was to solicit emotion from his listeners, not to impart information for them to act on. Expository evangelistic speaking involves emotion. If you are not emotionally sold on Christ, you won't sell your audience on Him. However, it's not emotion based on manipulation; it's authentic emotion generated by the text.

Expository evangelistic speaking gives information on which an intelligent decision can be made. God is not asking for our opinions on our lost condition. He has said we are lost. The unbeliever then has a decision to make about the facts of God's Word. You, the expositional evangelistic preacher, speak from the inspired, authoritative manual—God's Word. The facts can either be received or ignored. They can't be denied.

It guards against false theology.

God's Word is accurate and reliable. Expository evangelistic speaking makes sure we are saying what the Word says, not something we would like it to say. The truth rests on God's Word. A cliché or familiar statement *may represent* biblical theology, but sometimes it doesn't.

Evangelists have said, "Across the world, people are crying out for God. They are seeking after Him and saying, 'How can I know Him?'" This is *not* what Scripture teaches. Romans 3:11 says, "There is none who seeks after God." God seeks men. Men don't seek God. Now we see where John 6:44 fits: "No one can come to Me unless the Father who sent Me draws him." But doesn't Hebrews 11:6 say, "He is a rewarder of those who diligently seek Him"? God has to start the process. Left to his own, a person will not seek God. Once God starts the process, if the person responds by seeking after Him, God will reward that seeking by bringing him or her to a saving knowledge of Christ. First-century Cornelius is a prime example. Scripture portrays him as "a just man, one who fears God and has a good reputation among all the nation of the Jews" (Acts 10:22). God rewarded his seeking by sending Peter who shared with him the gospel of grace.

God's way of seeking people is not always the same. Sometimes He seeks us through creation: "For since the creation of the world His invisible attributes are clearly seen, being understood by the things that are made, even His eternal power and Godhead, so that they are without excuse" (Rom. 1:20). Sometimes He seeks us by exposing us to another believer. But the point is that we don't seek God; God seeks us. Expository evangelistic speaking guards against that kind of false theology.

Some evangelists have said, "If you don't know the date you were saved, you're not saved." They then beg, "If you don't know when that was, get saved *today*." Scripture never says we have to know the date we were saved. That is false theology. We have to know we are trusting Christ alone to save us. There was a precise moment we crossed from darkness into light, but whether we know when that particular moment occurred is not the issue. If we are trusting Christ alone to save us, we are saved regardless of whether we know the precise moment of our salvation.

"Invite Christ into your heart," other evangelistic speakers beckon. They mean well, but that phrase is never used of salvation in Scripture. People who misunderstand the phrase think that by saying a prayer in which they "invite Christ into their heart" they are saved. The word Scripture uses is "believe"—which means understanding that Christ died for me, arose, and that I have to *trust* Christ alone to save me. To imply that people are saved by saying a prayer in which they invite Jesus into their hearts may be as damaging as saying we are saved by good behavior. It is also confusing to children and others who think in concrete terms. They cannot picture how Jesus can physically walk into their hearts. Expository evangelistic preaching guards against false theology. It makes us examine everything we say with the standard, "Is this what the Bible says?"

It edifies believers.

When one preaches an evangelistic message, usually some believers are also in attendance. Expository evangelistic speaking also helps them.

As an expositor, you are committed to unfolding a text to the understanding of the people. Each time the Word is explained, God uses it to take out of a believer's life what should not be there and put in what should be there. So even while you are trying to reach non-Christians, the Word also ministers to believers.

Another way expository evangelistic speaking equips believers is in teaching them how to evangelize. After I speak in an outreach, believers often say to me, "It helps me so much to see how you do it." They usually refer to the Scripture I used that addresses pertinent questions non-Christians have, the extent I go to in order to make the gospel clear, helpful illustrations I use, and even the way I try to combine grace and truth. Watching a mechanic overhaul a car can help us learn car repair; observing an evangelist can help us learn how to evangelize.

If expository evangelistic speaking did nothing more than bring non-Christians to Christ, that would be enough. But the results affect both Christians and non-Christians. Non-Christians are introduced to Christ while Christians are brought closer to Him.

Conclusion

Expository evangelistic speaking is largely unheard of today. But since God uses His Word to bring people to Christ, it's the Word we need to preach. The benefits of expository evangelistic speaking warrant its use. We need to appeal to unbelievers through the unfolding of the Scriptures. Doing so benefits both non-Christians and Christians.

REFLECTING...

1. In one sentence, explain why the careful handling of Scripture is so essential.

2. What are four additional benefits of expository evangelistic speaking?

3. What three truths does the Holy Spirit want to convict the world of?

4. Give an example of false theology that expository evangelistic speaking will guard against.

5. How does expository evangelistic speaking edify believers at the same time it reaches unbelievers?

Chapter 6

What Challenges Face an Expository Evangelistic Speaker?

OPPORTUNITIES ARE OFTEN BESET with problems. A day at an amusement park may mean adjusting to undesired crowds. A new promotion at work might entail nights away from the family. The luxury of a new car may also result in higher insurance costs. The benefits are there, but so are certain problems.

So it is with expository evangelistic speaking. It is an opportunity that has its benefits—but also difficulties.

Some of these challenges were addressed in the examination of why there is so little expository evangelistic speaking. Putting a few of these challenges before us can equip us for what we will face in putting together an expository evangelistic message.

Few passages contain the complete plan of salvation.

To begin, we have the problem addressed earlier—the limitation that comes from having few passages that give the whole plan of salvation. Three subjects must be addressed each time you give an evangelistic message: 1) We are sinners; 2) Christ died for us and rose again; 3) We must trust Christ. Unless one speaks from an exceptionally long passage of Scripture, there is not a single verse or small section of text that addresses all three.

Isaiah 53:5–6 is an effective passage from which to deliver an evangelistic message. It tells me I'm a sinner. He was "wounded for our transgressions . . . bruised for our iniquities." It explains Christ died for me. "The

Lord has laid on Him the iniquity of us all." It does not tell me of my need to trust Christ.

John 5:24 can be equally effective. Christ said, "Most assuredly, I say to you, he who hears My word and believes in Him who sent Me has everlasting life, and shall not come into judgment, but has passed from death into life." This passage explains that we are sinners by using the phrase "and shall not come into judgment." It stresses the need for faith: "He who hears My Word and believes." It does not tell me Christ died for me and rose again.

The speaker needs to address whatever the text does not. There is always a logical, common sense way to do so. If every text explained the three subjects that must be addressed in every evangelistic message, expository evangelistic speaking would be much easier.

Few passages are specifically directed to non-Christians.

The scarcity of passages addressed to non-Christians is another problem. The one book of the New Testament in which the author defines his purpose as that of telling readers how to receive eternal life is the Gospel of John: "[B]ut these are written that you may believe that Jesus is the Christ, the Son of God, and that believing you may have life in His name" (20:31). The word "believe" occurs ninety-eight times in the book.

We come to Christ by believing—recognizing that we are sinners for whom Christ died and arose, and by trusting Christ alone to save us. The plan of salvation can certainly be found in other places in Scripture, but the Gospel of John is the only book specifically directed at non-Christians. That's one reason why the Gospel of John is the easiest book from which to speak an expository evangelistic message. John addresses the same audience we are addressing—unbelievers. Jay Adams comments, "It is not without reason that the Gospel of John has been used more frequently than any other to bring people to a saving knowledge of Jesus Christ; it was written for that purpose. The Spirit, who produced the Bible, will bless its use when the preacher's intent is the same as His own."[1]

Most New Testament books are addressed to believers, not unbelievers. Suppose one speaks to unbelievers from Ephesians 2:1–10, an excellent passage for explaining God's grace toward sinners. To be contextually accurate, one cannot say, "Paul wrote this passage to tell you how to come to Christ." He wrote the passage to remind the Ephesians of how *they* came to Christ. One could appropriately say, "By reminding the Ephesians of how they were saved, Paul clearly tells you how you can be saved." To be contextually accurate, we have to bear in mind that Paul was speaking to Christians, not non-Christians, as he wrote his epistle.

First John 4:9–10 are excellent verses from which to deliver an evangelistic message:

In this the love of God was manifested toward us, that God has sent His only begotten Son into the world, that we might live through Him. In this is love, not that we loved God, but that He loved us and sent His Son to be a propitiation for our sins.

Unlike the Gospel of John, 1 John was written to tell us how to draw close to the One who saved us. John states his purpose in 1 John 1:3–4:

That which we have seen and heard we declare to you, that you also may have fellowship with us; and truly our fellowship is with the Father and with His Son Jesus Christ. And these things we write to you that your joy might be full.

John and 1 John are great companion books because John was written to speak about salvation while 1 John was written to speak about fellowship. John was written to tell us how to come to the Savior. First John was written to tell us how to draw close to our Savior.

To be an expositor who handles the Word carefully, we need to keep the author's original audience or intent in mind when speaking. For instance, in 1 John 4:9–11, John was explaining that as children of God we should love one another as He has loved us. What is the greatest manifestation of His love? Exactly what John says—the cross. You could accurately say, "In a paragraph where John spoke of our need to love others as God loved us, he tells us what the greatest manifestation of God's love was." But the scarcity of passages where the purpose is to confront non-Christians makes expository evangelistic speaking more difficult. Most Scripture is directed toward Christians and concerns what God wants to take out of our lives that should not be there and put in what should be there. Thus, speaking to believers is easier for an expositor than speaking to non-Christians.

Explaining complex phrases to non-Christians is not always easy.

Another challenge for an expository evangelistic speaker is explaining a complex phrase or passage to those unfamiliar with expository speaking.

My wife came from a background where the preacher was an orator. He was good at telling stories and quite dramatic in his presentation. But he was not an expositor. When she first heard expository speaking, she wasn't sure she liked it. It didn't seem quite as interesting as what she had had become accustomed to growing up. Now she becomes frustrated listening to one who is not an expositor. She wants the speaker to be enthusiastic, but she wants him to be enthusiastic about the text. She wants to leave knowing she's heard from God and that she now understands a portion of Scripture better than she did before. But the taste for expository speaking

45

has to be acquired. The listener has to be even more interested and patient if the passage the speaker is explaining contains a complex verse.

In the story of Nicodemus, we read, "Most assuredly, I say to you, unless one is born of water and the Spirit, he cannot enter the kingdom of God" (John 3:5). For the sake of the text and the clarity of the gospel, you have to explain what is meant by water. Otherwise, one could mistakenly believe baptism is a requirement for salvation. I believe that the water John refers to is the water of physical birth. Christ explained, "Most assuredly, I say to you unless one is born again, he cannot see the kingdom of God" (v. 3). Nicodemus, with physical birth in mind, asked, "How can a man be born when he is old? Can he enter a second time into his mother's womb and be born" (v. 4)? Christ answered, unless one is born of water and the Spirit, he cannot enter the kingdom of God. I believe Christ was saying that we have been born of water in order to live, and then of the Spirit in order to live forever.

Taking time to explain a difficult verse (not difficult perhaps to our mind, but difficult to the mind of our listeners) is a problem expositors face. It can be done without boring the audience, but it's an obstacle you confront.

We encounter a similar problem when speaking from Titus 3:3–5:

> For we ourselves were also once foolish, disobedient, deceived, serving various lusts and pleasures, living in malice and envy, hateful and hating one another. But when the kindness and the love of God our Savior toward man appeared, not by works of righteousness which we have done, but according to His mercy He saved us, through the washing of regeneration and renewing of the Holy Spirit.

The phrase "the washing of regeneration" could make one think baptism saves. However, Titus is referring to the work of the Holy Spirit in imparting new life. The fact that Paul wanted to portray the work of the Holy Spirit in cleansing the believer at salvation is appropriately supported in John 7:38–39. Christ declares,

> "He who believes in Me, as the Scripture has said, out of his heart will flow rivers of living water." But this He spoke concerning the Spirit, whom those believing in Him would receive; for the Holy Spirit was not yet given, because Jesus was not yet glorified.

Again, to be an expositor, we have to explain a difficult verse while speaking to unbelievers. It can be done, and done well, by a simple statement such as, "When God saves us, He cleanses from our sin, not with water, but through what the Bible calls the Holy Spirit." Explaining complex phrases to a non-Christian is an issue expositors face.

Another example is Romans 5:6: "For when we were still without strength, in due time Christ died for the ungodly." That verse, along with the next two verses, is a good passage to use in presenting an expository evangelistic message. But to adequately handle the text, we need to at least say a sentence or two about the meaning of the words "in due time."

Those words contain the idea "at the appointed and proper time." God, unlike us, is always on time. At a time appointed by God, He acted on our behalf. He did for us what we could not do for ourselves. The phrase "in due time" can be dealt with quite easily. But as a speaker, you would have reason to wish that the phrase were not there. An expositor speaking to a non-Christian audience confronts that difficulty.

Allow me one more example. Christ said to Zaccheus, "Today salvation has come to this house, because he also is a son of Abraham" (Luke 19:9). God's blessings were given to Abraham in the Old Testament. He promised to make of him a great nation. Anyone who received those blessings was called a son of Abraham. The way you became a son of Abraham was to place your trust in the promised Messiah who would die for your sins. That day Zaccheus placed his trust in Christ and became a son of Abraham.

As a speaker, you must keep your non-Christian audience engaged. You also hope you will not lose them while explaining Luke 19:9 in the above way. Once again, though, an expository evangelistic speaker could wish that phrase did not have to be dealt with in a passage so effective for evangelistic speaking.

The structure of a particular passage can make explaining it more difficult.

God hasn't structured every verse the way you might prefer for use in speaking to non-Christians. Hebrews 2:14–15 is a good example:

Inasmuch then as the children have partaken of flesh and blood, He Himself likewise shared in the same, that through death He might destroy him who had the power of death, that is, the devil, and release those who through fear of death were all their lifetime subject to bondage.

Contained in this passage are four truths about death that are very powerful in speaking to unbelievers.

1. Death is of the devil.
2. The fear of death enslaves all of us.
3. Christ died.
4. Because He died, we no longer have to fear death.

The problem is that these four truths are in this passage but not in that order. Let's go back and put the portion of Scripture alongside each fact and the verse where it is found.

Death is of the devil. "Who had the power of death, that is, the devil" (v. 14b).

The fear of death enslaves all of us. "And release those who through fear of death were all their lifetime subject to bondage" (v. 15).

Christ died. "Inasmuch then as the children have partaken of flesh and blood, He Himself likewise shared in the same, that through death He might destroy him who had the power of death, that is, the devil" (v. 14).

Because He died, we no longer have to fear death. "That through death He might destroy him, who had the power of death, that is, the devil, and release those who through fear of death were all their lifetime subject to bondage" (vv. 14b–15).

If you presented them in that order, you would go from the end of verse 14 to verse 15 and then back to verse 14. You can do that and stick to the text. There is nothing wrong with doing so. But any expositor would prefer that the phrases were written in that order.

Conclusion

The challenges faced by expository evangelistic speaking are not insurmountable. However, part of solving any problem is facing it. We need to face the problems in expository evangelistic speaking and then ask, "How do we solve those problems?" We then arrive at solutions that allow us to speak the text and at the same time remain relevant to unbelievers. Difficulties faced in expository evangelistic speaking are overcome with know-how and experience.

REFLECTING...

1. Name four problems that an expository evangelistic speaker faces.

2. What is the easiest book of the Bible from which to preach an expository evangelistic message? Why?

3. Why do expositors have to keep the author's original audience or intent in mind?

4. Why is speaking to believers easier for an expositor than speaking to unbelievers?

5. What two things play a major role in overcoming the challenges faced in expository evangelistic speaking?

Chapter 7

How Do You Develop Your Evangelistic Speaking Skills?

WHEN LEONARDO DA VINCI was a young pupil, his elderly, well-known teacher asked him to finish a painting the teacher had begun. The young painter stood in awe of his master's skill and respectfully declined. But his teacher would accept no excuse and said, "Just do your best." Trembling, da Vinci took his brush and began. With each stroke, his hand grew steadier as the genius within him awoke. Soon he was so caught up in his work, he forgot his timidity. When the painting was finished, the frail and weak master came into the studio to see it. Embracing his student, he exclaimed, "Son, I paint no more."[1]

Even though Leonardo da Vinci had underestimated his own ability, it was there; it just had to be developed.

Speaking is a skill. Like all skills, it has to be developed. To develop it, several things are needed.

God-given Ability

Let's start where the ability originates. It is God-given, not man-produced. As much as I want to help you become an effective speaker, I cannot develop what God has not given.

My wife is a talented soloist. When she sings, people exclaim, "Sing some more." Her music lifts me, moves me. But if I sing, people exclaim, "Sing no more!" Even though the desire might be there, the ability isn't. As much as I love music, I'm not a soloist. Singing is not an ability God has given me.

Speaking, like singing, is a God-given ability. A person must have a certain amount of ability to stand up in front of people and proclaim a message. One might be timid, but underneath that timidity there must be a God-given ability waiting to be developed. I've met those who can speak one-to-one with ease and effectiveness but cannot speak publicly. The comment often made about such a person is, "He's great one-on-one. He's just not a public speaker."

How does one know if he has that undiscovered or undeveloped ability?

It usually comes down to one word—desire. Speakers who speak well at some time or another *desired* to speak. Even though they may have first been intimidated by the thought, an inner compulsion kept driving them. As they took their ability, laid it at God's feet, and said, "Help me," God took it from there to develop the ability He had given. People with the ability to speak are people who *want* to speak.

I make my living speaking. But in high school, when I stood up to speak, I was extremely nervous. I wanted to get my words out, but they just wouldn't come. I struggled with shame and self-doubt. At that point it wasn't due to the speech defect I mentioned earlier. It was just the thought of speaking in public. But I still wanted to do it.

A word of caution! This does not mean that to be an effective evangelistic speaker you must have the spiritual gift of evangelism, although that definitely helps. For those with the gift of evangelism, relating to non-Christians and speaking in a way they understand may come easier. But it's not a necessity. If you have the desire to speak, develop your ability, and identify well with your audience, you can be an effective communicator. I've known many who claim no gift in evangelism but are very effective in communicating to unbelievers.

Clear Thinking

Learning how to speak doesn't start with the mouth; it starts with the mind. Years ago in a class at Dallas Theological Seminary, Dr. Haddon Robinson made this profound statement: "Learning how to speak is learning how to think. If you think clearly, you will speak clearly."

What is unclear in the mind of the speaker is confusing in the mind of the audience. Confusing speakers are often unclear thinkers. The mouth releases what the mind has processed. It's trite but true: A mist in the pulpit is a fog in the pew.

Years ago, I asked an intern, "What is the connection between these two points of your message? I'm not following you." He answered, "I'm not sure either." We laughed together as he understood my point. I said, "If it is not clear in your mind, it won't be clear in the mind of the audience."

The mind has to interact with the text and then ask the "whys," the "wheres," and the "wherefores." It has to address what the text says, what it doesn't say, and why it doesn't say it. It must answer questions such as, "Is this something I need to explain or is this something I can assume the audience already knows? Does it matter if they don't know this? How do I illustrate this? What analogies do I use? How can I summarize this thought in one sentence? What is my aim in this message and who is my audience?"

No one else can process these thoughts for you. Others may be able to assist and can even help sharpen your ability to think. But sooner or later the thinking you do in putting together a message has to be thinking you do for yourself. This ability to think, and to think clearly, is what will make you a clear speaker.

One way a speaker develops his skills is by reading a lot. As we read, we learn, we interact with the author's thinking, and we're stimulated to think for ourselves. Reading develops a mind that needs constant challenge.

Time and Experience

God-given ability and a good mind are not sufficient in and of themselves. A speaker needs time to embrace all kinds of situations and settings. Speak before one audience and then another. Do it in a small setting; do it in a large one. Speak to those ranging in age from nine to ninety in the same audience. Speak in front of teens. Give a message to a group of retirees. Speak in church settings. Present a message in a civic auditorium. Do it when the program has been carefully planned. Should you discover the program has not been thought through, speak with the same enthusiasm. Speak before audiences varying in receptivity.

Time that allows for varying situations and settings is essential. What does time produce? Experience! Experience too valuable to assess! Soon you are not one who has spent years *discussing* evangelistic speaking; instead you have spent years *doing* it. Experience teaches you what classroom lectures cannot. Developing your evangelistic speaking skills does not happen overnight. It doesn't happen over several nights. It's a lifelong process. As with other skills, the more you speak, provided you are willing to learn as you go, the better you will become. Time and experience come together to produce a skilled speaker, a speaker who has exercised and developed his ability and mind.

Teachability

Let's go back to the phrase "provided you are willing to learn." Teachability complements the first three elements in developing skills as an expository evangelistic speaker. None of the preceding has any value if you do not have a teachable spirit. Examine the book of Proverbs closely. You will find the emphasis is not on a person who talks; it is on someone who listens. Proverbs begs, "Listen to counsel and receive instruction, that you may be wise in your latter days" (19:20). In any area, the ability to receive instruction makes us better.

The ability to receive instruction is essential in speaking because speakers have a certain amount of ego, which is one reason they are not afraid to speak in front of people—speakers like being in front of people. The ability to move an audience stimulates them. There is nothing wrong with that, unless the ego is an unteachable one. Without a teachable ego, nothing that man or even God Himself says will make a difference.

A. W. Tozer was noted for his observation, "It is doubtful whether God can bless a man greatly until He has hurt him deeply."[2] This is where brokenness enters in. Broken people are the most teachable. The consequences of brokenness, however it has occurred, bring them to the point of saying, "What do you have to teach me?" instead of, "I have something to teach you." Always broken, always teachable, they are always learning. God in His multiple ways does the teaching.

Teachability has much to do with humility. A spirit of humility makes a speaker more concerned about what he may be doing wrong instead of what he is doing right. The question, "Where is improvement needed?" is always on his mind. He's not so impressed with what he is; he's more concerned about what he can become.

Brokenness allows us to reach out to others. We want to learn from communicators we respect. We not only accept feedback, we seek it. Others are impressed when we acknowledge that they have something to teach us. Even someone who has less ability as a speaker can help us because we value that person's observations. Humility allows us to ask about every speaker we hear, "Is there something effective she does that I could benefit from?" The speakers we learn from cover a wide range. Even those who don't address an audience properly can teach us what not to do.

I heard a young speaker who demonstrated great potential. He clearly evidenced the ability to speak. But he was making mistakes experienced speakers learn to avoid. I said to someone who knew him, "He's quite a speaker." They answered, "Yes, he is. He'd be better, though, if he let someone work with him. But he has an attitude that he already knows it all." I left burdened that his lack of humility, contributing to a lack of teachableness, will prevent him from becoming a better speaker. Ultimately, this will keep him from fully realizing his God-given potential.

Be a teachable person. Speaking will become a lifelong learning experience that may be rewarded by achieving a level of expertise you did not realize possible.

Hard Work

Effective speaking is not an easy task. Some messages come together quickly; most do not. The work it takes to put together a good message can be tiring and strenuous. To take a message from start—that is, deciding on the passage I'm going to speak from—to a completed manuscript, requires twenty to thirty hours of hard work. That's one reason someone without a good work ethic should not even consider the speaking profession. Putting together a message can be enjoyable, but it's not a leisure activity. It's work done in the trenches, not the recliner. I have often heard Dr. Robinson remark, "Thinking is hard work. Thinking about thinking is harder work." As a speaker, you are not only thinking but also trying to get the audience to think with you. That can be exhausting.

Little did I know when I started out in the speaking profession how much my dairy farm background would help me. I've never known a nine-to-five job. Dad woke us up at 5:00 a.m., gave us ten minutes to be downstairs and ready to head for the barn. Many days ended at 9:00 p.m. The good work ethic I learned on the dairy farm has been of immense value to me in speaking.

It's not just the preparation that's tiring. The message itself, properly delivered, is emotionally and physically exhausting. A respected speaker once concluded what others have affirmed: By the time a speaker has delivered a thirty-minute message, he's done the emotional equivalent of four to six hours of physical labor. The preparation of the message and the delivery of the message can be reduced to two words: hard work.

Keeping in shape physically will dramatically affect your speaking ability. I once heard a doctor remark that no group should be more concerned about preserving physical health than men and women who make professional use of their speaking and singing voices. I heartily agree. I've been told that legendary football coach Vince Lombardi, who led the Green Bay Packers in the 1960s, was once asked why he pushed his team so hard toward physical conditioning. His reported response was, "Fatigue makes cowards of us all." Fatigue also produces poor speakers, affecting, among other things, a speaker's enthusiasm.

For years I've enjoyed running on the treadmill an average of three miles a day. I had no idea when I started how much it would help my speaking, not to mention keeping me in shape physically. I am able to think faster and better, and feel more alert both in my study and in the pulpit. Speaking and preparing to speak, though still demanding physically, are not as tiring as they would be if I did not keep fit physically. The older I become, the more important physical fitness is in maintaining a steady speaking career. Hard work demands that we keep in shape physically, and speaking is hard work.

Conclusion

The car vibrates. You slow down. Dust rises behind your vehicle. The children in the back seat wake up. "Where are we, Dad?" How did a road so smooth suddenly become so bumpy? The sign along the highway reads: "under construction." You left the paved highway to travel for a few miles on a road that is being repaved. It is still under construction.

That is what a preacher of the gospel is. He is a person under construction. But when these five essentials—God-given ability, clear thinking, time and experience, teachability, and hard work—come together in his life, there will be consistent improvement. And the improvement will result in a speaker who becomes an increasingly effective preacher of the gospel. In time, he will be referred to not as a speaker but as a communicator—a very experienced one.

REFLECTING...

1. What five things are helpful in developing your evangelistic speaking skills?

2. Learning how to speak is learning how to think. How does clear thinking affect clear speaking?

3. In what specific ways do time and experience develop your evangelistic speaking skills?

4. How and why is teachability essential in developing evangelistic speaking skills?

5. What makes preparing and delivering an evangelistic message such hard work?

Chapter 8

Where Does Evangelistic Speaking Start and Why?

IF A PERSON ASKED, "How can I become an effective expository evangelistic speaker," where would you tell him to start? Chances are, you would tell him to enroll in a good Bible college or seminary. You might suggest he listen to a few tapes from speakers skilled in expository evangelistic speaking. You could explain the need to take a text of Scripture and study it thoroughly. Or you might recommend that he pick up a book like this one and digest it chapter by chapter.

None of those are the place to start. In fact, one does not have to be a Bible college or seminary graduate to give an expositional evangelistic message. People in the workplace can do a commendable job. There are two other essential starting points.

The first is obvious but needs to be said: *We need to know God.* It's difficult to speak of God if we don't know Him well as a result of studying His Word and walking with Him. Knowing Him intimately helps us speak with passion. Others need to know Him, and we want them to meet Him *today*. That is why our daily time with Him through Bible study and prayer is critical. It is not time we have; it is time we take in order to intimately know Him.

The other starting point also should be obvious but is often overlooked: *We need to know the people to whom we are speaking.* Please understand that loving them is inherent in knowing them. The saintly Scottish preacher Andrew Bonar listened to a well-known preacher proclaim the Word. Afterward, Bonar asked the preacher, "You love to preach, don't you?" The famous preacher replied, "Yes, I do." Bonar then asked, "Do you love the men to whom you preach?"[1]

In evangelistic speaking we are not speaking to Christians; we are speaking to non-Christians. If we don't know non-Christians, we'll have great difficulty speaking to them. To know God but not the people we are speaking to makes it difficult to communicate His thoughts to them.

That's why expository evangelistic speaking doesn't begin in a study surrounded by books. It begins on a sidewalk surrounded by the type of people we are preparing to address. The people we meet on the sidewalk are representative of those who will be our audience.

What do you need to know about non-Christians?

How they think

First, as conversations unfold, we will discover their thought processes. As unbelievers, they do not approach life from a Christian worldview. They approach it from their own. So we must learn to look at life through *their* eyes. Unbelievers often view God as unfair. Why does God let those who do wrong prosper and those who do good suffer? Some see Him as cold and calloused. Otherwise, why would children, or anyone, for that matter, be the victim of an explosion that He could have stopped? How can He claim to be loving and yet seem eager to send people to hell? Some struggle not with the nature of truth, but with the belief that there is any such thing as truth. Not every non-Christian thinks that way, but many do.

Unbelievers' thoughts about God often reflect their thoughts about life. You will find as you speak to them that they view life as confusing, disappointing, and not very satisfying. Addictions are a futile attempt to escape their own harsh reality. They view those who do well as lucky. Life is about chance and coincidence more than it is about choice. "Do unto others before they do unto you" is their mode of operation.

Many non-Christians are convinced they have not needed God before and they don't need Him now. In their minds, their own efforts brought them to where they are. For other non-Christians, God might be an integral part of their lives, but they are trying to merit His approval, hoping in the end that their good works will outweigh the bad.

For long-time believers, it has been a while since we thought that way. We need to go back and think the way we did as a non-Christian, not the way we do now. Nothing helps us more in this regard than spending time with unbelievers.

How they talk

When speaking to non-Christians, it helps to say things the way unbelievers say them. When they speak of going to heaven, they sometimes say, "I think I stand a whole lot better chance than a lot of people I know." When being defensive, or perhaps braggadocios, about their lack of church attendance, they comment, "I live a whole lot better without going to church than many who go." They are quick to refer to a church as "that place" and to the Christians who gather there as a "bunch of misguided religious fanatics." Spiritual things might be "God stuff," and struggles with Christ are "Jesus issues." To them, Christians may be people who "don't care a lot" and missionaries may be considered a "bunch of beggars." Remember, they talk this way because they've never met the Savior and are not indwelt by the Holy Spirit. Some of us spoke the same way before we met the Lord.

How they talk reveals their attitude, not just their word choice. They may be animated or apathetic. Their voice may show confusion or expose bitterness. Listen to how they talk. When we speak, especially if we're quoting them, we want to say things with the same emotions they use. They need to know we not only understand what they are saying but that we understand the feeling attached to their words. We must not use curse words, but the way we speak must demonstrate that we understand what the curse words they use reveal about them. The more time we spend with them, the more we see their attitude.

What they talk about

Knowing how unbelievers talk is helpful, but we also need to know what they are talking about. Conversations may range from their most recent raise to the newspaper's most recent rumor. You'll learn the names of public figures they trust and the names of those they don't. If a public figure is immoral, as long as he's doing a good job for the nation, non-Christians might not be concerned. Knowing when and why an unbeliever's conversation changes from the past weekend to the next weekend can be revealing. Notice what portion of their talk surrounds the secular. It is a contrast to the amount of our talk that surrounds the spiritual. A little thing to us may be a big gripe to them and vice versa.

What happens when we know how they think, talk, and what they talk about? When we speak to them, we are speaking to people we understand. We had lunch with them, hit tennis balls to them, or car-pooled to work. They are no longer strangers. Our comfort level in knowing what they are like has risen considerably. Even though we take a different position on God and life than they do, we are not ignorant of them. When non-Christians are assured we understand them, they are more likely to be interested in what we want to say to them.

Where do you find time to spend with non-Christians?

How does a speaker who is not in the secular workplace find time to spend with non-Christians? Most people active in church-related work don't have enough time for the people they presently minister to, let alone those they occasionally minister to. Three ideas are helpful.

It's part of discipleship.

Look beyond the people behind your message to the purpose behind your life. Do you consider yourself a disciple of Christ? Hopefully, the answer is yes. The first thing Christ taught His disciples was evangelism. He urged, "Follow Me, and I will make you fishers of men" (Matt. 4:19). He took them from catching something that became dead, to taking those spiritually dead and seeing them become alive. What a high perspective on life. But that's what God desires us to do, regardless of our profession—plumber or preacher, machinist or missionary, one who operates a backhoe or one who pilots a plane. Spending time with non-Christians should be a life issue, not just a speaking issue. As Robert Coleman says in *The Master Plan of Evangelism*, "Evangelism is not an optional accessory to our life. It is the heartbeat of all that we are called to be and do."[2] The basis of spending time with non-Christians is bigger than simply being a speaker; it's the fact that we have been called to be a disciple.

Remember who God is.

Don't forget who God is: He's a God who seeks the non-Christian. Christ said, "For the Son of Man has come to seek and to save that which was lost" (Luke 19:10). Come before Him and say, "Show me how and where to meet non-Christians." He'll answer in greater ways than you anticipate. God's mind is superior to ours. He can bring ideas to mind we have never considered and cause things to happen for our advantage and opportunity.

Work non-Christians into your schedule.

Don't make spending time with non-Christians harder than it is. You don't have to take time out of your schedule. Just work them into your schedule. Look at everything you do from building a backyard fence to playing a backyard game—everything from work to leisure. Then ask, "Can I do this, or enjoy this, with a non-Christian?" If non-Christians are not part of our lives, it's not because there is not a place for them. Christian speakers do things most people do, all of which provide opportunities to interact with non-Christians.

Speakers eat. If they are not careful, they eat too much! Restaurants can provide an opportunity for meaningful and, at times, extended discussions with unbelievers. Treating non-Christians to a meal can demonstrate appreciation for them and provide opportunities for the gospel. Even when dining with believers, unexpected things may happen. Tammy and I, along with some Christian friends, were enjoying dinner at a Mexican restaurant in Dallas. We noticed our waiter was wearing a WWJD (What Would Jesus Do?) bracelet. We also noticed that when he brought the ticket for our meal he had drawn the Christian icthus sign next to his name. When he came to collect our money, I said, "We noticed your WWJD bracelet and the fish symbol. Are you a Christian?" When he said, "Yes," I asked, "When did you become a Christian?" He answered, "I've been one since birth." I told him I was in the ministry and gave him a copy of our *May I Ask You a Question?* tract explaining that it had been a tremendous help to many. I then said, "Let me ask you a question. If you were to stand before God and He were to ask you, 'Why should I let you into heaven?' what would you tell Him?" He answered, "I don't know what I'd say because I haven't been to church very much." Because he was in a rush to take care of other people, there was no opportunity to talk. But I urged him to read the booklet, assuring him he could know for certain he was going to heaven and that it had nothing to do with going to church. Eating at restaurants where non-Christians work affords opportunity.

Christian speakers also get their hair cut, cars repaired, shirts laundered, and appliances repaired. All provide opportunities to interact with non-Christians. I'll go extra miles to do business with non-Christians when it offers an opportunity for the gospel. Years ago when Tammy and I moved to our present suburb, we wanted a hair stylist within a short distance of the house—as long as she or he was a non-Christian. We found Melanie, a great hair stylist. Tammy and I both interacted with her on separate occasions. We could sense she did not know where she was spiritually and did not understand the gospel of grace. The contact began a relationship out of which Tammy invited her to lunch. There at the lunch table she explained to Melanie the message of grace and salvation through Christ alone, and Melanie trusted Christ. If you walk into her hair salon today and ask, "If you stood before God and He were to ask you, 'Why should I let you into heaven?' what would you say?" she would probably answer, "How do you know Larry and Tammy Moyer?"

I could supplement this concept with stories about the many opportunities we've had with home repair specialists, car mechanics, dry-cleaning personnel, service station attendants, and grocery store clerks. The confused answers they give when asked about spiritual things clearly show the way non-Christians think. As they try to earn approval with their friends, they likewise try to earn approval with God.

Speakers also need to unwind. Being a lover of the outdoors, I like to unwind by going hunting. I have had the opportunity to share the gospel while hunting with a non-Christian. On what used to be my dad's farm in Pennsylvania, I was walking along the edge of a meadow when I met another hunter. Not having met me, and concerned I might be a trespasser, he asked if I had permission to hunt there. When I replied, "Yes," he asked, "Are you Larry Moyer?" The present owner had told him I had permission to hunt the farm. As we talked, I learned he knew I was a preacher. He began to discuss spiritual struggles he was having. I asked, "Do you feel like you've come to a point in your life where you know you're going to heaven?" Although he hesitated, he responded positively. That allowed me to share the simplicity and freeness of the gospel. It also started a relationship. "If you are up here and want someone to drive with you to a speaking engagement, could I do that?" he asked. Sometimes God adds opportunity upon opportunity. Months later I called him and invited him to ride with me to Virginia where I was speaking. As a result of that trip, and him listening as I trained believers in evangelism, he trusted Christ. If you spoke to him today, he'd tell you that he had never understood the gospel. As he told me, "I never knew you had to trust a person—Christ—to save you."

What did being with that former non-Christian teach me? It allowed me, out of experience, to say to unbelievers, "Sometimes we tell people we know we are going to heaven but in our hearts we aren't certain." Many unbelievers can identify.

Even the hardships of life give opportunity for the gospel. Years ago, I was driving to the office when a car passed me illegally on the right causing a collision. Fortunately, no one was hurt but there was severe damage to the right front end of my car. I had my car fixed at a friend's body shop in a neighboring town. When it was fixed, the owner of the body shop had Paul, one of his employees, return my car to my office and pick up the loaner he gave me. When Paul walked into the office, I was on a long-distance call. He asked my assistant, "What do y'all do here anyway?" She responded, "It's a Christian ministry. Would you like to hear more about it?" He answered, "No." When I got off the phone, he wanted me to examine the car before he left. As we circled the car, I referred to the good job they did. Then he asked, "Are you a minister or preacher?" I said, "Yes." He said, "Man, I've got to talk to someone. I've got to get my life straightened out." I said, "Do you have time to talk right now?" He answered, "Probably not." I said, "Let me get you one of our *May I Ask You a Question?* booklets." I went inside to get it, and when I returned he seemed more responsive. I asked, "Why don't we go inside and talk for a few moments if you have time?" Even though he'd previously said he didn't have time, he suddenly seemed eager to talk.

When we sat down in my office, he told me that twenty years earlier his wife and child were killed in a car accident. He'd only been to church twice since. "You know who I blame?" he asked. "Yes," I said, "You blame God." Over time, he'd gotten over some of his bitterness. He had remarried, but that marriage fell apart and he said that he never wanted to marry again. I told him how hard it was for my father when my brother died, and I mentioned how hard it must have been to part with a child and a wife. I also explained that my father-in-law had been killed in a car accident. I then said, "Many times God uses all those situations, and through the pain, He brings us to Himself." The most important thing of all is that we know for sure we're going to heaven. He said, "I would sure love to know that." I asked, "Well, what do you think you have to do to get to heaven?" He answered, "Well, be good, be kind, that sort of thing." Then he said, "For example, if I'm driving down the road and I see a turtle cross the road, I have to stop and help the turtle cross the road so it won't be hurt. That's the kind of person I am." I laughed on the inside, but said, "I commend you for your kindness toward turtles, but I need to tell you that God will not accept that as a basis for entrance into heaven." He said, "I was afraid you were going to say that."

I went through EvanTell's *Bad News/Good News* presentation of the gospel and we interacted all the way through the tract. At the end, he confessed he'd never understood that before. I then asked if he would like to pray right then and tell God he was trusting Christ as his Savior. He said, "Yes." There in my office he trusted Christ. I heard later from his boss about the differences he saw in Paul's life.

We learn from life's experiences. Experiences like these teach me the way non-Christians think and talk. They look at the smallest thing they've done (even if it's helping a turtle cross the road) as an opportunity to earn favor with God. They blame God for the hardships of life, but rarely credit Him for the good things. Spending an hour with a non-Christian is informative and is even used of God to develop a compassion for them. Hopefully they come to Christ, but even if they don't, they have helped you know them better and understand them more.

An advantage some speakers have is they often fly to their speaking engagements. Airplanes offer great opportunities to interact with non-Christians. Perhaps the fear of flying makes people approachable about spiritual things, or maybe they just feel the need to be friendly to a fellow passenger. Anyone who flies, who is evangelistic, will tell you of great opportunities they've had.

Once on the way back from New Jersey, I sat next to a thirty-eight-year-old man who was about to get out of the army. He asked me what I did. I answered, "I'm a speaker. I'm in the ministry." He said twice, "That is super." We got to talking, and I asked if he had any type of church background. He said he was a member of a Baptist church. I then asked, "When did you come to know the Lord?" He shook his head and said, "I don't think I have." As we proceeded to talk, he mentioned he'd just recently confessed to his wife that he'd been unfaithful to her while stationed overseas. He was remorseful and appreciated the fact that she wanted to make the marriage work. When he told her of his infidelity, she confessed to him that she'd been unfaithful to him ten years earlier, something he never knew. It was obvious how much it meant to him that not only could she forgive him, but also that he could forgive her, and that their marriage could be saved. As I talked with him, I said, "Your wife has forgiven you. It's obvious you have forgiven yourself. What about God? Do you know for certain that He has forgiven you?" He paused and then said, "I think so." I said, "God doesn't want you to think you've been forgiven. He wants you to know. He wants you to know beyond any doubt that when you die you'll go straight to heaven. Let me show you four verses in the Bible that will help you understand." I went through our *Bad News/Good News* method, but I could tell he wasn't tracking with me. I continued to explain it, and the light came on. He confessed he'd never understood the gospel. There on the plane, he trusted Christ. I questioned him to make sure he understood it and showed him the promise of John 5:24.

Since guilt is where so many non-Christians live, being around them reminds us what they are thinking. At the same time, as we ask God to do so, He develops in us a heart of compassion toward them.

Conclusion

Evangelistic speaking does not start in the study. It starts on the sidewalks and streets of life. To speak to non-Christians, we must know what non-Christians are like—how they think, how they talk, and what they talk about. Regardless of where we serve, opportunities abound to have contacts and conversations with non-Christians. Once we get to know our audience, we can then effectively speak to them.

REFLECTING...

1. Why do we need to know non-Christians in order to speak effectively to them?

2. What are the three things about non-Christians we need to know?

3. What was the first thing Christ taught His disciples?

4. In what ways do we make spending time with non-Christians harder than it needs to be?

5. What are ways you can work non-Christians into *your* schedule?

Chapter 9

When Are Good Times to Present an Evangelistic Message?

THE HAILSTORM STRUCK. BROKEN tree branches. Downed power lines. Damaged roofs. Everyone was discouraged. Except my friend. He makes his living as a roofer. Being a very caring person, he doesn't wish anyone to suffer. But bad weather keeps his business alive. If there were no damaged roofs, there would be less need for his service.

Every profession has its opportunities. Shopping malls capitalize on Christmas. Plumbers prepare to be extra busy as the temperature drops to zero and pipes freeze and burst. Contractors love to hear about the zoning of new subdivisions.

Evangelistic speakers are no exception. They too have their opportunities. In fact, the apostle Paul prayed for them. He requested that God might grant him a door for the Word (Col. 4:3). As a prisoner of the Roman Empire, he was probably handcuffed to a Roman soldier twenty-four hours a day. Undoubtedly, he had a chance to share Christ with those soldiers. Although he was their captive—handcuffed to a soldier—he also had a captive audience. At the same time, he did not want to be limited by the walls of a prison. He wanted to make it known to everyone that Christ's death on the cross was the only basis for a right standing with God. To that end, he prayed for a door for the Word.

Speakers who desire to speak evangelistically also need those doors of opportunity. Sometimes they come in expected ways; other times they are unexpected. What doors does God open for evangelistic speakers?

Holidays: When non-Christians are more attentive to spiritual things

One opportunity for speakers comes during holidays when non-Christians are more likely to attend church. The two that come to mind are Easter and Christmas. On these two holidays, non-believers tend to be more God-conscious and sensitive to spiritual things.

If you are a minister, you may be frustrated that, for many, Easter is the only time you see them. However, this is not a time to be sarcastic, like the pastor who said, "Let me take this opportunity to wish many of you a Merry Christmas. It's unlikely I'll see you again before then." Instead of seeing the day as a frustration, view it as an opportunity. Those who come to church only at Easter don't need to be made to feel guilty. They probably already do. Otherwise, it's unlikely they'd be there. Even if they are attending out of guilt, or some other reason, they have a certain reverence for the day and the Person it represents. You should use the opportunity to positively and gracefully explain the message behind the empty tomb.

Christmas affords the same opportunity. Some churches have found Christmas Eve even more effective than the Sunday closest to Christmas. It's easy to understand why. Put yourself in the shoes of a non-Christian. You somehow sense that you need to bring God into your holiday celebrations. The Sunday closest to Christmas may be difficult. Isn't Sunday morning the morning to sleep in? For others, the Sunday closest to Christmas may be a day for traveling.

Christmas Eve offers a solution. After all, the excitement of the next day will probably make sleep difficult anyway. I've observed churches that had double or even triple their normal Sunday morning attendance at a Christmas Eve service. This service is a wonderful time to be creative. Use drama and let variety spice the service. Put the entire program together with non-Christians in mind. The speaker's message should be no more than thirty minutes in length. By God's grace, you will have people realize that on the first Christmas, Christ came to them; on this Christmas, they can come to Christ. As Christmas morning approaches, instead of being excited about what is under the tree, they can be excited about the One who made the tree. A Christmas Eve service affords us the opportunity to ask non-Christians, "Why experience Christmas one day a year when through Christ you can experience it every day?"

Holidays and special events: Times when non-Christians can be encouraged to attend

Christmas and Easter are two obvious holidays for reaching out to unbelievers. There are others. Consider Mother's Day or Father's Day. Non-Christians who won't do anything for a relative any other day of the year will do something on Mother's Day or Father's Day. I've spoken on those holidays. One Father's Day, for example, a father said to his son, "Do you know what is the best Father's Day gift you could give me? Just come with me to my church this Sunday and then let me treat you to dinner afterward. That would be the best Father's Day gift I could receive." Imagine the impact an evangelistic message can have on such a day. These are times when relatives may not only come to church, they may even come to Christ.

New Year's Eve presents another opportunity. What week of the year is normally one of the more difficult for non-Christians? Counselors tell us that for many it's the week between Christmas and New Year's Day. With partying and gift giving over, non-Christians often ponder, "What's left?" Strained family relations, or the separation by death of loved ones, can make the holiday season painfully lonely. Still others experience the remorse of overspending. These and other scenarios can lead to acute feelings of aloneness and depression. They want the New Year to be different. They make New Year's resolutions. A New Year's Eve service presents the opportunity to tell them that the key to a different new year is not a resolution but a relationship. Why not start the new year by introducing them to the best friend they will ever have?

In addition to holidays are special events. High school graduation is a time for celebration. The people in our churches have influenced our teens. The teenagers have influenced them. Celebrate the momentous occasion as they leave high school and begin college or a career. Most non-Christian parents and grandparents are willing to attend a service where their child or grandchild is being honored. After all, it's not the church's teenager; it's *their* teenager—flesh of their flesh and bone of their bone. By saying a good word about their teenager, we build a bridge to say a great word about Christ.

What might we do? One possibility is to have a teenager give a testimony about how she came to know the Savior. It's important that the testimony be carefully written and given privately beforehand. A well-prepared testimony explains what life was like before meeting Christ, how she came to know Christ, and how her life is different with Christ. We then can follow that testimony with an expository message that promises God's guidance as we walk with Him and obey Him. It's not only an encouraging and needed word for the graduating teens, it's also an opportunity to say to all, "Before we can walk with Him and obey Him, it's essential to know Him. So could I take this opportunity to ask everyone here, 'Have you come to a point in your life that you know if you were to die you'd go to heaven?'" Then give a clear presentation of the gospel inviting those who don't know Christ to trust Him.

Baptismal services provide another opportunity. Baptism may mean little or nothing to non-Christians. But if their friend is a believer and is being baptized, the relationship may mean enough for a non-Christian to attend. I've witnessed occasions when a believer said to a friend, "I'm going to be baptized tonight at my church. It would mean a lot to me if you came to see me baptized." The friend attended out of respect for the relationship, not out of an interest in spiritual things. The point is, he or she was there. Many baptisms include special verses from Scripture that are significant to the person being baptized but speak to the unbelievers as well. Often the question is asked about who they are placing their faith in. Other services provide some time for each person being baptized to give a brief testimony. The relationship between friends can make the service much more inviting to the non-Christians.

Most non-Christians view baptism as an entrance requirement for heaven. What an opportunity to explain the opposite—that eternal life is never conditioned on baptism. Instead, it's a gift, because the price has already been paid by a Savior who died as our substitute. Going into the water does not make a person a Christian. Trusting Christ does.

The more direct we are, the better. It is appropriate to say, "If you are here and do not know for sure that you are going to heaven, please understand, baptism is an outward sign of an inward decision. Being baptized does not get you to heaven. Instead, if you are here today and do not have a personal relationship with Jesus Christ, we are encouraging you to trust Christ. He who died for you and rose again is the only way to heaven."

Weddings present opportunities as well. Perhaps a Christian couple is burdened for non-Christian relatives. They want unbelievers to know something greater than the joy of a wedding; they want them to know the joy of the Lord. An evangelistic message that explains how the couple came to Christ can invite others to come to the Savior.

Another suggestion, but one that involves sadness, is funerals. This difficult time must be handled with sensitivity. Nevertheless, when handled properly, funerals present an opportunity for the gospel. Those who attend a funeral are grieving the loss of a loved one. But there is not a person there who is not thinking of their own mortality. They are aware that sooner than they think, others may be attending their funeral.

If the deceased is a believer, it's a time for praise and celebration. Deceased believers have graduated to a better place where they are experiencing the greatest happiness they've ever known. They are living life in God's presence. God wants everyone in the audience to one day join them. That allows the speaker to pose the question, "What do you have to do to get to heaven?" We might begin by talking about what doesn't get you to heaven—being a good or moral person, church attendance, baptism, keeping the commandments, or taking the sacraments. If the person who died was a fervent believer who did all those, you might even commend her for that. Then explain, "But if she were alive today, she would tell you that these are not why she's in His presence. She's there because of something she understood and wants all of us to know." Then give a clear presentation of the gospel, explaining the free gift of salvation.

What if the person did not know the Lord? How can we speak with truth and grace? We cannot give false hope. The person may have died without trusting Christ; then again, on his deathbed something could have happened that we will find out about in eternity. We don't know. But think about it. Like the rich man who died and wanted to warn his relatives about hell (Luke 16), the deceased who died without Christ would want his relatives and friends to know of their need for Christ. So a speaker can say, "I have an obligation this morning. It's an obligation before God and before the one whose life we are remembering and honoring. It's an obligation to say what I feel God and (the deceased) would want me to say. I believe God and (the deceased) would want you to know the most important truths of the Bible. They're often called the bad news and the good news." Then you might even use EvanTell's *Bad News/Good News* approach to present a clear presentation of the gospel. I have been encouraged over the years by church leaders and lay people who have told me they have done just that at a funeral.

While some come to Christ at funerals, more people come to Christ in the days, weeks, or months *after* funerals. I believe the reason is that funerals are emotionally difficult. Grief can be enormous. In fact, in dealing with people who come to Christ at funerals, we have to be careful to be certain they are doing it out of conviction, not out of emotion. It's after the grief subsides that they reflect even more on the message given at the memorial service. That's why a speaker who communicates in a truthful but caring way often has an opportunity later to lead people to Christ. Numerous non-Christians have said things to me such as, "I attended the funeral of a friend of mine. It really made me start thinking."

Presenting a series surrounding needs non-Christians have

Pastors who carefully think through their year often prepare a preaching calendar. As the year progresses, they may make some changes. It's something they direct; it doesn't direct them. A preaching calendar enables them to plan not just a single message but a *series* of messages. A series allows one to think of needs Christians and non-Christians alike have. The pastor can also decide if, at particular points in the series, he should deliver the message or invite a gifted lay person to do so.

For example, consider a series on the family. A series such as "The Home: Castle or Chaos" enables us to speak about relationships, husbands, wives, children, and forgiveness. The list is almost endless and yet centers on the relationships most important in our lives. How does such a series reach out to non-Christians? In order to be the family they were created to be, they need to know the One who started the family. The originator of the family is the One who best knows how to make it work. So what does His Word have to say about knowing Him and living for Him in the home?

Another subject that concerns non-Christians as well as Christians is money. Some have named it the number one cause of domestic unhappiness. It's been observed that some spend so much time trying to make a killing they forget to make a living. A series titled, "How to Manage Money Instead of Letting Money Manage You" speaks to a real need in the area of finances. It also provides the opportunity to explain that what matters to God is not what you have but who you know. By reaching out to non-Christians on the temporal issue of money, you can speak to them about the eternal issue of their relationship with God.

Loneliness. There's another need—the need for a friend. It has been noted that in one year the average person today meets more people than people did in an entire lifetime one hundred years ago. Yet loneliness today is a problem for many. There's a big difference between being lonely and being alone. The presence of other people doesn't necessarily solve loneliness. A person of considerable means stated, "I have found that when you have the big house, the four cars, the country club, and the enormous overhead, there is still that awful loneliness." Each person needs to know that the worst loneliness there is, is not being separated from a friend but being separated from the Friend of sinners. Sin is the cause; salvation is the cure. Once we have a relationship with Him, we have someone who is there in our loneliest moments. Salvation becomes the bridge to our most important relationship.

The list of needs to address is long: peace of mind, living after divorce, coping with disappointment and discouragement, finding hope in a hopeless society, living a purposeful life. Those issues, properly handled through an expository evangelistic message, allow us to point non-Christians to the One who knows our even greater relational needs because He's the One who created us. Because God created us, He knows how to help us. Best of all, He knows how to save us. It also allows us to explain to non-Christians, "When Christ is all you have, you discover Christ is all you need."

When confronted with a crisis or emergency that attracts local or national attention

Recall the crises and emergencies that have faced our country over the past fifty years. The most recent come to the forefront and the most distant ones fade, but they are still memorable. The cyclone that hit Myanmar and the earthquake that struck in China in 2008. The disastrous hurricanes of 2005. The devastating tsunami in Southeast Asia in 2004. The horrendous September 11 attack on America in 2001 and the resulting wars in Iraq and Afghanistan. The hostage crisis in Iran. The explosions and loss of the space shuttles Challenger and Columbia and their crews. The attempted assassination of Ronald Reagan and the assassination of John F. Kennedy. Unbelievers look at these events and want to know, "What does God have to say about this? How does God feel? Why didn't God prevent it? Does God really care?" Because clergy represent God to some lost people, tragedy can be an opportunity for the Lord.

Sometimes events are national in scope and grip every neighborhood in the same way. Other times they are local. News reports once told of a hunter in Wisconsin who gunned down six other hunters as they approached his deer stand, complaining they were trespassing. In that area, the news was so gripping that residents could concentrate on nothing else. Although people in Dallas, Texas, were concerned, it did not grip them with the same intensity. A sensitive speaker has to answer the question, "Is this of such importance to my audience that I should set aside what I was going to speak on and speak on this instead? Should I miss this opportunity?"

A speaker does not need to have an answer for every crisis. He can't. Even the Bible, from which he's giving an expository evangelistic message, doesn't contain all the answers. It has been well said, "When we go through hard times, God doesn't promise answers. He promises Himself." An expository evangelistic speaker might not be able to provide an answer, but he can say whatever the Bible says, provide the comfort the Bible provides, and point people to a loving and caring God. We do not know why such tragedies occur, but God cared enough to take our place on a cross. There is no doubt He loves us. Despite all the things He allows, the cross says in the loudest way possible, "I love you! I love you! I love you! I love you!"

It is helpful in addressing tragedy to recall how Christ viewed current events of His time. When someone told Jesus about Galileans whose blood Pilate had mingled with their sacrifices, Jesus said,

> "Do you suppose that these Galileans were worse sinners than all other Galileans, because they suffered such things? I tell you, no; but unless you repent you will all likewise perish. Or those eighteen on whom the tower of Siloam fell and killed them, do you think that they were worse sinners than all other men who dwelt in Jerusalem? I tell you, no; but unless you repent you will all likewise perish." (Luke 13:2–5)

In the first event, pilgrims from Galilee had come to Jerusalem for one of the feasts. As they presented their offerings, Pontius Pilate murdered them. Jewish blood was mingled with that of the slaughtered beasts. Imagine something so cruel and grotesque. The second event was a national tragedy as opposed to a violent act. A tower in Siloam fell, killing eighteen people. Jesus' point was that being killed or not being killed was no measure of a person's righteousness. "Unless you repent you will all likewise perish." By "perish" He possibly had in mind the forthcoming fall of Jerusalem, not to an eternal hell.

Christ was using current events to relate biblical truth. That's a model worthy of repeating. Crisis and emergencies that attract local and national attention can be effectively used to reach out to non-Christians.

What if the crisis or emergency takes place on Saturday with little time to prepare? It's far better to step into the pulpit on Sunday with little preparation than to ignore something so heavy on the minds of non-Christians. Take the opportunity to speak to the issue. Churches immediately after the September 11, 2001, tragedy experienced a windfall in attendance. Countless non-Christians sensed something was terribly wrong. The magnitude of the tragedy surfaced deep fears. Their security had been threatened. People were looking for assurance and comfort. In such times, a church leader should rise to the moment and introduce people to the God of all comfort. The importance of eternal security and the assurance of knowing Christ and the reality we would be with Him forever. What an opportunity to explain to non-Christians, "The time to know Christ and be certain of our relationship with Him is not tomorrow, it's today!"

When confronted with a moral issue

Moral issues and questions also provide an opportunity to speak. Abortion—is the destruction of a fetus murder? What about rape? Is abortion acceptable when a woman becomes the victim of an immoral and violent act? Homosexuality—didn't God make people with their sexual preferences? Why be judgmental of those whose desired partner is of the same sex? Euthanasia—if a person wants to die, aren't we doing her a favor by helping her? Why prolong his agony instead of assisting him in ending it? Capital punishment—isn't "an eye for an eye and a tooth for a tooth" an Old Testament principle, not a New Testament one? Where does forgiveness fit in? If a person takes a life, are we necessarily right in taking his or hers?

We have to speak with truth about all those issues even though the truth may be unpopular or even offensive. The apostle Paul said, "For if I still pleased men, I would not be a bondservant of Christ" (Gal. 1:10). Christ was noted for, and we must also speak with, truth and grace (John 1:14). We do so by reminding the audience that to God, sin is sin. The way we feel about homosexuality in particular is the way God feels about our sin in general. Such issues therefore give us opportunity to say, "Sin is offensive to God—whether it's immorality or an unkind word or thought." We dare not say "They are sinners." We must conclude that we are sinners, and that sin, whatever it is, was paid for by Christ on a cross. In so doing, we have spoken not only with truth but also with grace.

An expository evangelistic message on these issues might bring those involved to Christ. What often happens, though, is that it brings others to

Christ with different issues because they heard a message that deals with the seriousness of sin and the forgiveness and salvation God offers. One pastor had about twenty homosexuals attending his church as he spoke lovingly and courageously on the issue of homosexuality. He told me, "We saw a few come to Christ. But we saw a number of others come to Christ who were not practicing homosexuals. They saw their own sin as being as serious before God as anyone else's."

When confronted with a religious issue

Some issues are religious rather than moral in nature, such as an issue involving a cult. Years ago, David Koresh attracted national attention as he herded his followers together in Waco, Texas, as officers from the Bureau of Alcohol, Tobacco, and Firearms surrounded them. The death of women and children left unanswered questions. Who was in the right? Did the government handle the situation properly? What was the truth about what was said and what wasn't said? Were the people there of their own free will or were they David Koresh's hostages? Where does religious freedom begin and end?

Two movies, *The Passion of the Christ* and *The Da Vinci Code*, afforded great opportunities for evangelism. The first supported the biblical picture of Christ while the second opposed it. Both allowed us to say, "Here is what the Bible says."

Other relevant topics are religion and politics, the separation of church and state, and the sin and hypocrisy of televangelists. Even the term "born again" can become a religious issue when it's used of a prominent person in spreading his faith. How do we use the term, and what does the Bible mean by it?

When do we state, "This is right and this is wrong?" Only when the Scriptures say so. Often issues become so convoluted that doing so becomes difficult. But when we address religious and moral questions as accurately as we can, we present ourselves as a people current with our times and relevant to our audience. It also gives us the opportunity to say, "Here's what we don't know from the Bible, but here's what we do know." These issues give us the opportunity to say, "Before we focus on others, before we focus on society, we must step up to the mirror and look at ourselves." Don't start with the question, "Where do they stand before God." Instead, start with the question, "Where do I stand before God?" A clear presentation of the gospel can then turn someone from an outward focus to an inward focus, and ultimately to a relationship with God.

Conclusion

Doors of opportunity could be holidays, special events, particular needs, crises, and moral or religious issues. Some are expected; others are unexpected. All have one thing in common: They present natural opportunities to speak to an issue with eternal consequences. Directing an audience from what we know to Whom they *need* to know is the greatest favor we can do for them.

REFLECTING...

1. Name four good opportunities to present an evangelistic message.

2. What are three holidays or special events when non-Christians can be encouraged to attend?

3. What three needs do non-Christians have that we could address through a single message or a series of messages and use to bring an evangelistic message?

4. What insight does Christ's use of current events (Luke 13) provide as to how we can use current events to speak evangelistically?

5. What are two moral or religious issues our society has faced within the past year that could be addressed through an evangelistic message?

Chapter 10

What Are False Assumptions to Be Avoided?

PAUL HARVEY ONCE REPORTED an interesting thing that happened years ago during the America's Cup competition in Australia. The Italian team went to the outback on their day off to see if they could find a kangaroo in the wild. They had been outfitted by the designer Gucci with jackets, wallets, and luggage. Near the end of their search, much to their surprise, a kangaroo jumped out of the brush and was struck by their jeep. As the kangaroo lay there, presumably dead, an idea struck them. They put the driver's jacket on the animal and took a picture of a Gucci-clad kangaroo. As they prepared to snap the picture, the kangaroo, which had only been stunned, jumped up and hopped into the brush wearing the jacket. You can imagine the driver's regret when he remembered that his keys and wallet were in the jacket.[1] Assuming the animal was dead proved to be costly.

False assumptions can be costly in the speaking world as well. At the least, a wrong assumption hinders our communication; at worst it can cost us our audience.

In expository evangelistic speaking there are things we cannot assume. Some are due to the nature of the audience—unbelievers. Some are due to the very nature of expository evangelistic speaking.

Don't assume their interest.

Don't assume that your audience is eager to be there or that listening to you is high on their priority list. They may be present because a friend pressured them to come. Therefore, everything from your first comments to the introduction of your message must gain that person's attention.

To communicate, we must connect. Unbelievers aren't coming to hear us with the same level of interest as a believer who is eager to hear what the Word says and believes that we have something that will help them.

Therefore, the first words out of our mouths are crucial. The non-Christians may not have intended to come to a service or event. Therefore, one of our goals must be to make them glad they did. We'll discuss later how to effectively make your first words meaningful and attention grabbing. Understanding the significance of gaining the interest of our audience makes us better speakers to anyone anywhere. The better we are at speaking to non-Christians, the better we are as a speaker to Christians, too. If we develop a pattern of stepping before people and gaining their attention instead of assuming it, we've developed a good habit.

Don't assume your listeners have a knowledge of the Bible.

A second thing we cannot assume about our listeners is that they have a knowledge of the Bible. In fact, we cannot even assume they can locate a particular passage in the Scriptures. As an expositor, I want my audience to leave knowing where God said what I am just repeating. Chances are, they do not have a Bible and, even if they do, it is doubtful they know how to find a particular book. Warren and David Wiersbe, in *The Elements of Preaching*, comment, "Most of the people who listen to us preach don't spend many hours in Bible reading or Bible study. Some, unfortunately, never pick up the Bible from one Sunday to another. Young believers have a difficult time finding the different books of the Bible."[2]

Solving this problem is not difficult. Address the audience and say, "If you don't have a Bible with you, may I encourage you to look on with someone sitting near you. If a husband and wife here have two Bibles, would you be so thoughtful as to glance around and, if you see someone without a Bible, share one of yours with them?" That way, Christians can look around and see if anyone needs a Bible without appearing "holier than thou." And non-Christians without a Bible are free to look at someone else's without feeling embarrassed.

However, keep in mind that even when someone loans them a Bible, they still might not know where to find the passage we are speaking from. In speaking to Christians, we can say, "Turn to John 20:24." To a non-Christian audience, we have to say, "Once you have the Bible in front of you, turn to the back part. That's called the New Testament. Now turn to the fourth book. That's called John. Now turn to chapter 20 and verse 24." In so doing, we've told them how to find the right part of their Bible, the right book, the right chapter, and the right verse. If there are Bibles at their seat, which is always preferable, we can direct them to the page number. Another possibility is to reproduce the passage and hand it to them as they walk into the auditorium.

New believers have told me that prior to coming to Christ they didn't know the Bible had a table of contents with the books and page numbers listed. Nor did they know what the colon in a verse reference meant, such as when one refers to Romans 5:1. It is imperative to keep in mind our audience is non-Christians and they won't know the Bible. Even Christian audiences will have varying levels of familiarity with it.

The audience's lack of Bible knowledge affects us in other ways. For example, once I direct them to the passage I am speaking from, I stay there. I have found it time-consuming and a hindrance in communication to have the audience turn to a second passage. If I make reference to another passage, I choose to explain it instead of having them turn to it.

Referring to a supportive passage may be helpful, but remember the point I just stressed—you need to explain it and not assume your audience understands. I once heard an evangelistic speaker remark, "Remember Nicodemus in the Bible. Remember the woman at the well. Christ told them both that He was the only One who could give them eternal life." I assure you that a large number of non-Christians in his audience did not have the slightest idea of who he meant by Nicodemus or the woman at the well. If we refer to Bible characters, we have to give a synopsis of who they were. Mention some Old Testament story and there's a good chance, unless it's an obscure one, Christians have heard it fifty times. Non-Christians in the audience may not have heard it even once. In making a reference to the Garden of Eden, it's best to refer to the first man and woman God made instead of saying "When God made Adam and Eve." That way, even if they don't know their names, they will know who you mean. In directing your audience's attention to Joshua or Moses, it's helpful to describe them as "leaders frequently mentioned in the Old Testament" and then reference their names.

Don't assume their knowledge of Christian terminology.

It's equally important not to assume that unbelievers understand terms that Christians are familiar with. When we ask unbelievers to place their faith in Christ, we are asking them to trust in Christ alone as their only way to heaven. As Romans 5:1 teaches, "Therefore, having been justified by faith, we have peace with God through our Lord Jesus Christ." Unless the meaning of "faith" is explained, they may misunderstand. Misunderstandings can allow your listeners to define faith in their own terms. Faith to them may be living a God-honoring life or depending upon Him to meet their finances, provide their groceries, or keep their car running. They may feel that by following God and living a life of dependence upon Him, they can merit heaven. Ask some non-Christians, "Do you have faith in Christ?" They will respond, "Oh, yes, I couldn't get through life without Him." Ask that same person, "Do you know you're going to heaven?" They might say, "Well, I think so."

When we speak of the hope of eternal life, we are referring to the absolute certainty that when we die we will be in His presence. Hope to non-Christians may be "maybe I'll make it, maybe I won't." Ask them if they know they are going to heaven and they will frequently answer, "I'm working at it." Unless it's explained, the idea of eternal life being a gift with no strings attached might elude them. Don't assume they understand the "hope of eternal life."

Terms that Christians understand, non-Christians may not. We need to assume the need to explain every term. That way, if we err, we err on the side of clarity, leaving less room for misunderstanding. We don't want their misunderstanding to be the result of our not communicating.

Don't assume they accept your underlying presuppositions.

When I stand before a Christian audience, I can assume they are in agreement with some basic presuppositions about God, His Word, and life. That is not necessarily so with non-Christians. I saw a bumper sticker that read: "Life is hard but God is good." I would agree. Life can be very hard but indeed God is good. As I pondered that statement as an evangelist, though, I thought how quickly some non-Christians would disagree. They might say, "Life is hard and so is God." After all, isn't it God who allows babies to be born with deformities, allows adults to die at an early age, and stands by with His arms folded while terrorists destroy people by the thousands?

We call God forgiving, but, as one non-Christian told me, "I always pictured God with a big heavy bat ready to clobber me for everything wrong I'd done." Instead of God being a holy God who rewards righteousness and punishes iniquity, the non-Christian often concludes that He is a God who lets the righteous suffer and the wicked prosper. Bad people seem to fare better than good people. A believer's underlying presupposition might be that people who go to church are happier than those who don't go. The unbeliever's presupposition might have nothing to do with happiness. They may feel the reason Christians go to church is because God has given them a list of do's and don'ts. If they want to keep on His good side, they better be there whenever the doors are open.

This means that speakers must use whatever authority necessary to support their conclusions. That authority may be the Bible. God said it; that settles it. Depending on what conclusions I ask my audience to accept, though, it may be another source. If explaining the growth of crime in major cities across the United States, *U.S. News and World Report* might be our authority. Comments from the mayor of a city might give weight to our conclusion about family values. A story in the daily newspaper might support our conclusions about the callousness of the human heart.

Do not assume that stating a fact makes it a fact in your hearers' minds. Instead we must ask, "What support must I give to make what's believable to me, believable to them?"

Conclusion

False assumptions can be costly. How do we benefit as a speaker by not assuming people's interest, knowledge of the Bible, knowledge of Christian vocabulary, or acceptance of our underlying presuppositions? We make absolutely certain that we are speaking to their level. If our assumptions are unnecessary, we've lost nothing. But if our assumptions were necessary and ignored, we may lose our audience—an audience we are approaching with eternity in mind.

REFLECTING...

1. What are four things you should not assume when speaking to a non-Christian audience?

2. In what specific ways does your ability to speak effectively to non-Christians make you a better speaker to believers?

3. How is directing a non-Christian audience to a particular passage in the Bible different from directing a Christian audience to the same passage?

4. What are a few examples of Christian terminology that may be misunderstood by non-Christians?

5. What are a few examples of presuppositions that Christians accept but non-Christians may not?

Chapter 11

What Are Different Ways to Give an Evangelistic Message?

HAVE YOU EVER WATCHED an elephant at a circus? His foot is tied to an eighteen-inch stake. With little effort he could pull the stake out of the ground. I've been told, though, that the reason he doesn't try is that he tried it when he was a baby and was unsuccessful. So he's concluded that it can't be done. He has allowed his past limitations to control him.

Expository evangelistic speaking has its limitations. These limitations grow out of two problems. First, as mentioned earlier, an evangelistic message must tell people three things: 1) we are sinners; 2) Christ died for us and rose again; and 3) we must trust Christ. There are few passages of Scripture in which these three elements are discussed in the same passage. Second, the only book in the New Testament where the author states his purpose as being to tell you how to receive eternal life is the Gospel of John, which says, "But these are written that you may believe that Jesus is the Christ, the Son of God, and that believing you may have life in His name" (20:31). So how does one present an expository evangelistic message? The possibilities are not as limiting as you might think. There are different ways to pull the stake out of the ground and remain an expositor. Six possibilities allow us to be true to the text and relevant to a non-Christian audience.

Select passages from the book of John.

Let's begin with the obvious. That is, select verses or passages from the book of John. Since John's purpose in his book was to tell non-Christians how to receive eternal life, an expository evangelistic speaker is addressing the same audience as John. However, even in John some passages are easier to communicate to non-Christians than others, mostly due to the simplicity or complexity of the passage. It must continually be foremost in our minds that in evangelistic speaking, we are speaking to a non-Christian audience. I've found the following passages to be some of the easiest: John 1:11–13; 3:1–15; 3:16; 3:17–18; 4:5–29; 5:24; 6:35–40; 8:1–11; 10:7–18; 11:1–27; 14:1–6; 16:8–11; 20:24–29.

Select passages that remind believers of how they were saved.

A second possibility opens up many New Testament epistles to the expository evangelistic speaker. The epistles were not written to tell us how to enter the Christian life, although some passages do address the subject. Instead, they were written to tell us how to live it. However, since the author often reminds believers of how they were saved, we can use them to tell the audience how they too must be saved. For example, Paul wrote to several congregations in the province of Asia, where Ephesus was the capital. The first half of the book of Ephesians addresses doctrines central to the Christian faith. The latter half describes how these truths should be reflected in a believer's behavior.

Paul reminds believers of how they were saved. When they were dead in trespasses and sins, God, through His mercy and grace, saved them so that they might be proofs of His workmanship (Eph. 2:1–10). Therefore, as we speak from this passage, we might say, "By reminding the believers of how they were saved, Paul tells us how we too can be one hundred percent certain that we have eternal life." In so doing, we have not changed the purpose of the passage; instead, we have made it meaningful and relevant to non-Christians.

Another passage is Titus 3:3–5, where Paul presents the darkest picture of what we were—foolish, disobedient, deceived, serving various lusts and pleasures, living in malice and envy, hateful and hating one another. He then presented a radiant picture of who God is: "but when the kindness and the love of God our Savior toward man appeared . . ." This passage allows us to speak to a non-Christian audience about where all of us are before we come to Christ. The same kindness and love received by Titus's audience is available to us.

Also consider 1 Peter 3:18: "For Christ also suffered once for sins, the just for the unjust, that He might bring us to God, being put to death in the flesh but made alive by the Spirit." In addressing suffering, he reminded readers that it was better to suffer for doing good than for doing evil (1 Pet. 3:13–17). That became a bridge to explain that Christ understands suffering—because He too suffered. Peter explained, "For Christ also suffered once for sins, the just for the unjust, that He might bring us to God." What an opportunity to explain the gospel. One can raise the question, "Does Jesus Christ really understand suffering?" The answer is "Yes"—here's how and why.

Unlike the Gospel of John, the book of 1 John was not written to tell us how to receive eternal life. Instead, it was written to tell us how to get close to the One we came to—how to have fellowship with Him: "That which we have seen and heard we declare to you, that you may also have fellowship with us; and truly our fellowship is with the Father and with His Son Jesus Christ" (1 John 1:3). What does John beg us to do as we draw close to Him? One thing he mentions is that we are to love others as He has loved us. How was that love manifested? He answers in a way that allows us to easily and powerfully explain the gospel:

> In this the love of God was manifested toward us, that God has sent His only begotten Son into the world, that we might live through Him. In this is love, not that we loved God, but that He loved us and sent His Son to be the propitiation for our sins. (1 John 4:9–10)

This passage allows us to answer for non-Christians the question, "How does God demonstrate love?" In so doing, we can be true to the text and context and relevant to non-Christians.

Where is the gospel defined in the New Testament? Paul reminds the Corinthians of the gospel God declared to him (1 Cor. 15:1–8). He says, "I delivered to you . . . that which I also received" (v. 3). He then summarizes the gospel with four verbs:

> Christ *died* for our sins, according to the Scriptures.
> He was *buried*.
> He *rose* again the third day according to the Scriptures.
> He was *seen*.

Burial is proof that He died, and the fact that He was seen is proof He arose. So the gospel in its simplicity is this: Christ died for our sins and rose from the dead. Therefore, 1 Corinthians 15:1–8 answers the question, "What is the good news God has for anyone anywhere?" Once again we have taken a passage written to believers and made it relevant to a non-Christian audience.

Another possibility is Hebrews 9:27–28. The author of Hebrews explains the greatness of Christ's sacrifice over the sacrifices of the Old Testament. He then speaks of our problem and Christ's solution. We read, "And as it is appointed for men to die once, but after this the judgment, so Christ was offered once to bear the sins of many. To those who eagerly wait for Him He will appear a second time, apart from sin, for salvation." We have the opportunity to explain the gospel to non-Christians through a passage addressed to Christians.

As you speak through a series in a particular book, alert the audience beforehand. Encourage them to bring their non-Christian friends. Then explain that particular passage with non-Christians solely in mind.

Select passages that deal with a major soteriological doctrine.

A pastor friend of mine once said, "There's a dearth of truth in the church today." I agree. People need to be reminded of the truth they embraced when they came to Christ, so that "we should no longer be children, tossed to and fro and carried about with every wind of doctrine " (Eph. 4:14). Major doctrines can be presented in such a way that they are instructional to the believer and meaningful for the non-Christian. Let's consider four of these doctrines.

Justification

Through the substitutionary death and resurrection of His Son, God declares sinners 100 percent righteous the moment we trust Christ to save us. As sinners, we deserve to die. But God places our sins upon Christ and places Christ's righteousness on us. Through that imputed righteousness we stand as perfect before God as His own Son stands. Romans 4:5 says, "But to him who does not work but believes on Him who justifies the ungodly, his faith is accounted for righteousness." Romans 5:1 explains, "Therefore, having been justified by faith, we have peace with God through our Lord Jesus Christ."

Justification answers the question: How can a person stand perfect in the sight of God? If we explain justification by answering that question or using verses such as Romans 4:5 and 5:1, we present an evangelistic message to the unbeliever. At the same time, we instruct the believer. If we present that question before non-Christians, they are likely to think, "I did not know one *could* stand perfect before God." The question is intriguing, and the answer is simple and exciting.

Propitiation

A holy and righteous God was satisfied with His Son's death. Nothing else could have satisfied God's anger against our sin. Our good works, baptism, and keeping of the commandments were not sufficient. Furthermore, no sinner could satisfy God's anger against sin. A sinner cannot die for a sinner anymore than one murderer can die for another murderer. It took someone completely perfect. Jesus Christ was the only one who qualified. The moment His Son died, a holy God said, "I'm satisfied. I'll accept my Son's death as payment for their sins." First John 2:2 tells us, "And He Himself is the propitiation for our sins, and not for ours only but also for the whole world." So propitiation answers the question, "How can I be certain God is satisfied with me?" Explaining propitiation in a way non-Christians can understand it explains the depth of it to the believer as well.

Redemption

God delivered us from slavery to sin by the payment of His own blood. He had to crucify His Son when He should have crucified us.

Knowing that you were not redeemed with corruptible things, like silver or gold, from your aimless conduct received by tradition from your fathers, but with the precious blood of Christ, as of a lamb without blemish and without spot. (1 Pet. 1:18–19)

Redemption answers the question: "How much does it cost to be saved?" The answer is, "It cost God everything; it costs us nothing." Once again we have an opportunity to explain the gospel and appeal to non-Christians by teaching a major doctrine to believers.

Reconciliation

God took those who were His enemies and made it possible for them to be His friends. The apostle Paul explains God's reconciling work:

Now all things *are* of God, who has reconciled us to Himself through Jesus Christ, and has given us the ministry of reconciliation, that is, that God was in Christ reconciling the world to Himself, not imputing their trespasses to them, and has committed to us the word of reconciliation. Now then, we are ambassadors for Christ, as though God were pleading through us: we implore *you* on Christ's behalf, be reconciled to God. For He made Him who knew no sin *to be* sin for us, that we might become the righteousness of God in Him. (2 Cor. 5:18–21)

Reconciliation answers the question: "How do you get on God's good side?" This becomes a need-oriented question for non-Christians who know and feel they have wronged God. Explaining reconciliation will tell a non-Christian how to come into eternal relationship with God. It also teaches the believer an important doctrine about spiritual growth.

Believers need to be taught life-transforming doctrine. By teaching doctrine in a way that is interesting and relevant to unbelievers, we are able to increase the family of God as well as build up those who are already in it.

Select passages that answer specific questions non-Christians are asking.

Non-Christians have questions. The answers we offer them need to come from the Word. When we use the Scripture to answer these questions through an expository message, we introduce unbelievers to Christ. A secondary advantage is that believers learn how to respond to the questions non-Christians ask.

Question: "How do we know there is a God?" No text answers that better or more directly than Romans 1:20: "For since the creation of the world His invisible attributes are clearly seen, being understood by the things that are made, even His eternal power and Godhead, so that they are without excuse."

This verse does not merely say there is a God. It says there is a God Who has no equal: "even His eternal power and Godhead." One cannot look at creation and say, "There is a God," then point to an idol he has carved and say, "Here he is. I made him." Instead, he has to say, "God made me." Creation holds everyone accountable. An expository evangelistic message that answers the question, "How do we know there is a God?" can take a non-Christian from the creation to the Creator to Christ.

Question: "How can God condemn those who have never heard?" Two passages answer that question: Romans 1:18–20 and Romans 2:14–16. Two words summarize these passages: creation and conscience. If a person acknowledges through creation and conscience that there must be a God, will God respond? We know from Hebrews 11:6 that God is a rewarder of those who diligently seek Him. Cornelius, described in the book of Acts, is a good example. Cornelius was "a devout man and one who feared God with all his household, who gave alms generously to the people, and prayed to God always" (10:2). Through Peter, God honored Cornelius's seeking and brought him the message, "Whoever believes in Him will receive remission of sins" (v. 43). An expository evangelistic message on Romans 1:18–20 and 2:14–16 will answer a question non-Christians have and reach out to them with the gospel.

Select passages that answer questions of interest to non-Christians.

There are questions non-Christians ask openly. There are other questions that are not always voiced but are of *interest* to them. For example, many non-Christians are of the opinion that to get to heaven you have to keep the Ten Commandments. Most would admit, though, that nobody keeps them perfectly. This raises the question, "How many of the Ten Commandments do we have to keep to get to heaven?" An expositional message on Romans 3:20–23 answers that question. We learn that all have sinned and fallen short of the glory of God. The Ten Commandments can only tell us that we are sinners. They cannot do anything about it. "By the deeds of the law, no flesh will be justified in His sight" (Rom. 3:20). An expositional evangelistic message on this passage answers a question of interest to non-Christians.

Question: "What must I do to get to heaven?" Some non-Christians don't think about the hereafter, but many do. What better passage to address this question than the dramatic story of the Philippian jailer who met the Savior through Paul and Silas (Acts 16:25–34)? A non-Christian hearing such an expositional message can find deliverance from his own imprisonment in sin.

Some non-Christians are convinced that God loves people in general. Their question is, "Does He love *them*?" How can they be certain? Romans 5:6–8 answers that question. Paul addresses the issue of what has made possible God's all-sustaining grace that even allows us to glory in tribulation. He goes back to the cross and contrasts the people we would die for and the people He died for. We probably would not die for a righteous man—one who obeys the law. We respect such a man, but it is unlikely that we would die for him. We might die for a good man—someone who mows our yard or loans us his car while ours is in the repair shop. But Christ died for sinners. What we might do for the best, He did for the least. Since there is no one outside the purpose of His death, no one is outside the scope of His love. An expositional evangelistic message exclaims, "God loves *you*."

Question: "What does the Bible say about death?" This question is of interest to non-Christians because death is a moment everyone has to face. One passage that can address this question is Hebrews 2:14–15:

Inasmuch then as the children have partaken of flesh and blood, He Himself likewise shared in the same, that through death He might destroy him who had the power of death, that is, the devil, and release those who through fear of death were all their lifetime subject to bondage.

An evangelistic message on this passage allows us to present the bad news and good news about the event we all eventually will face.

Ask a non-Christian, "What word most characterizes your life?" Some might answer "guilt." They are plagued by all the places they wish they had never gone, all the people they wish they'd never met, all the words they wish they'd never said, all the things they wish they'd never done. They wonder, "How do I get rid of this guilt?"

When Peter explains forgiveness to Cornelius he gives a pertinent problem a personal answer (Acts 10:34–43). An expositional evangelistic message allows us to explain, "What God did for Cornelius, He can do for you."

There are questions that interest non-Christians even though they may not ask them. Those questions concern everything from guilt to the grave. Take a passage of Scripture that addresses those questions, handle it properly in context, and you are reaching out to unbelievers where they are.

Select passages that deal with objections non-Christians have.

What often hinders Christians in evangelism? They are afraid they cannot answer the questions and objections non-Christians have. Those objections often are not that difficult to answer. Sometimes the answer can come through an expositional message.

One caution. Our desire is to be an expositor. We are not presenting our own thoughts; we're presenting God's. Be careful not to say, "God wrote this passage to answer that objection." Most likely He didn't. Instead, present the passage in a way that says, "God wrote this passage to (explain the context)." Then say, "In so doing, He also addressed a struggle or objection many of us have to the Christian faith." That way, we have not twisted the passage out of context but have made it relevant to non-Christians.

Objection: *"But we are all going to the same place."* Years ago, a person said this to me about death: "I don't think you go anywhere. You just lie in the ground." That was the "same place" in his mind for all. The Bible is clear. We don't all go to the same place. There is either life with God or separation from God. The passage that allows you to explain that truth is Luke 16:19–31, the story of the rich man and Lazarus. Once again, preach the Bible in context. In context, Christ was addressing the covetousness of the Pharisees. So He tells a story about a rich man who in death had nothing and a poor man who in death had everything. We can use the objection, "But we are all going to the same place" in our introduction to draw non-Christians into the message. Then explain how Christ, through a story told to rebuke lovers of money, sheds light on that thought. The introduction would explain why non-Christians need to listen. The message would explain the text in its context.

Objection: *"I'm already a member of a church."* We can counter that objection through an expositional evangelistic message on Luke 18:9–14. A Pharisee directs God to his good deeds and religious achievements; a tax collector brings to God his repentance, his admission that he is a sinner. The context fits the unbeliever's objection beautifully, for Jesus "spoke this parable to some who trusted in themselves that they were righteous, and despised others" (v. 9). What an opportunity to explain through an expositional evangelistic message that the issue is not what we've done for Him but what He has done for us.

Objection: *"I'm too bad to be saved."* I heard this frequently the first time I spoke in Russia. Seventy years of atheism caused many to think they were too bad for God to save. I didn't have to tell them they needed to be saved; I had to assure them they *could* be saved. One passage of Scripture ideal for addressing this objection is 1 Timothy 1:15–16:

> This *is* a faithful saying and worthy of all acceptance, that Christ Jesus came into the world to save sinners, of whom I am chief. However, for this reason I obtained mercy, that in me first Jesus Christ might show all longsuffering, as a pattern to those who are going to believe on Him for everlasting life.

Through his own testimony, Paul assures his readers that God saved him to prove He can save anyone.

Objection: *"How can I possibly live the Christian life?"* Some non-Christians don't deny they need Christ. Their objection lies in the fear that they could not live the Christian life. We can address this with an expositional evangelistic message on Ephesians 2:8–10:

> For by grace you have been saved through faith, and that not of your-selves; it is the gift of God, not of works, lest anyone should boast. For we are His workmanship, created in Christ Jesus for good works, which God prepared beforehand that we should walk in them.

Good works are not something we do for God. They are something God performs through us. We can introduce the message with the idea that Christians and non-Christians have a similar struggle. Once we come to Christ we are to live like Christians, but we aren't sure we can do that. Paul reminded the people in Ephesus that we aren't saved by our good works. Instead salvation is a gift. But once we receive that gift, Paul explains how we can live the life God wants us to live. After the introduction, we can look at what Paul says about coming to Christ and then living for Christ.

Objection: *"I'm just not ready."* Any passage about the brevity of life and suddenness of death allows us to address the issue. One possibility is James 4:13–14:

> Come now, you who say, 'Today or tomorrow we will go to such and such a city, spend a year there, buy and sell, and make a profit; whereas you do not know what will happen tomorrow. For what is your life? It is even a vapor that appears for a little time and then vanishes away.

What is the passage saying? The one thing no one is promised is to-morrow. We have no more days to live than the days God gives us. So whatever agreement we want with God then has to be made now. Planning that leaves God out is foolish.

Objection: *"I'm too busy. I don't have time to think about all this right now."* No passage I know of purposefully addresses this objection. But it is addressed, and it's done so through a passage where Christ warns about the danger of covetousness (Luke 12:13–21). Christ is addressing an inheritance dispute. He weaves into His answer a parable about a farmer who in being careful about life became careless about God. Christ minced no words in calling him a fool. The passage makes the application clear that until one knows he is going to heaven, nothing else matters.

Objection: *"I'm doing the best I can. I live a good life."* What better text to answer this objection than Matthew 7:21–23:

> "Not everyone who says to Me, 'Lord, Lord,' shall enter the kingdom of heaven, but he who does the will of My Father in heaven. Many will say to Me in that day, 'Lord, Lord, have we not prophesied in Your name, cast out demons in Your name, and done many wonders in Your name?' And then I will declare to them, 'I never knew you; depart from Me, you who practice lawlessness!'"

In His Sermon on the Mount, Christ warned that becoming a Christian is not something we have to do but Someone we have to know. It's not doing something that gets us to heaven. It's trusting Someone. The "will of my Father" as it relates to eternal salvation is explained in John 6:40: "And this is the will of Him who sent Me, that everyone who sees the Son and believes in Him may have everlasting life; and I will raise him up at the last day." An expositional message from this passage explains that our best effort is not good enough. Eternal life is not found in something, but in Someone.

Conclusion

An expository evangelistic message is not as limiting as it may seem. Approaching a message through one of these six ways let's us be true to the text and relevant to the non-Christian. Some might address the issue through a front door, others a side door, and others a back door. But in every way, we are coming through the door of the Word—the door that God uses to bring people to Christ.

REFLECTING...

1. What are six ways of giving an expository evangelistic message?

2. If we use a passage addressed to believers to give an evangelistic message, what is important about the way we use that passage?

3. What two major doctrines can be made relevant to a non-Christian audience?

4. What are four questions non-Christians have that can be answered through an expository evangelistic message?

5. What are four objections non-Christians have that can be addressed through expository evangelistic speaking?

Chapter 12

How Do You Appeal to Unbelievers in a Non-Evangelistic Setting?

SUDDENLY THEY SHOW UP. Not uninvited but unexpected. Not just several people but several families. They are prepared to hear you. The problem is, you are not prepared to speak to them. Your whole message, start to finish, was prepared for believers, not unbelievers. If you're a pastor of a church growing through conversion, this experience should become more of a rule than an exception.

Not every message a pastor gives can be directed to non-Christians. If it were, he would have a church full of infant Christians—individuals who know how to enter the Christian life but never learn how to live it. At the same time, if believers have genuine relationships with non-Christians, there should be unbelievers frequenting the church service on a regular basis. Therefore, how does one appeal to non-Christians in a non-evangelistic setting such as a Sunday morning service where the message is directed toward believers, not unbelievers? Church leaders throughout the nation have found several ideas beneficial.

Appeal to them through your manner, not just your message in the pulpit.

It's not only what we say that appeals to non-Christians, it's how we say it. Even in a message directed to believers, how we say what we say can make an eternal difference.

We must be enthusiastic and excited about what we are saying. I heard an unbeliever say of a speaker, "I love to listen to him. He's so enthusiastic."

The speaker's enthusiasm caught the non-Christian's attention. If what we are saying excites us, the non-Christian gets the impression it may be something that he ought to understand too.

We must also be approachable. Remember, unbelievers often have deep hurts. They need to talk to someone. That someone might be you. As they listen they might think, "Can I talk with him? Would he keep what I say confidential? Can I be open with him?" Beyond what you say, they observe you as a person. If they are thinking, "He doesn't strike me as the kind of person I could talk to," we are not likely to appeal to them.

Beyond being approachable, we must be caring. "Do I really matter?" and "Does he really care?" are questions heavy on their minds. When a non-Christian responded to a message I preached in Montana, I expressed a desire to meet with him one on one. He said, "Would you mind if I spoke to the pastor? I've been coming here three Sundays and feel like I know him better." I did not take that as a negative reflection on me. (In fact, he even said, "Please understand, that's nothing against you.") I took it as a positive reflection on the pastor. I know the pastor well. This man was not the first person to say that of him. His caring demeanor appeals to unbelievers even when his message is to believers.

The message is not the only place to make an appeal.

Sometimes we need what Winston Churchill called "the genius to recognize the obvious." We overlook some of the simplest and most natural ways to make an appeal to non-Christians.

It can be done in the way we take up the morning offering. I heard a pastor say to his people, "In a moment we are going to take an offering for the expenses of the ministry. If you are visiting this morning, we request that you *not* place anything in it. Instead of giving a gift to the church, we'd like you to *receive* a gift Christ has for you. Jesus Christ paid for our sins on a cross by dying as our substitute, taking our punishment, and rising again the third day. Through personal trust in Christ, we can receive His gift of eternal life. Instead of giving, just sit and meditate upon what God would like to give you. Right here this morning you could receive that gift. Would the ushers please come to take up the offering?" I thought, "What a natural, honest, and direct way to make an appeal to non-Christians."

It can be done the way we *introduce* a passage of Scripture. For example, suppose we are speaking from 1 Corinthians. It would be both natural and effective to say, "I always enjoy speaking from the book of 1 Corinthians because the person God used to write this portion of Scripture was a man by the name of Paul. Prior to coming to know Christ, Paul called himself a blasphemer, a persecutor, and a violently arrogant man. He had every reason to think 'I'm too big a sinner for God to save.' But he recognized that Christ did not die on the cross for some people, He died for everyone.

Because He paid the price for our sins by dying in our place and rising again, God can now extend the gift of eternal life to anyone who will put his or her trust in Christ. So if you think you are too big a sinner for God to save, rest assured that as we study this passage in 1 Corinthians you will see that is not true. If God could save Paul, He can save you."

Another possibility is to make a connection with the particular passage. Suppose we are speaking on spiritual gifts from 1 Corinthians 12. Before reading a particular portion of the chapter, we could introduce it by saying, "This morning we are going to talk about spiritual gifts. The Bible says that when we come to Christ, God gives us particular abilities by which we can build up and encourage one another as believers in Christ. Not all of us have the same spiritual gift, but the moment we come to Christ, God gives us at least one spiritual gift. We are studying this morning what these special God-given abilities are. It's important to find out what your spiritual gift is and then let the Lord use it to help others. However, if you have not trusted Christ as your personal Savior, before you think about your spiritual gifts, I would encourage you to think about the *eternal* gift God has for you. Don't think about how to serve the Lord before you make certain you know the Lord. Two thousand years ago, Jesus Christ died on a cross for your sins, taking the punishment for everything wrong you've done. The third day He rose again. Because the price for your sin has already been paid, God can now give you eternal life completely free. All you have to do is trust in Christ alone as your only way to heaven. Before you think about the spiritual gifts God gives you when you come to Christ, be sure you've received His gift of eternal life. You need to know beyond any doubt that if you were to die you'd go to heaven. Now let's read together this passage from 1 Corinthians 12."

Appeal to them in the way you illustrate your message.

Non-Christians relate especially well to pastors who effectively use illustrations. Unbelievers do not understand the Bible, but they do understand life. A pastor who uses illustrations effectively tells the non-Christian that he understands not only the Scriptures, but life as well.

Years ago, I was speaking in a church on the subject of marriage and the family using Genesis 2:18–25. I was addressing the subject, "Why did God start it all?" I explained that one of the reasons God instituted marriage was for companionship. God plainly said, "It is not good that man should be alone." I then addressed the subject of loneliness, giving the illustration of a twenty-nine-year-old single man from Topeka, Kansas, who said, "For myself, I can only describe the word 'loneliness' as being a gut-level sick feeling at the pit of your stomach. It's so far within yourself you fear you are in a trap and will never be set free." After the service, a non-Christian sought me out and said, "You couldn't have described me any better. That quote really penetrated." I had the privilege of taking him aside and leading him to the Lord.

Be careful to avoid phrases like "Many times in our lives as Christians" unless it's absolutely necessary. The illustration you are about to use may be true of people *everywhere,* not just believers. I once spoke from James 1:1–12 on how to live for Christ when life turns upside down. As I introduced my message on trials and hardships, I used the illustration of a boy whose baby brother was killed in an automobile accident. Looking toward heaven he said, "God, when my brother died, my mother prayed for you to let him live. He was only two years old. You could have let him live but didn't. How could a two-year-old have sinned so much that you had to punish him? You let him die, and you broke my mother's heart. How can I love you?" That is an illustration that unbelievers can relate to. To have said, "Many times we as Christians think what a young boy actually said…," would have damaged its appeal to non-Christians.

People everywhere love stories. A speaker who effectively uses illustrations relates to unbelievers even when his message is to believers.

Appeal to them through the conclusion of your message.

A conclusion of a message has to appeal for action. God does not want everyone there merely to hear what has been said. He wants them to *act* on it. Suppose we are speaking on John 13:1–17, where we read that Christ washed the feet of the disciples. Although it has nothing to do with how to get to heaven, what would be more appropriate than to conclude by saying that a mark of greatness in God's eyes is not how many servants we have but how many people we serve? Give ideas as to how they can reach out and serve this week. Then say to non-Christians in the audience, "But one caution. Maybe you do not know for sure that if you were to die today, you'd go to heaven. Before you think about how you can serve the Lord, I'd like to encourage you to think about how the Lord has served you. Two thousand years ago, Jesus Christ, the perfect Son of God, did for you and me what we would never do for one another. He died on a cross to take the punishment for our sins and rose again the third day. Because the price for your sin has been paid, you can receive the gift of eternal life. If you have not received that gift, I would love to talk with you and help you arrive at that point where you know beyond any doubt that if you were to die, you'd go to heaven. Please see me before you leave today. Do not even think about serving the Lord until you understand how He has served you."

We may be speaking on the garments of love as they are listed in Colossians 3:12–14. As we conclude, we appeal to believers to wear those garments daily. It would then be appropriate to say, "But do you know what excites me about these garments? Jesus Christ wore every one of these as He walked among people like us. He was compassionate, kind, humble, meek, longsuffering, and forgiving. The best proof is what He did for us on a cross years ago. Because we are sinners, we deserve to be punished for our sins by eternal separation from God. But because of the love He had for us, He humbled Himself, came and died on a cross as our substitute. He took the punishment we deserve. His resurrection on the third day proved He had conquered sin and death. Through trust in Christ as our Savior, we can be forgiven of all sin and receive the gift of eternal life. If you have not received that gift, please do so today by trusting Christ as Savior. Remember, the garments He is asking us to wear are the ones He wore Himself." This is an appropriate appeal, fitting to the text and to non-Christians. One word of caution: If you can tie your appeal to something in your message, by all means, do so. If you can't do it naturally, don't try. If it's awkward, you will sense it and so will the non-Christian.

There's another way we can appeal to unbelievers at the conclusion of a message to believers. Once we close our message, as heads are bowed in prayer, it's appropriate to say, "My message today has been to believers. Maybe you're here and you don't know for sure if you were to die you'd go to heaven. God makes the gospel so simple. You come to Him as a sinner, recognize Christ died for you and was raised from death, and put your trust in Christ alone as your only way to heaven. If you have not trusted Christ as your personal Savior, I would not only invite you to do so, I would invite you to do so *today*. Once you've trusted Him, you will know beyond any doubt that if you were to die you'd go straight to heaven." Then encourage anyone who would like to talk with you after the service to meet you at the front, in a side room, or wherever you prefer.

What determines whether we appeal to unbelievers at a particular spot in the message, the conclusion of the message, or at the very end as heads are bowed and eyes closed? Again, the rule of thumb should be to do what is natural to the situation and the subject. There are times we may do all three. Bear in mind that just because a person is a non-Christian does not mean he is foolish or non-thinking. If the appeal is not natural in where and how it is done, as stated earlier, the speaker can sense it, and so can an unbeliever.

The speaker is not the only one who can make the appeal.

A church of any size has more than one person involved in the service on Sunday morning. As the pastor prepares to speak to believers, these people can be of tremendous assistance in appealing to lost people.

The choir or worship team can do it through selecting a song with a message to non-Christians. Dawn Rodgers and Eric Wyse wrote a song entitled "Wonderful, Merciful Savior." Imagine non-Christians sitting in a service directed to believers but hearing words like these: "Wonderful, merciful Savior, Precious Redeemer and friend, who would have thought that a Lamb could rescue the souls of men. Oh, You rescue the souls of men. Counselor, Comforter, Keeper, Spirit we long to embrace, You offer hope when our hearts have hopelessly lost our way. Oh, we've hopelessly lost our way." What better way to appeal to unbelievers?

The worship leader can even do it in the way he introduces a particular song. In a service that uses a mixture of hymns and choruses (which many today are finding effective) the leader might choose one of the all-time favorite hymns, "Amazing Grace," and introduce it by saying, "There are moments in life when we wonder if we've gone too far for God to help us, if we've done too much wrong for Him to forgive us. Because of the life we're living, we wonder if He'd even accept us. John Newton wrote the song we're about to sing. His mother, a very godly person, died when he wasn't quite seven years old. His father remarried, and after several years of formal education away from home, John left school and joined his father's ship. At the age of eleven, he began life as a seaman. His early years were marked by rebellion and debauchery. He served on several ships and worked for a period of time on the islands and mainland of the West African Coast collecting slaves for sale. Then he became captain of his own slave ship. That capturing, selling, and transporting of slaves to the plantations from the West Indies to America was a cruel and vicious way of life.

"On March 10, 1748, while returning from England to Africa during a very stormy voyage, it appeared all would be lost. Newton picked up a book called *The Imitation of Christ* by Thomas à Kempis. The Holy Spirit used the message of that book, a frightening experience at sea, and the prayers of his mother before her death to sow the seed for his eventual conversion. Shortly thereafter, he trusted Christ as his personal Savior and became one of the great evangelical preachers of the late eighteenth century.

"If you have not trusted Christ as your personal Savior, think on these words carefully and listen as we sing them. Jesus Christ saved John Newton, and He can save you. He died on a cross in our place, taking the punishment for our sins, and rose again so that through personal trust in Him we can receive the gift of eternal life.

"If you have not trusted Jesus Christ as your personal Savior, do so today. Then you, too, will be able to sing with John Newton, 'Amazing Grace, how sweet the sound, that saved a wretch like me.'"

A person who gives a five- to seven-minute testimony can also make an appeal to unbelievers. People know that their brothers and sisters have come to Christ but seldom know the circumstances. On a fairly regular basis, have individuals give a testimony that clearly presents the gospel to non-Christians. One word of caution—believers often don't know *how* to give an effective testimony. When I hear them give their testimonies, I know something has happened to them. But if I were a non-Christian, I wouldn't know how to make it happen to me. That five to seven minutes is so critical it's important to have people write out their testimonies, allow you to read them and make suggestions, and then re-write them. Through a clear testimony the unbeliever comes to understand how he, too, can come to know the Savior.

Conclusion

Speaking to non-Christians in a service directed toward Christians is an exciting frustration. It's a frustration in that the entire service is not directed to non-Christians. But it's an exciting one because there are so many easy, sensible, and relevant ways to present the gospel.

Variety is often called the spice of life. It also is the spice of evangelism. When one uses varied ways to appeal to non-Christians in a non-evangelistic setting, he often makes an eternal difference in the lives of those who don't know Christ. After all, if we take seriously the brevity of life, it is important that we relate to non-Christians in one way or another in every single service. We speak to dying people. That unbeliever who sits in your service today may not be alive to sit in any service tomorrow. The time to appeal to them is now.

REFLECTING...

1. What are five ways of appealing to unbelievers in a non-evangelistic setting?

2. How can your manner in the pulpit appeal to non-Christians?

3. If we don't make an appeal to non-Christians in the message itself, what are other ways and places to do it?

4. How does the effective use of illustrations appeal to non-Christians?

5. If the speaker does not make the appeal to non-Christians, who else can do it?

Chapter 13

Have You Thought about the Service, Not Just the Sermon?

LET ME POSE A question. Suppose you have put together, with God's help, one of the most effective evangelistic messages ever given. Your message accurately reflects the text. You are about to preach His Word, not yours. Your introduction grips people. It's one of the best you've ever done. It leaves them wanting to know what you are going to say. The illustrations are as perfect as they come. Each one beautifully illustrates your point. Your word choices are effective. They are relevant to your audience. Your message has a great central idea. Easy to remember; impossible to forget. The humor is fitting and communicative. The audience will laugh, but as they laugh they will listen and be convicted. Your conclusion leaves no doubt what you are asking of each person.

Now here is the question: What can hinder the effectiveness of that message? I didn't ask what can kill the message. That's possibly too strong. Instead, I've asked, "What can hinder its effectiveness?"

The answer: the program. We can have the best evangelistic message ever given, but if the program does not enhance the service, the impact of the message can be severely and adversely affected.

What does one have to think of in terms of the program surrounding an evangelistic message? Basically, you must consider three areas.

The Perspective

The evangelistic service is not for Christians, although that's who the majority in attendance will be. Nevertheless, the service is for non-Christians. With that audience identified, you must aim directly at them. That begins by watching your language. Be relatable with your speech.

Speak in a warm, caring way. This is not a time when a pastor speaks to his parishioners. It's a time when a person speaks to his friends. A natural, conversational tone—a non-preaching voice—goes a long way. Personalize your prayers. To the non-Christian, God is already far away. Make Him approachable. He is our friend, so in public prayer we need to use language to which non-Christians can relate. Imagine yourself as a non-Christian. As they hear us pray publicly, we say:

> Dear God, thank you for giving us the life and breath to be here today. And thank you that when we speak to you, we can simply talk from our hearts. Some of us here tonight are lonely. We don't feel like we've lost a friend. We feel we've never had one. Some of us here feel like we're heading in the wrong direction, but we're not sure how to turn things around and we wonder if it's even worth it. Some of us are not sure about you. Even in a prayer like this we feel like we're talking to a wall, not a person. Some of us are afraid of you—afraid of who you are and afraid of what you might do with us since you're probably not too pleased with where we've been and what we've done. Some of us are hurting so badly we don't even know how to talk to you about those hurts. Our laughter on the outside is just a cover-up for the hurt on the inside. But God, if you would just somehow talk to us during this service and help us listen, you could make a difference. So help us to listen, help us to learn, O God, just help us. In Jesus' name, amen.

If I were a non-Christian, I'd think, "Wow. I didn't know you could talk to God like that. Maybe He's not as removed as I've made Him." The point is, our prayers need to be personal and meaningful. Keep them brief and conversational in tone.

The right perspective includes dress. It cannot be said enough: We are speaking to non-Christians, not Christians. What does 1 Samuel 16:7 teach us? "But the Lord does not see as man sees; for man looks at the outward appearance, but the Lord looks at the heart." Both parts of that Scripture are just that—Scripture. Yes, God looks at the heart. But it is just as true that man looks at the outward appearance. Don't misunderstand. You are not trying to impress. You are trying to express—truth. Doing so in a professional manner helps greatly. Professional dress communicates, "This truth is of great importance. It's not to be taken lightly." Therefore, everyone on the platform—song leaders, soloists and speaker—must use the "one step above the audience" rule (see chapter 23).

The People

If the speaker is the key person, the worship leader is next. After all, people see him before they see you. He sets the tone of the service, affects the attitude of the people, and prepares them for the message.

This means that he must be enthusiastic, happy, and positive. Imagine a speaker, sober-faced and sad, who stands before people and says, "I'm so glad to be here. I used to abuse alcohol and drugs and was suicidal. Then I came to Christ." One cannot help but wonder if coming to Christ made him sadder or happier. The countenance of the worship leader must communicate that he's excited to be there and that the audience ought to be too. Immediately he lifts people, inspires them, and makes them glad they came. He causes them to think, "I hope the speaker is as enjoyable as he is." Normally, this kind of worship leader is a people person. He likes being around people. You can sense it, and so can others.

The right worship leader knows how to welcome people, not embarrass them. He doesn't have the guests stand, which I assure you they don't want to do. They usually prefer to feel welcome but not recognized publicly. Sometimes it is best to have the instrumentalist play an upbeat chorus while everyone says hello to one another. Properly done, it can enhance the atmosphere of the service. The song leader is the key. Does he instruct the audience to just say hello or does he communicate, "Let's meet some wonderful people—the people who are on all sides of you"?

He also needs to be flexible. Programs are put together by people. Since people aren't perfect, programs usually aren't either. Besides that, any number of things can go wrong. A microphone can malfunction. A breakdown between the song leader and the musicians becomes obvious. In one service, a person in the front row had a heart attack and had to be tended to. An insincere non-Christian may become boisterous and distracting and have to be dealt with appropriately. It's not what happens that will affect the program as much as how the worship leader responds. The right response can relax and help people. An inappropriate response can offend them.

The Program

The right program involves four essential aspects.

Order

The order of the program needs to show thought. Why does a particular song precede a testimony or vice versa? Does the program appear as though it was put together five minutes ago or five days ago? Remember, non-Christians may be unbelievers, but they are not unthinking. If the program appears thrown together instead of put together, they can sense it. Since the speaker's message is directed to non-Christians, the program should be too. A song or testimony that is particularly for Christians doesn't prepare the audience for a message directed to non-Christians.

Special music, congregational songs, and testimony should speak to the audience the speaker is going to address.

Flow

Good programming requires a smooth flow. As a well-fitting glove slides onto a hand, one part of the service should slide into the other. Non-Christians are a watching audience more than a reading audience. What they watch on television is done smoothly and professionally. Avoid breaks and dead time. From start to finish, there should be a momentum all the way through the message and into the invitation. That's why announcements should be kept away from the service. Few things are more interruptive in a service that is going smoothly than an abrupt change for the announcements that pertain to the week ahead. Announcements are rightly called "flow killers."

Some ask, "When is it appropriate to read the Scripture that the expositor will explain?" The best time is when we get up to give our message. That way, the passage is set before the people as the speaker explains it and is fresh on their minds as he begins his message. It also tends to help the flow of the service.

If possible, avoid an offering. That might delightfully surprise non-Christians who are concerned that the only thing the church is out for is their money. If it is necessary, make sure it flows properly into the program. It can be done as the soloist ministers in song, causing attention to go properly to the soloist, not improperly to the ushers. Also stress that the offering is not for guests. Its purpose is for those who are members of the church.

Pace

In one word: fast. The pace of an evangelistic service is faster than the pace of a normal worship service. If the song leader announces, "And now Joe Smith will tell us through song what God has done for him," Joe Smith should be stepping behind the microphone as the song leader says his last words. He ought not to be walking from two rows back to the platform. The pace should be so fast that the service can easily be confined to an hour—and half of that is the message itself. You want non-Christians to leave wishing it had been longer, not shorter, desiring more, not less.

Music

Absolutely nothing prepares the audience better for a message than music, properly used. Immediately you may ask, "Hymns or choruses?" You've started at the wrong place. The place to start is in the content of the hymn or song. Whatever you choose, it needs to communicate to non-Christians. A song that speaks about being glad to be redeemed cannot truthfully be sung by a non-Christian. Choose songs that call attention to God and His grace and love—the things you want unbelievers to be thinking about as they prepare for the message. You want songs directed to who God is, not who we are. We are addressing non-Christians, so we ought not to choose songs that speak of the need for revival among believers or a closer walk with God. The unbeliever needs to come to Him before he can walk with Him.

Don't embarrass non-Christians with the fact that they don't know the words or are unfamiliar with a songbook. Put the words on a screen overhead so they cannot only sing with everyone else but they can look up to a screen instead of down at a songbook. They need to sing up and out, not down and in. Since the pace of the service is fast, for the most part, the pace of the music should be fast too.

Special music is helpful as long as it is well done and professional in nature. I've never forgotten the time I was scheduled to speak and a soloist who preceded me said, "This is not very good because I'm not a very good soloist. But since I'm doing it for the Lord, it doesn't matter." First of all, not having special music is better than having poor special music. Second, if she has done the best she can, she is better off to just do it and not apologize for it. Furthermore, although not intending to do so, she made the Lord look of less importance. Would she have said the same thing if singing in the presence of a king? Of course not. So why say it when singing in the presence of the King of kings?

Most important of all, the whole program must be bathed in prayer. God is the power. We are only instruments. Each word said, each note played, and everything else must be done with the utmost dependence on God, for if He doesn't work, it will all be in vain. In an evangelistic service, we are not working through Him, He is working through us.

Conclusion

Christmas morning arrives. You are excited to find a gift with your name on it. The package makes it enticing. The gift is wrapped in such an attractive way that you are excited to know what's inside.

Package an evangelistic service properly. Guests might be excited to know what's inside the package. When, through the program and the message, they meet the One who is at the center of the package, all the time spent in preparation will be well worth the effort.

REFLECTING...

1. When putting together an evangelistic message, why does the service need to be given as much consideration as the sermon?

2. What are three areas we should consider in regard to the service?

3. How can the language we use even in our public prayers help or hurt our appeal to non-Christians?

4. Why is the worship leader important for having the proper service?

5. What are the four things that must be considered in regard to the program?

PART II
Looking at Our Message

Chapter 14

What Is This Thing Called Sin and How Do You Explain It to an Unbeliever?

SIN IS OFTEN ENJOYABLE. A small boy prayed, "Lord, if you can't make me a better boy, don't worry about it. I'm having a good time as it is."[1] Enjoyable as it may be, sin is deadly. So deadly it will send a person to an eternal hell. Unless people understand sin's consequences, they may not see their need of Christ.

L. A. Banks, in *Great Themes of the Bible*, told of a time when D. L. Moody was visiting inmates in a prison. He asked each prisoner "What brought you here?" He received replies such as, "I don't deserve to be here," "I was framed," "I was falsely accused," "I was given an unfair trial." Not one would admit his guilt. Finally, Moody came upon a man with his face buried in his hands, weeping. He asked, "What's wrong?" The prisoner answered, "My sins are more than I can bear." Moody responded, "Thank God for that." Moody then had the privilege of introducing him to Christ.[2]

When we come to God, we must come to Him as sinners. Effectiveness in evangelistic speaking demands that we understand the issue of sin and how to explain that to a non-Christian audience.

What prevents non-Christians from seeing themselves as sinners?

There are many answers to this question, but two are paramount. One is pride. Pride makes us focus on what we've done right, instead of what we've done wrong. The University of Wisconsin once asked each person applying for admission to complete a personal data sheet. In response to the request to list personal strengths, an eighteen-year-old answered, "Sometimes I am trustworthy, loyal, helpful, friendly, courteous, kind, obedient, cheerful, thrifty, brave, clean, and reverent." When the same form requested a list of personal weaknesses the same applicant wrote, "Sometimes I am *not* trustworthy, loyal, helpful, friendly, courteous, kind, obedient, cheerful, thrifty, brave, clean, and reverent."[3] Our list of weaknesses are as long as our list of personal strengths. But we prefer to focus on what we've done right instead of what we've done wrong.

How many times in confronting unbelievers about their sinful condition before God have you received the response, "I've done a lot of things right in my time. The Lord knows I'm trying to do what is right." Their focus is on what they've done right, not what they've done wrong.

A second problem is comparison. Non-Christians place themselves alongside others, choosing those who, in their opinion, live worse than they do. They conclude, "I'm not nearly as bad as a lot of people I know." They seldom question whether or not they are using the right standard. They've chosen the standard that they desire to use—the one that makes them look better than others.

So how should we explain sin to unbelievers in such a way that they see themselves as wretched before God?

One caution: We cannot do the Holy Spirit's work. Seeing ourselves as God sees us is a spiritual issue. "But the natural man does not receive the things of the Spirit of God, for they are foolishness to him; nor can he know them, because they are spiritually discerned" (1 Cor. 2:14).

The Holy Spirit has to do the convicting. As mentioned earlier, one of the things the Holy Spirit convicts us of is sin, particularly the sin of not believing in Christ. Referring to the Holy Spirit, Christ says, "And when He has come, He will convict the world of sin, and of righteousness, and of judgment" (John 16:8). He continues, "of sin, because they do not believe in Me" (v. 9). Faith in Christ and His sin payment is the answer to their sin problem. Therefore, the Holy Spirit wants to convict them of their sinful state. Unless the Holy Spirit works they will never see themselves as sinners.

What is the Bible's explanation of "You are a sinner"?

In confronting issues of pride and comparing ourselves with others, God does two things. First, He focuses on His standard, not ours. His standard is not goodness. If it were, God could grade on a curve and we might be good enough. Instead, God's standard is perfection. The most moral, well-behaved person has fallen short of that standard.

The predominant New Testament Greek word for sin is *hamartia*. It means "missing the mark." That is the word used in Romans 3:23: "For all have sinned (*hamartia*) and fall short of the glory of God." One lie, one unkind thought, one moment of lust and we have missed His standard of perfection. We all have fallen short of His mark.

Solomon observed, "For there is not a just man on earth who does good and does not sin" (Eccl. 7:20). He uttered that same truth when he dedicated the temple and confessed, "When they sin against You (for there is no one who does not sin)" (1 Kings 8:46). Solomon warns us to avoid people who find pleasure in exposing the shortcomings of others. Why? Because we ourselves have done what we accuse others of doing. He says, "Also do not take to heart everything people say, lest you hear your servant cursing you. For many times, also, your own heart has known that even you have cursed others" (Eccl. 7:21–22). David confessed, "For in Your sight no one living is righteous" (Ps. 143:2). Since God's standard is perfection, no one stands righteous in His sight.

If someone were perfect, we might overlook him. We often miss what is right before our eyes. But God doesn't. He doesn't overlook anything or anyone. What does He observe? "The Lord looks down from heaven upon the children of men, to see if there are any who understand, who seek God. They have all turned aside, they have together become corrupt; there is none who does good, no, not one" (Ps. 14:2–3).

God's standard is perfection. No one measures up. A non-Christian must therefore be challenged to place himself alongside Christ. He cannot use his neighbor, his spouse, a co-worker, or a respected preacher. The standard is perfection as seen in the person of Christ.

The second thing God does to confront our pride is point to our rebellion against Him. A prominent word used in the New Testament to show our rebellion is the Greek word *adikia*, often translated "unrighteousness." *Adikia* covers many offenses, from immorality to a violation of governmental laws. We are the opposite of who God is. What He says not to do, we do. What He says to do, we don't do. We are stubborn and rebellious.

Few passages in the Bible address our rebellion any more specifically than Romans 1:28–32:

> And even as they did not like to retain God in their knowledge, God gave them over to a debased mind, to do those things which are not fitting; being filled with all unrighteousness, sexual immorality, wickedness, covetousness, maliciousness; full of envy, murder, strife, deceit, evil-mindedness; they are whisperers, backbiters, haters of God, violent, proud, boasters, inventors of evil things, disobedient to parents, undiscerning, untrustworthy, unloving, unforgiving, unmerciful; who, knowing the righteous judgment of God, that those who practice such things are deserving of death, not only do the same but also approve of those who practice them.

What proof does God give?

To show us that we have missed His standard and rebelled against Him, God uses the law, particularly the Ten Commandments, to show us how we have fallen short. Romans 3 reminds us of the purpose of the law: "For by the law is the knowledge of sin" (Rom. 3:20).

Review the Ten Commandments (Exod. 20:1–17). God commands, "You shall not take the name of the Lord your God in vain." Every time we use the name of God in an irreverent way, we are proven to be sinners. We have missed the mark. God commands, "You shall not bear false witness against your neighbor." Every time we lie about someone, we have proven we are sinners. We have missed the mark. God commands, "You shall not covet your neighbor's house; you shall not covet your neighbor's wife . . . nor anything that is your neighbor's." When we covet what someone else has, we have proven we are sinners. We have missed the mark. The Ten Commandments show us the specifics of how we have fallen short. The law cannot remove our sinful condition, but it does prove the sinful condition we are in. No one can read the Ten Commandments objectively and not conclude, "I have sinned."

What is the speaker's explanation of "You are a sinner"?

The two ideas the Scriptures use to prove we are sinners are the same two ideas the speaker should use—missing the mark and rebellion. To illustrate this, we should use the same standard the New Testament uses: the Ten Commandments. Regardless of what kind of message we are giving as an evangelistic message, there is always the opportunity to tell people: 1) we have missed the mark; and 2) we have rebelled against God.

By directing a non-believer to the Ten Commandments, we address both the issues of pride and the temptation to compare ourselves with others. We have directed them to God rather than to goodness or perfection. No one measures up. We all have fallen short whether we have sinned once or one hundred times. God's standard is not the preacher or the pope; God's standard is perfection as seen in Christ alone.

We also address rebellion. What God says don't do, we do. What God says do, we don't do. Years of speaking to non-Christians have proven to me that one of the best ways to show a sinner his sin is to do what the New Testament does—use the law. Through the law, the whole world stands guilty before God (Rom. 3:19). Should an unbeliever not be familiar with the Ten Commandments, it takes but a moment to explain what they are and why God gave them. Using commandments such as "You shall not take the name of the Lord your God in vain" and "You shall not covet" allows everyone to see themselves as sinners. As they live and move in the workplace, they break His commandments every day.

We need to feel free to speak of hell, but we must do it with compassion.

If we do not feel a tinge of sorrow that a non-Christian could spend eternity there, we need to ask God to give us that remorse. Hell should never be mentioned with a spirit of revenge as though to say, "You'll get what you deserve." It needs to be stressed with a depth of sorrow that says, "God doesn't want you to go there."

What about those who, when confronted with the Ten Commandments, deny their wrongs or minimize them? They don't see themselves as rebellious against God.

Once more, it is not for us to do the work of the Holy Spirit. They may attempt to live in denial, but that's all it is—an attempt. They must deal with their own conscience:

> For not the hearers of the law are just in the sight of God, but the doers of the law will be justified; for when Gentiles, who do not have the law, by nature do the things in the law, these, although not having the law, are a law to themselves, who show the work of the law written in their hearts, their conscience also bearing witness, and between themselves their thoughts accusing or else excusing them. (Rom. 2:13–15)

How does an *expositor* explain "You are a sinner"?

This book is dedicated not merely to evangelistic speaking, but *expository* evangelistic preaching. In expository evangelistic speaking, we are speaking from a particular text of Scripture. Suppose we are speaking from a passage that addresses the substitutionary death of Christ or the need for faith but does not tell us we are sinners. The passage says nothing about our rebellion or missing the mark. What do we do?

As expositors, we need to point the listener to his or her sinful condition at some point in the message. The best place to do this depends on and is determined by the particular message being given. With the issues of missing the mark and rebellion, it can be done easily and quickly.

For example, suppose we are speaking from a passage that addresses the death of Christ on our behalf, such as John 3:16. At the appropriate point in the message, we can say:

> Now why does the passage speak of Christ's death for us? Because we must all understand—we are sinners. Now frankly, we don't like to look at ourselves that way. We like to look at ourselves as good, moral, religious people. But the word "sin" means to miss the mark. God set a standard for getting into heaven. He says we must be perfect. It doesn't matter how good we've been or how religiously we have lived; we cannot be as perfect as God demands. We have rebelled against Him. We lie, cheat, have wrong thoughts,

are unkind, have moments of jealousy or hatred, and use His name in an irreverent way. God, being a holy God, has no other choice than to punish sin. The punishment for sin is death. That death is not only a physical death, it is eternal separation from God in what the Bible calls hell. This sentence explains that Christ took that punishment for us.

In a few moments we have addressed what the passage we chose did not—the problem of sin and its consequences.

Conclusion

Sin is missing the mark. Sin is rebellion against God. The law, particularly the Ten Commandments, shows us we are guilty of both. We must give the proof the New Testament gives—the Ten Commandments. Unless our audience sees themselves as sinners, they will never see their need of a Savior.

REFLECTING...

1. What are the two biggest reasons why people have trouble seeing themselves as sinners?

2. What are the two things God uses to enable us to see ourselves as sinners?

3. What proof does God give to show us we have missed the mark and rebelled against Him?

4. Should the text we have selected not explain our sinful condition, what do we do?

5. How does a clear understanding of the depth of our sin pave the way for the good news we have for unbelievers?

Chapter 15

What Is Our Message for Non-Christians?

IT HAS BEEN SAID, "The better you know what you're talking about, the more simply you can put it."[1] God wants us to keep our message to non-Christians simple and understandable. To do so, we need to know what our message is.

You may ask, "Isn't our message to non-Christians the gospel? After all, Mark 16:15 tells us to 'Go into all the world and preach the gospel to every creature.'"

Most certainly, our message is the gospel. But what is the gospel? D. L. Moody once said, "I do not think there is a word in the English language so little understood as the word gospel."[2] Approach a gathering of believers and ask the question, "What is the gospel?" The variety of answers you receive validates the confusion.

Why the confusion?

One reason for this confusion is that the word "gospel" is sometimes used generically to refer to any truth. "I'm telling you the gospel truth" may refer to a statement made about a friend, the weather forecast, a hard-to-believe fact, or a promise we intend to keep. Sometimes it is used as a synonym for the entire Bible. Hence, Genesis and Revelation, creation, and end-time events are all considered the gospel. Even in Christian circles, the first four books of the New Testament are often referenced as the "Gospels" of Matthew, Mark, Luke, and John.

But when God tells an evangelistic speaker to "Go into all the world and preach the gospel to every creature," He is referring to a very *specific* truth. Paul referred to it as the gospel of the grace of God. He testified, "But none of these things move me; nor do I count my life dear to myself, so that I may finish my race with joy, and the ministry which I received from the Lord Jesus, to testify to the gospel of the grace of God" (Acts 20:24).

How does God define the gospel?

Nowhere in Scripture are the historical elements of the gospel more clearly defined than in 1 Corinthians 15:3–5. What adds weight to Paul's definition of the gospel is that the gospel he defined came straight from God to him to the Corinthians. "For I delivered to you first of all that which I also received" (v. 3). "Received" is the same word Paul used when he said, "For I neither received it from man, nor was I taught it, but it came through the revelation of Jesus Christ" (Gal. 1:12). The gospel Paul received and declared was not the result of a church council decision or a product of his own imagination. Its origin was God.

Paul then continued, "That Christ died for our sins according to the Scriptures, and that He was buried, and that He rose again the third day according to the Scriptures, and that He was seen by Cephas, then by the twelve." Paul's definition of the gospel centered on four verbs:

Christ *died* for our sins according to the Scriptures.
He was *buried.*
He *rose* again the third day according to the Scriptures.
He was *seen.*

Let's look carefully at these four verbs.

"Christ *died* for our sins" according to the Scriptures. "For" is the translation of a Greek preposition that means "instead of" or "on behalf of." The idea is that had He not died, we would have. He died in our place. He was our substitute.

A *National Geographic* article once reported about a man who took his young son fishing but took only one life jacket. A storm arose; strong winds caused the boat to capsize. The father put the vest on his son and pushed him toward shore. The last words the son heard his dad say were "I love you." The father died in the son's place. Had the father not died, the son would have. The father saved his son by dying for him. Jesus Christ took our place. They hung Christ where they should have hung us. He died as our substitute, for our sins.[3]

"According to the Scriptures" means His death was a fulfillment of what was prophesied seven hundred years earlier. Isaiah prophesied, "But He was wounded for our transgressions, He was bruised for our iniquities" (Isa. 53:5).

"He was *buried.*" Note that Paul did not repeat the phrase "according to the Scriptures." His burial is proof that He died.

114

"He *rose* again the third day according to the Scriptures." Christ's resurrection, just like His crucifixion, was prophesied years earlier. David predicted the resurrection of Christ when he said, "For You will not leave my soul in Sheol, nor will You allow Your Holy One to see corruption" (Ps. 16:10).

"And that He was *seen*." Once again Paul did not repeat the phrase "according to the Scriptures." As Paul mentioned Christ's burial as proof that He died, he mentioned the fact that He was seen as proof He arose. No greater testimony exists in court than an eyewitness. In essence, Paul invites you into the courtroom and gives a list of those witnesses. These were not people prone to hallucinations. The Person they saw was real. Neither were these uninformed witnesses who did not know Christ and could have mistaken Him for someone else. They knew Him.

His burial is proof of death. The fact that Jesus was seen is proof of His resurrection. So the gospel simply stated is "Christ died for our sins and rose from the dead." Ten words stated so simply, a new convert can tell a friend. The Bible contains sixty-six books and can never be fully grasped in a lifetime. The gospel can be put in ten words and can be learned in a minute—*Christ died for our sins and rose from the dead.*

What are the ramifications of the gospel?

Looking at this definition more closely, we discover that the gospel has ramifications. For one, it concerns something Christ has done. It is past, proven, finished. The gospel is not about something God will do in a person's life. It is about something He *has already done*—more than two thousand years ago. There are many things God will do—bring contentment, provide inner peace, and give purpose for living. But they are not the gospel. The gospel concerns what has already been done—Christ died for our sins and rose from the dead.

The gospel also focuses on our relationship with God, not our relationship with others. God can reconcile marriages and help a couple who walked the aisle together to also walk life together. He can restore relationships in such a way that enemies become friends. These examples concern horizontal relationships; the gospel deals with our vertical one. Our primary problem is not that we are separated from one another. Our problem, first and foremost, is our lack of a relationship with God. Christ's death for our sins destroyed the enmity between God and us and allowed us a way whereby we could be His friends. He did for us what we could not do for ourselves. "Christ died for our sins" means that if we receive what He did for us, we can have a relationship with God and ultimately be with Him rather than separated from Him.

The gospel's emphasis is also eternal life, not temporal life. That is why a clear understanding of the gospel message is most needed in every culture. A person in India who comes to Christ may still die of leprosy. A new believer in Ethiopia may still die of starvation. An African Christian may still be the victim of AIDS. An American who comes to Christ may still lose his job or suffer a marital break-up. But the gospel centers on life in the hereafter. Its emphasis is eternal life with God. That eternal life begins the day one trusts Christ and continues forever in His presence.

That "Good News" of the gospel leaves a non-Christian without any excuse for not trusting Christ. Someone may doubt God's love because of the sudden death of a relative or friend, a prolonged hardship, or personal illness. But if a person questions God's love, one must *start* with the cross. The fact that Jesus died for us removes any and all questions about His love. He did for us what we probably would never do for another. "For scarcely for a righteous man will one die; yet perhaps for a good man someone would even dare to die. But God demonstrates His own love toward us, in that while we were still sinners, Christ died for us" (Rom. 5:7–8).

If an unbeliever doubts that Jesus Christ is God, all he has to do is go back to the empty tomb. The resurrection of Christ has been declared by many to be the most attested fact of history. John Singleton Copley, one of the great legal minds in British history and three time High Chancellor of England, wrote, "I know pretty well what evidence is, and I tell you, such evidence as that for His resurrection has never broken down yet."[4] There are thousands of references in secular history to that resurrection. Dr. Donald G. Barnhouse noted, "The angel rolled away the stone from Jesus' tomb, not to let the living Lord out, but to let the unconvinced outsiders in."[5] What makes that resurrection so important? The bodily resurrection of Jesus Christ from the dead is the crowning proof of Christianity.[6] His resurrection on the third day proved His victory over sin and the grave.

How does the gospel impact evangelistic speaking?

"The main thing is to make the main thing the main thing." What is the "main thing" of evangelistic speaking? What is our message for unbelievers? It's the gospel. Christ died for our sins and rose from the dead. That means regardless of what text we speak on to a non-Christian audience, *that* is our message for them. Christ died for our sins and rose from the dead.

As we bring an *expository* evangelistic message, the nature of the text determines where we explain "Christ died for our sins and rose from the dead." Depending on what passage of Scripture we speak from, we might not explain the gospel till the middle or even the end of our message. An expositor preaches the text. If the text speaks of our sinfulness, that has to be the thrust of an expositor's message. But at the most appropriate point, the speaker must announce the death and resurrection of Christ. If the text speaks about the need to believe, that must be the thrust of the speaker's message. But at the appropriate spot, he must direct his audience to the death and resurrection of Christ. How to do so will be addressed further in another chapter.

We stand before unbelievers to tell them the greatest truth they need to know—the gospel. If we do not present the gospel, we have not given an evangelistic message. Lewis Sperry Chafer, founder of Dallas Theological Seminary, is reported to have said about week-long crusades, which were common at that time, "The job of the evangelist is to preach the gospel night after night after night." When it comes to evangelistic speaking, it is the gospel that needs to be preached.

Making the substitutionary death and His resurrection clear before non-Christians is a moral issue before God. That message is so near and dear to God's heart, Paul even said, as he was inspired by the Holy Spirit, "But even if we, or an angel from heaven, preach any other gospel to you than what we have preached to you, let him be accursed" (Gal. 1:8). It is the one area in which we must not speak with confusion. When it comes to the gospel, we must "Be clear, be clear, be clear!" The better we understand our message, the more simply we can state it.

Conclusion

When non-Christians leave our presence, our message should have helped them in many ways. But first and foremost they must leave knowing that "Christ died for our sins, and rose from the dead." If we do not present that, we have not given an evangelistic message.

REFLECTING...

1. Where in the New Testament are the historical elements of the gospel clearly defined?

2. In ten words, what is the gospel?

3. Why does the gospel leave an unbeliever without any defense for not coming to Christ?

4. How does understanding "the main thing is to make the main thing the main thing" give direction and simplicity to an evangelistic message?

5. How does a correct understanding of the gospel make it cross-cultural?

Chapter 16

What Do We Mean by "Believe"?

DIRECTIONS ARE CRITICAL. WITHOUT them there is no way to arrive at a particular destination. My wife loves the story of a woman who frantically called the fire department and exclaimed, "Fire!, Fire!" The fireman answered, "Hurry, tell us, how do we get there?" She answered, "Don't you have that little red truck anymore?" Of course they had the truck. What they needed was directions.

Directions to God are simple. There is only one way. We come through Christ. His words were unmistakably clear. "I am the way, the truth, and the life. No one comes to the Father, except through Me" (John 14:6). The question is, "How do we get to Christ?"

The answer is "believe," a word used ninety-eight times in the Gospel of John, the one book specifically written to tell us how to receive eternal life (John 20:31). John's recurring theme is this: "He who believes in the Son has everlasting life" (3:36). The question is, "What does believe mean?" Confusion often surrounds word choices.

Take the word "box." To some it's passive, to others, active. Adults think of a container that holds winter clothing for half the year and summer clothing the other half. Children think of a four-by-six structure in the back yard that contains sand and muddied toys. Others think of it in the restrictive sense, as in the imagery of "don't box me in." An athlete thinks of raising his fists before his opponent and driving home that knockout punch. Our life experiences often conjure up what we mean by "box."

Let's take another word: "pad." A cook thinks of the item he places underneath a hot pan to keep it from searing the table. A pet lover thinks of a soft rug his pet sleeps on. An NFL player thinks of the cushion underneath his jersey that protects him from the hard blows of the opposing team. Once again, our life experiences conjure up what we mean by "pad."

The word "believe" holds similar problems that can lead to confusion. To some, "believe" means nothing more than hope or speculation. "I believe I can be there by five o'clock." "I believe I know how to find your house." "I believe I laid it on the top shelf of the guest room closet." "I believe you are better at that than I am."

To others, "believe" is an intellectual assent to a set of facts. "I believe that advertisement is right—that company makes the best passenger truck on the market." "I believe that store has better customer service than their competitor. I know because I shop there regularly." "I believe what he said. He has never lied to me."

So what does the Bible mean by believe?

Believe means to accept as true.

If you look up the word *pisteuo* (believe) in a Greek lexicon, it will say, "be convinced of something, give credence to." We must be convinced that it is an historical fact that more than 2,000 years ago Jesus Christ died on a cross and rose the third day. History proves it. The cross and the empty tomb are two of the most attested to facts of history. But reading those facts is not enough. We must accept them as being true.

Note that we are not merely accepting as true that He died and arose. We are acknowledging that He did it *for us*. It was a substitutionary "instead of us" death. He did not die to show us how to love each other enough to die for them. Nor did He die to show us how to die sacrificially, without revenge or hatred. Instead, He died *in our place*. The nails that should have been driven through our hands and feet were driven through His.

Outdoor Life magazine once told of a thirty-six-year-old mother who, along with her three children, was horseback riding in the Similkameen backcountry, thirty miles northwest of Princeton, British Columbia. All four felt a mixture of excitement and freedom as they traveled the vast wilderness. As they were headed to a cabin where they would join the rest of the family for a camping vacation, the horses became increasingly nervous. It became clear why when a cougar jumped from the undergrowth at Steve, the six-year-old son. The cougar soon had the child in a clawed death grip. The mother, a knowledgeable outdoors woman, knew her son would be dead in seconds from a broken neck or crushed artery. She leaped from her horse and, with adrenaline-fueled strength, broke off a limb from a nearby tree and clubbed the cat away from her little boy.

The lion then turned his attention to her, opening a terrible gash in her arm with one blow. The mother screamed for the older children to pick up the bleeding son and run to the campground for help. An hour later, help returned. The mother's question, as she continued to resist the cougar, was, "Are my children all right?" On hearing they were okay, she whispered, "I am dying now." The rescuers shot the cougar and rushed to the mother's aid, but she was beyond help. She traded her life for that of her son, who survived. She was awarded the Star of Courage posthumously by the Governor General of Canada.[1]

Christ died in our place. The punishment we should have received He suffered for us. He became our substitute. Christ saved us by dying for us. The third day He arose, proving that He had conquered both sin and death.

Believe means to trust.

Ask some people, particularly ones from a religious background, "Do you believe Christ died for you and rose again?" They may answer, "Yes." At the same time they might express a conviction that without being baptized one cannot be saved. The problem is, they are not *believing* in the biblical sense of the word. Once again, pull a Greek lexicon off the shelf and look up the word *pisteuo* (believe). Along with "be convinced of something, give credence to," you will see "trust." If we *believe* in the biblical sense of the word, that means we are trusting Christ to save us—not our good life, church attendance, baptism, sacraments, or keeping the commandments.

No better word brings out the meaning of "believe" to a twenty-first-century audience than the word "trust." We must be sensitive to the fact that some people believe in Christ in the sense that they accept Him as an historical figure who died and arose. But they are not trusting Him to save them, which is what the biblical word involves.

I flew to Washington, D.C., to speak at Capital Bible Seminary. En route, I had the opportunity to speak to an associate pastor of a church in the D.C. area. As we talked about spiritual things, I said, "Let me ask you the test question. If you stood before God and He were to ask, 'Why should I let you into heaven?' what would you tell Him?" He answered, "All I'd say is, 'the blood of Jesus Christ.'" As we talked, it was clear to me that he understood eternal life was free and had trusted Christ to save him.

I then explained why I asked—that I don't take anyone's salvation for granted. He answered, "I certainly understand." He then told me of a preacher in his denomination whom they invited to speak at their church. As they talked with him, they gathered he was not certain he was going to heaven. So they asked him, "Do you know for sure you're going to heaven?" The preacher said, "Of course not. No one can know that." As they continued questioning him, it became obvious he did not understand eternal life was a gift. He even became defensive about his personal salvation. He "believed" Christ died and arose but had not trusted Christ to save *him*.

Someone might respond, "So he *didn't* believe in the biblical sense of the word." They're right. But the easiest way to cause a person to understand is to use the word "trust." I've often said to someone, "I think you do believe. You believe Jesus Christ was a historical figure who died on a cross and arose and even that He did it for you. But I have reason to believe you are trusting in your good life to save you." Repeatedly, I've had people say, "Oh, you're right." I then explain, "But that's what I want you to understand. To believe in the Bible means you must trust in Christ alone to save you." As we speak evangelistically, we must consistently ask our audience, "Will you trust in Christ alone to save you?" Use the word "trust."

For years I have cautioned believers not to use the following phrases in their one-to-one evangelism. It's equally important not to use them in evangelistic speaking.

Invite Jesus into your heart.

The Bible does not use this phrase. Even Revelation 3:20, which some use to support this wording, is addressed to believers, not unbelievers. The issue is not inviting Jesus into your heart but trusting Christ to save you. Once you trust Christ, He is already in your heart. There is no need to invite Him in.

Give your life to God.

This too is not a phrase the Bible uses for salvation. The issue is not you giving Him your life; it's Him giving you His. "And this is the testimony: that *God has given us* eternal life, and this life is in His Son" (1 John 5:11, italics added). There is nothing eternal about your life. When you trust Christ, you begin to live forever because you have His life inside of you.

Would you like to pray to receive Christ?

Again, this is not a phrase the Bible uses. The issue is not saying a prayer. It's trusting Christ. Prayer may be how you tell God what you are doing. But saying a prayer does not save. It's trusting Christ that saves. I've often encouraged people that I've led to Christ to pray and tell God what they are doing. I have found that verbalizing it to God helps them verbalize it to others. But I always caution them, "It's not the prayer that saves, it's trusting Christ that saves."

Accept Christ.

The danger with this phrase is that the unbeliever may accept Christ the way we accept one another—as a person. He may accept Christ as a person who historically lived and died and not trust in Christ to save him. When it says, "But as many as *received* Him," he explains, "to those who *believe*" (John 1:12, italics added). Once again, use the word "trust."

122

Believe means to trust in Christ alone.

Trusting Christ saves. But inherent in trusting Christ is a third idea: We must trust in Christ *alone* to save us.

What were Christ's words from the cross? "It is finished" (John 19:30). "Finished" is the translation of a Greek word *tetelestai,* which means "paid in full." Receipts for taxes during New Testament times have been recovered with the word *tetelestai* written across them, meaning "paid in full." Jesus Christ before an Almighty God did not make the down payment for our sins. He made the full payment.

Therefore, we are saved only when we trust Christ *alone* to save us—not Christ plus something, such as good works or church attendance, but Christ alone. The message behind the gospel is that we must be satisfied with the thing that satisfies God. If we are satisfied with Christ *and* our church attendance to give us a right standing with God, we have not believed on Christ.

Suppose we throw away Christ's substitutionary death and resurrection for a life of good works that we depend on to save us. Or suppose we throw away Christ by depending on Christ *and* our good works to save us. In which one have we disregarded what Christ did on our behalf? Both. Unless we believe that Christ alone saves, we have not accepted as true Christ's declaration, "It is finished." We have not trusted Christ.

In one-to-one evangelism, I use three circles to help people understand that Christ alone saves. The thought behind them is equally important in evangelistic speaking. Inside the one circle I put a "W" to represent the good works they've done, whether going to church, living a good life, being baptized, loving your neighbor, etc. Inside the middle circle, I put "C + W" for Christ and works. Inside the next circle, I put "C" for Christ alone. So the three circles look like this:

Then I explain, "Some people trust in works to save them, such as the good things they've done; some trust in Christ plus works; and some trust in Christ alone. Where are you? It's alarming how many people point to "C + W."

Then I comment, "If you're trusting works to get you to heaven, you're saying, 'Christ's death was unnecessary.'" I even write the word "unnecessary" below the left circle. Then I continue, "If anything we do gets us to heaven, there was no need for Christ to die. In fact, if anything we do gets us to heaven, God made a fool out of His own Son because there was no need for Him to die. If you are trusting Christ plus works, you are saying that His death was disappointing." I write the word "disappointing" below the middle circle. Then I say, "It's like saying, 'He paid for those sins, I have to pay for these. He didn't get the job done. He disappointed God; He disappointed me.' If you trust Christ alone, you say that His death is sufficient." I write the word "sufficient" underneath the right circle. I then direct them to Christ's words "It is finished" (John 19:30). So now the circles look like this:

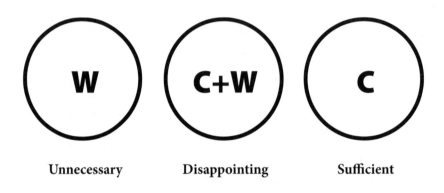

Unnecessary   Disappointing   Sufficient

I do not know how many I and others have been privileged to lead to Christ using these three circles to communicate the suffering of Christ's death for our sins. Whether we are a workplace leader or a church leader giving an evangelistic message to non-Christians, we must explain that God is asking us to trust in Christ alone to save us. Only when we trust Christ alone to save us are we satisfied with the thing that satisfies God. To believe in the biblical sense of the word is to trust in Christ alone as our only way to heaven.

Conclusion

Directions we give to people about how to come to Christ are the most critical of all directions. "He who believes in Him is not condemned; but he who does not believe is condemned already, because he has not believed in the name of the only begotten Son of God" (John 3:18). In beckoning unbelievers to believe, we must explain to them that God is asking them to trust in Christ alone to save them. They must come to God as sinners, recognize Christ died for them and rose again, and trust in Christ alone to save them. Then, and only then, are they forever justified in His sight.

REFLECTING...

1. What word is used ninety-eight times in the Gospel of John to explain how one receives eternal life?

2. What is the word that best communicates to today's audience what we mean by believe?

3. Why is it important to emphasize that we must trust Christ *alone* to save us?

4. How does the use of wrong phrases, such as "invite Jesus into your heart," take away from the clarity needed in evangelistic speaking?

5. How does our understanding of Christ's declaration of "It is finished" (John 19:30) help our understanding of the simple message of salvation?

Chapter 17

Where Does Repentance Fit?

THE EVANGELISTIC SPEAKER POSED the question, "How do you come to Christ?" He then gave the audience this answer. "You begin with repentance. You recognize you've been going the wrong direction. You make an about face and follow Christ. You then have to accept Him as your Lord and Savior. You have to let Him control all your thoughts and decisions. Unless you repent, you cannot come to Christ."

Several things are interesting about his answer. One is that changing the direction of your life preceded coming to Christ. Second, only when you changed the direction of your life could you come to Christ. Third, in coming to Christ you had to be willing to give Him complete control of your life. Fourth, nowhere was any comment made as to the freeness of salvation. He made no mention of the fact that we are accepted by God not based on what we've done for Him but based on what He's done for us. A fifth observation is perhaps the most striking of all. Nowhere did he ask the audience to do what the Gospel of John asks them to do: believe.

Interestingly, his entire answer was wrapped around repentance. Is repentance essential to salvation? What part does repentance play in presenting an evangelistic message? As we speak evangelistically, it is essential we have a biblical understanding of repentance.

We can make several observations upon a careful study of Scripture.

Repentance is essential to salvation.

We know from such a clear statement as Acts 17:30–31 that repentance is essential to salvation. In that passage we read,

Truly, these times of ignorance God overlooked, but now commands all men everywhere to repent, because He has appointed a day on which He will judge the world in righteousness by the Man whom He has ordained. He has given assurance of this to all by raising Him from the dead.

As Paul spoke to the people of Athens from Mars Hill, he placed their gods against His—the resurrected Christ. Instead of thinking of God as something they had carved, they had to recognize God as the one who carved them. Since God would judge the whole world by His Son, men *everywhere* are commanded to repent.

Consider Peter's response to questions raised about the promise of the Lord's return. To those becoming disgruntled, Peter explained, "The Lord is not slack concerning His promise, as some count slackness, but is longsuffering toward us, not willing that any should perish but that all should come to repentance" (2 Pet. 3:9). Note again the emphasis on "all." Repentance is seen not as something men might do, but as something men must do. Whatever it means, it is essential to salvation.

Repentance implies faith or is associated with faith.

The book of John tells us how to receive eternal life (20:31). Ninety-eight times the word "believe" is used. The most familiar verse of that book reads, "For God so loved the world that He gave His only begotten Son, that whoever believes in Him should not perish but have everlasting life" (3:16). How many times in the Gospel of John is the word "repent" used? Not once. Therefore, we can safely conclude that when used in a salvation context, repentance either implies faith or is associated with faith.

The words of Paul and Peter that we've just examined offer good support. Peter testified to Cornelius: "To Him all the prophets witness that, through His name, whoever believes in Him will receive remission of sins" (Acts 10:43). Peter clearly understood that belief in Christ was the sole requirement for an eternal right standing with God. Yet, as mentioned above, he stresses the need to repent (2 Pet. 3:9). Paul likewise understood believing as the sole condition of a right standing with God. He stated, "And by Him everyone who believes is justified from all things from which you could not be justified by the law of Moses" (Acts 13:39). Four chapters later, though, he stresses the need for "all men everywhere to repent" (17:30).

Repentance either implies faith or is associated with faith. That explains why, when used in a salvation context, repentance includes believing and at other times it's distinct from believing. In Mark 1:15 we read, "The time is fulfilled, and the kingdom of God is at hand. Repent, and believe in the gospel." That also explains why it is only used once in the epistle to the Romans: "Or do you despise the riches of His goodness, forbearance, and longsuffering, not knowing that the goodness of God leads you to repentance" (Rom. 2:4). Lewis Sperry Chafer makes this excellent comment:

> In like manner, the Gospel of John, which is written to present Christ as the object of faith unto eternal life, does not once employ the word repentance. Similarly, the Epistle to the Romans, which is the complete analysis of all that enters into the whole plan of salvation by grace, does not use the word repentance in connection with the saving of a soul, except in 2:4 when repentance is equivalent to salvation itself.[1]

When used in a salvation context, to repent is to believe in Christ. That's why we do not need to apologize for not using the word "repentance" in evangelistic messages. When we call upon a non-Christian audience to trust Christ, we have called upon them to repent. We have called upon them to do what the Gospel of John asks—believe.

Repentance means to change your mind, not your life.

The two principal Greek works translated "repent" are *metanoia* and *metanoeo* (a third word, *metemelomai,* is used six times but only once in a salvation-related context). When the object of repentance is *stated,* it has one of five objects: God (Acts 20:21), idols (Rev. 9:20), particular sins (v. 21), deeds (16:11), dead works (Heb. 6:1). When the object is implied, it is often the Person of Christ, as in Acts 2:38: "Then Peter said to them, 'Repent, and let every one of you be baptized in the name of Jesus Christ for the remission of sins; and you shall receive the gift of the Holy Spirit." It is evident from these passages that a change of mind is what is involved—a change of mind regarding Christ, idolatry, particular sins, deeds, or the inability of one's good works to save him. William Evans makes this helpful comment:

> Thus, when Peter, on the Day of Pentecost, called upon the Jews to repent (Acts 2:14–40), he virtually called upon them to change their minds and their views regarding Christ. They had considered Christ to be a mere man, a blasphemer, an imposter. The events of the few preceding days had proven to them that He was none other than the righteous Son of God, their Savior and the Savior of the world. The result of their repentance or change of mind would be that they would receive Jesus Christ as their long promised Messiah.[2]

Raised in a religious home, I was of the opinion that my good living, honesty, church attendance, and baptism would save me. As I studied the

Scriptures, it became clear to me that eternal life was a gift. Good works or religious efforts could not earn it. Dropping to my knees by my bed as a young person, I changed my mind. I repented of my thinking that good works would save me, and I trusted Christ as my only way to heaven.

Those who define repentance as changing one's life often ask, "What about Acts 26:20?" There we read that Paul "declared first to those in Damascus and in Jerusalem, and throughout all the region of Judea, and then to the Gentiles, that they should repent, turn to God, and do works befitting repentance." Some ask, "Isn't there a 'turning' here and a bringing forth of 'works befitting repentance'?"

Two observations need to be made. First, the context makes it clear that repentance is changing one's mind about the Person and work of Christ. To repent, in the context of Acts 26 and other passages, does not speak to the issue of changing one's life but changing one's mind—from disbelief to belief in Christ as the promised Messiah. Two verses later we read,

> Therefore, having obtained help from God, to this day I stand, witnessing both to small and great, saying no other things than those which the prophets and Moses said would come—that the Christ would suffer, that He would be the first to rise from the dead, and would proclaim light to the Jewish people and to the Gentiles. (Acts 20:22–23)

Second, the Greek word translated "befitting" means "corresponding to" or "worthy of." They were to do works that demonstrated how appreciative they were of their salvation. But to handle the text properly, one cannot make fruit a *condition,* so as to say, "No fruit means no repentance." More than one person in the New Testament did not live such a life as a believer.

Changing one's life is not the issue, and understandably so. God offers His gift with no strings attached: "He who believes in Me has everlasting life" (John 6:47). To make changing one's life the first issue is an unbiblical presentation of the gospel; it confuses salvation and sanctification—entering the Christian life with living it. One enters the Christian life through simple trust in Christ. When one comes to God as a sinner, recognizes Christ died for him and arose, and trusts in Christ alone to save, both faith and repentance have taken place. We are entirely His. We then live the Christian life by walking in obedience to Him. Our salvation, though, is never conditioned on that obedience. That's why when we say, "You must come to Christ as Lord and Savior" that is most appropriate if we mean we must acknowledge the fact that He is Lord God Almighty. But if we mean that we must make Him Lord of every area of our lives, we have confused salvation and sanctification. Making Him Lord of every area of our life is part of growing as a disciple. It has nothing to do with salvation.

We cannot change our life before coming to Christ. The grip of sin and temptation is so strong that apart from Him there is no victory. Only after coming to Him, and relying upon Him and His indwelling strength day by day, can we say no to sin and yes to a life of righteousness. As the apostle Paul says,

> And do not present your members as instruments of unrighteousness to sin, but present yourselves to God as being alive from the dead, and your members as instruments of righteousness to God. For sin shall not have dominion over you, for you are not under law but under grace. (Rom. 6:13–14)

God never says, "Clean up your life and come to Me." God says, "Come to Me." It is through coming to Him that He helps us clean up our lives, by taking out of our lives what should not be there and putting in what should be there.

So repentance, as it relates to salvation, could be defined as "to change your mind about what is keeping you from trusting Christ and to trust Him alone to save you." Once we have trusted Christ, both repentance and faith have taken place.

Tears are not the issue.

The confusion surrounding repentance also relates to the shedding of tears. Some would teach that if there are no tears, there is no repentance because there is no sorrow for sin. Some have incorrectly used 2 Corinthians 7:8–10:

> For even if I made you sorry with my letter, I do not regret it; though I did regret it. For I perceive that the same epistle made you sorry, though only for a while. Now I rejoice, not that you were made sorry, but that your sorrow led to repentance. For you were made sorry in a godly manner, that you might suffer loss from us in nothing. For godly sorrow produces repentance leading to salvation, not to be regretted; but the sorrow of the world produces death.

In this context Paul was speaking to believers not about salvation from damnation, but salvation from the consequences of sin in a believer's life. After a painful visit, Paul wrote a severe letter to the Corinthian believers. It is referred to in 2 Corinthians 2:4 but is now lost to us. Although he first regretted writing to them, that changed when his rebuke brought about repentance and a change of behavior. Paul was addressing Christians, not unbelievers.

The issue is, we must know that we are sinners regardless of how we feel about our sin. Christ attracted sinners and amazed scribes and Pharisees (Mark 2). When asked how He could identify with those whom others felt were despicable, He replied, "Those who are well have no need of a physician, but those who are sick. I did not come to call the righteous, but sinners, to repentance" (v. 17). The difficulty the scribes and Pharisees had was admitting they were sinners, not how they felt about their sin. Additionally, it is only *after* we come to Christ that we develop a sorrow for sin as we discover more about His righteousness and our unrighteousness. If as believers we do not feel worse about sin now than when we came to Christ, it is doubtful that we have grown as Christians.

Conclusion

We tell a non-Christian audience that to come to Christ they need to do what the Gospel of John asks them to do—believe. When an unbeliever comes to God as a sinner, recognizes Christ died for Him and arose, and trusts in Christ alone to save, both repentance and faith have taken place. Repentance historically has been overladen with confusion, misunderstanding, and unbiblical teaching. To present a clear gospel we should explain His substitutionary death and His resurrection for sinners, and the need to receive the gift of eternal life by simple trust in Christ. When unbelievers trust in Christ alone to save them, they demonstrate repentance and faith.

REFLECTING...

1. Why is it understandable that the Gospel of John does not use the word "repent"?

2. Why is it important to understand that repentance means to change your mind, not change your life?

3. In one sentence, define the word "repentance."

4. Why is it unnecessary to use the word "repentance" in evangelistic messages?

5. Why should we feel worse about sin now than when we came to Christ?

Chapter 18

How Do You Combine Grace and Truth?

HAVE YOU NOTICED HOW extreme we are? We spend too freely or we are too stingy. We neglect our family or act like the family is the only thing that matters. We are either too firm with our children or not firm enough.

The same tendency toward the extreme happens in speaking. We can be so truthful that we lack grace in the way we present truth. I've heard evangelistic speakers characterize non-Christians as rebellious, self-centered, God-defying, and lost—all of which they often are. But it was said in such a way that I wondered if the speaker had any compassion for them. I've heard other speakers speak with so much grace that they never addressed the truthfulness of a person's lost condition. One speaker argued that Christ never referred to anyone as a sinner. That claim is biblically inaccurate as proven by Christ's statement "For I did not come to call the righteous, but sinners, to repentance" (Matt. 9:13).

Christ was a man of grace. But He was also a man of truth. "And the Word became flesh and dwelt among us, and we beheld His glory, the glory as of the only begotten of the Father, full of grace and truth" (John 1:14).

One place where the balance between truth and grace is evident is Christ's conversation with the Samaritan woman (John 4). He demonstrated grace when He took her from the physical water, which could not satisfy, to the spiritual water that could. He said to her, "If you knew the gift of God, and who it is that says to you, 'Give me a drink', you would have asked Him, and He would have given you living water" (v. 10). He demonstrated truth when, to her claim, "I have no husband" (v. 17), Jesus responded, "You have well said, 'I have no husband', for you have had five husbands, and the one whom you now have is not your husband; in that you spoke truly" (vv. 17–18).

Another example of His balance between grace and truth is found in John 8. A woman caught in adultery is brought before Him. He was calling sin what it is: sin. In no way was He minimizing what she had done. In fact, He was so truthful that He also revealed her accusers' sin veiled in self-righteousness. He said to her accusers, "He who is without sin among you, let him throw a stone at her first" (v. 7). That statement would have demonstrated grace to the woman. Had I been in her shoes, I would have been comforted by His disdain for my accusers' self-righteous attitude.

Disdain for their attitude and grace toward her would have been evident in His body language. That grace reached a climax when He stooped and wrote on the ground, "as though He did not hear," and said to her, "Neither do I condemn you; go and sin no more" (v. 11).

Scripture consistently presents Christ as a Person of both grace and truth. His truth told sinners what they needed to know. To those who spoke disparagingly of His being born of a virgin and despised His claims to be God, He said, "You are of your father the devil" (8:44). His grace welcomed sinners with unconditional love. He promised, "The one who comes to Me I will by no means cast out" (6:37).

Only in demonstrating such a balance are we Christ-like in our presentation. How does an *evangelistic speaker* demonstrate grace and truth? Three suggestions.

Examine your personal life.

Speakers are called to present Christ, but not all speak with the proper motive. When the apostle Paul was in prison, some took advantage of his confinement to gain the spotlight. He testified, "Some indeed preach Christ even from envy and strife, as some also from goodwill: the former preach Christ from selfish ambition, not sincerely, supposing to add affliction to my chains" (Phil. 1:15–16). He concludes, "whether in pretense or in truth, Christ is preached; and in this I rejoice, yes, and will rejoice" (v. 18). Paul was not condoning their motive. He was condoning their message in spite of their motive.

Although our motives at times may not be the best, that does not dismiss the need for speakers to be people of good character. Christ likeness in our character should be reflected in the way we come across as speakers. If we are negative and judgmental in our demeanor, we will be negative and judgmental in our messages. We will take what could be a positive passage and give it a negative twist. Some speakers don't feel they have fulfilled their role unless they make people feel guilty about everything and anything. They stress hell more than heaven. A preacher who is negative in the way he attempts to motivate his staff is not likely to have much grace in his evangelistic message. By contrast, the kind of speaker who "sees no wrong" in most other things, will most likely "see no wrong" in his messages.

Hence, instead of speaking truthfully and directly about the consequences of sin, this type of speaker will tend to comfort the sinner when he needs to make him uncomfortable.

We must model Christ, not just present Christ. I've urged those who desire to be evangelistic speakers to take the Gospel of John and meditate on a chapter a day and to keep this question foremost in mind: "How do Christ's conduct and conversations reflect grace and truth?" I have done that, and it proved to be one of the most spiritually helpful things I've done. It's been particularly helpful in the way I come across as an evangelistic speaker. I noticed things about Christ's approach when He came in contact with people. I saw Christ speak the strongest to the Pharisees and Sadducees whose religious arrogance merited His directness. I saw Him "come up from underneath" those overburdened by their sin, rather than "down on top" of them. That told me not only how I should come across in my messages, but also how to come across in my walk as a believer. God wanted me to walk for the unbeliever, not just talk to the unbeliever. The balance between grace and truth demonstrated in our personal lives will in many ways be the balance between grace or truth demonstrated when we speak.

Examine the thrust of the Gospel of John.

Now look at the Gospel of John from another angle—a much needed one. The one book written to tell us how to receive eternal life is the Gospel of John. John declares that as his purpose: "And truly Jesus did many other signs in the presence of His disciples, which are not written in this book; but these are written that you may believe that Jesus is the Christ, the Son of God, and that believing you may have life in His name. (John 20:30–31). When we study John, it becomes evident that God is not trying to scare us out of hell with bad news but inviting us to heaven with Good News.

Did Christ speak of hell? He certainly did. Although there is no reference in the Gospel of John to hell, two things are worth noting.

First, Christ spoke of condemnation.

"For God did not send his Son into the world to condemn the world, but that the world through Him might be saved. He who believes in Him is not condemned; but he who does not believe is condemned already, because he has not believed in the name of the only begotten Son of God." (John 3:17–18)

Second, other Gospels mention the stern warnings Christ gave about hell. Examine the following:

Matthew 23:33—*Serpents, brood of vipers! How can you escape the condemnation of hell?*

Mark 9:43–48—*If your hand causes you to sin, cut it off. It is better for you to enter into life maimed, rather than having two hands, to go to hell, into the fire that shall never be quenched—where "their worm does not die and the fire is not quenched." And if your foot causes you to sin, cut it off. It is better for you to enter life lame, rather than having two feet, to be cast into hell, into the fire that shall never be quenched—where "Their worm does not die and the fire is not quenched." And if your eye causes you to sin, pluck it out. It is better for you to enter the kingdom of God with one eye, rather than having two eyes, to be cast into hell fire—where "Their worm does not die, and the fire is not quenched."*

John's thrust, therefore, becomes very interesting. Christ spoke long and directly about hell most often to those whose religious arrogance needed a firm rebuke. But His emphasis, as seen in the Gospel of John, was to invite us to heaven with Good News. Look at the repeated emphasis of that book:

John 3:14–16—*And as Moses lifted up the serpent in the wilderness, even so must the Son of Man be lifted up, that whoever believes in Him should not perish but have eternal life. For God so loved the world that He gave His only begotten Son, that whoever believes in Him should not perish but have everlasting life.*

John 4:13–14—*Jesus answered and said to her, "Whoever drinks of this water will thirst again, but whoever drinks of the water that I shall give him will never thirst. But the water that I shall give him will become in him a fountain of water springing up into everlasting life."*

John 5:24—*Most assuredly, I say to you, he who hears My word and believes in Him who sent Me has everlasting life, and shall not come into judgment, but has passed from death into life.*

John 6:50-51—*This is the bread which comes down from heaven, that one may eat of it and not die. I am the living bread which came down from heaven. If anyone eats of this bread, he will live forever; and the bread that I shall give is My flesh, which I shall give for the life of the world.*

John 7:37–38—*On the last day, that great day of the feast, Jesus stood and cried out, saying, "If anyone thirsts, let him come to Me and drink. He who believes in Me, as the Scripture has said, out of his heart will flow rivers of living water."*

John 8:51—*"Most assuredly, I say to you, if anyone keeps My word he shall never see death."*

John 10: 9–10—*I am the door. If anyone enters by Me, he will be saved, and will go in and out and find pasture. The thief does not come except to steal, and to kill, and to destroy. I have come that they may have life, and that they may have it more abundantly.*

John 11:25–26—*Jesus said to her, "I am the resurrection and the life. He who believes in Me, though he may die, he shall live. And whoever lives and believes in Me shall never die. Do you believe this?"*

John 12:47–50—*And if anyone hears My words and does not believe, I do not judge him; for I did not come to judge the world but to save the world. He who rejects Me, and does not receive My words, has that which judges him—the word that I have spoken will judge him in the last day. For I have not spoken on My own authority; but the Father who sent Me gave Me a command, what I should say and what I should speak. And I know that His command is everlasting life. Therefore, whatever I speak, just as the Father has told Me, so I speak.*

John 14:3–6—*And if I go and prepare a place for you, I will come again and receive you to Myself; that where I am, there you may be also. And where I go you know, and the way you know. Thomas said to Him, "Lord, we do not know where You are going, and how can we know the way?" Jesus said to him, "I am the way, the truth, and the life. No one comes to the Father except through Me."*

John 17:3—*"And this is eternal life, that they may know You, the only true God, and Jesus Christ whom You have sent."*

As mentioned earlier, we should speak about hell. I've been told that D. L. Moody once shared the gospel with a young man. The man had difficulty grasping what Christ had done on the cross and even the reality of heaven and hell. At one point he said to Moody, "If I could see heaven for five minutes I would believe." Moody responded, "If you could see hell for five seconds you would believe." Hell is real. At the same time, though, we must speak of hell out of compassion for those who might go there. Some have said we should not preach hell unless we can do it with tears. One might argue whether actual tears are necessary, but we must appreciate the point: speak about hell with sorrow for those who could go there.

At the same time, our emphasis should be on inviting people to heaven with Good News. Hell is a place they don't need to go. Heaven is a place they should not miss out on. Why? Because heaven is more than a place. It has to do with a Person. Who we are going to be with—Jesus Christ Himself—is what will make heaven what it is.

When the focus of our message is inviting people to heaven with Good News, we are doing what the Gospel of John does. And we do so with grace and truth. The truth about hell is there, but it is accompanied by the truth of heaven and the grace of God that invites them there.

Conclusion

Balance is imperative in evangelistic speaking. We must not declare truth at the expense of grace. Nor should we declare grace at the expense of truth. We must be both graceful and truthful. When our audience hears us they should feel as if they have not just heard Christ; they have seen Him modeled. Such speech glorifies the Savior. It can be said of us, as was said of Christ; that we were "full of grace and truth" (John 1:14).

REFLECTING...

1. What two suggestions for balancing grace and truth would help any evangelistic speaker?

2. Where is one example of how Christ spoke with grace and another example of how He spoke with truth?

3. How does "negativism" or "positivism" in our demeanor affect the way we come across as speakers?

4. Why is the Gospel of John particularly helpful in determining how we should come across as evangelistic speakers?

5. If we are expository evangelistic speakers, how should the mood of the text affect our message?

Chapter 19

How Short Is Short?

SPEAKERS ARE TO SPEAK on eternity, not *for* eternity. George Burns reportedly said, "A good sermon ought to have a good beginning and a good ending. And they ought to be as close together as possible."

A lady once approached me after speaking and gave me what I considered a compliment. She said, "That was nice, informative, and short." What struck me was not her use of "nice" and "informative" but her use of "short." Effective evangelistic messages, whether given in the church or in the workplace, are not those that make the listener wonder, "When is he going to stop?" They make the listener exclaim, "Is he through already?" Martin Luther said it well, "Start fresh. Speak out. Stop short."[1]

In regard to the length of an evangelistic message, several questions need answering.

Why does length matter?

To determine why length matters, consider three factors. First, we are speaking to people not accustomed to sitting and listening to a message. If they have done so, it's probably not something they enjoyed. Even as I wrote this chapter, someone commented to me about a particular speaker, "His messages are too long." Our audience's attention span is relatively short. One might ask, "But what about those who sit and watch a two-hour movie?" The answer is obvious. Watching a two-hour movie is vastly different from listening to a one-hour message! I have never met one non-Christian who was discouraged because the speaker finished before he expected him to. I have met those who were pleasantly surprised.

Second, our preference is not that a non-Christians listen to us once; we'd prefer they return to hear us or someone else again—and again. Few people come to Christ the first time they hear the gospel. I've spoken with many who told me that they heard the gospel ten to fifteen times before trusting Christ. They are more likely to return if the message they hear is brief rather than lengthy.

Finally, the number one concern of people in the twenty-first century is not money, it's time. This is becoming increasingly true across the world. El Salvador's standard of living is much lower than that of the United States. But as I trained speakers there in evangelistic speaking, my interpreter told me something enlightening. He said, "The number one concern of our people is time." Therefore, when we keep the message short, we demonstrate sensitivity. The length of our message communicates, "I realize that you do not have all day to hear what I'm about to say."

What is the proper length?

Speaking in over a thousand outreaches over more than forty years has given me a clear answer. I refuse to speak more than thirty minutes to a non-Christian audience regardless of where that audience is located. If I can't say it in thirty minutes, I can't say it. The only exception would be when I'm speaking through an interpreter. Even then I'll keep as close to thirty minutes as I possibly can. Speaking through an interpreter cuts your speaking time by approximately one-third. That means, since your speaking time is shorter, your words have to be carefully chosen.

Understand that I'm speaking about the length of the message itself. In a church setting, I'll read the passage I'm speaking from prior to beginning my message. At the close of the message, I'll give an invitation of some kind or another, such as an invitation to meet me in a side room. The thirty minutes does not include the time it takes to read the passage or give an invitation. Thirty minutes is the actual message length.

Someone might ask, "Isn't the length of the message something you ought to let the Holy Spirit determine?" The answer is "yes." But the same Holy Spirit who directs you in what to say can help you to say it in thirty minutes. When an audience grows tired of a message due to its length, we ought not to attribute that message length to the Holy Spirit. More likely it is the human spirit that is at fault. God, through the Holy Spirit, wants to help us keep our message to a length that encourages the listener's attention.

What encourages brevity?

Preparing long messages is easy; preparing short ones is more difficult. Someone asked Woodrow Wilson, "How long does it take to prepare a ten-minute speech?" He answered, "Two weeks." They asked, "How long for a one-hour speech?" The president replied, "One week." They then asked, "How long for a two-hour speech?" He answered, "I'm ready now."[2] It takes more effort to prepare a shorter message than a longer one.

What encourages a speaker to devote the time, thought, and work necessary to keeping a message within thirty minutes?

One is the biblical exhortation to "Do unto others as you would have them do unto you." No one enjoys hearing a speaker whose message length reminds you of the mercy of God—it endures forever! It does not matter who the speaker is, eventually you glance at your watch and wonder when he is going to conclude. If you don't enjoy listening to long-winded speakers, why be one?

Cultivate the proper mindset: one of humility. It is easy to think people are dying to hear us. Only part of that is right. People are dying! They might enjoy hearing us speak, but they care more about the length of our message than we might think. Haddon Robinson has appropriately said, "When preachers stand up in the pulpit, they face audiences with their guard up. A few in the congregation wait eagerly for the sermon to begin. Most wait eagerly for the sermon to conclude."[3] Humility keeps us from crediting ourselves with being more exciting than we really are.

Brevity and effective speaking are connected. The art of effective speaking is not so much knowing what to put into a message but what to leave out. For an expository evangelistic speaker, the Word is like a buffet. There is more that can be said from one single passage than we have time to say. The more we develop skill in speaking, the more we will examine what can be *excluded* instead of what can be included. Speakers put it in; communicators take it out. The most effective communicators ask what *must* be said, not just what *can* be said. Developing your skills in speaking will be one of your biggest steps in learning how to keep a message to thirty minutes.

A shorter message is more direct because it requires more thought, preparation, and time allocation. We come across as someone who has something to say, we say it, and then we sit down. We not only know what we are going to say at each juncture of our message but how long we have to say it. Any speaker knows it takes more work to put together a shorter message than a longer one. We must carefully consider how much time we give to the introduction, how many illustrations we need, and how long we have to conclude our thoughts. The amount of time we give to each point of our message is critical.

Conclusion

Mark Twain is reported to have said, "Few sinners are saved after the first twenty minutes of a sermon."[4] One could argue about the "twenty minutes" standard. However, one cannot dispute that brevity enhances a message. Audiences are not asking us to say everything we can possibly say. They want us to think through our message and say it as succinctly as we can. The ability to say what needs to be said within the amount of time a non-Christian can digest it makes an effective communicator. Time is important to our audience and therefore needs to be important to us.

REFLECTING...

1. What should be the maximum length of an evangelistic message, regardless of when it is given?

2. Give two reasons why the length of the message matters.

3. How does a spirit of humility enhance brevity?

4. How are brevity and effective speaking related?

5. Why do shorter messages take more work than longer messages?

Chapter 20

How Do Illustrations Help?

TWO SPEAKERS. BOTH ARE eloquent. Every word is enunciated properly. Their voices are pleasant and conversational. Everything from their demeanor to their delivery conveys that they are keenly aware they are talking to people—people with real needs and problems. Both are biblically correct. Both conclude within thirty minutes. But why did one speaker's message seem like only ten minutes while the other one kept you looking at your watch?

Most likely, the speaker that kept your attention spiced his message with illustrations. You saw his children playing in the yard. He reminded you of a conversation you had with your wife on the sofa. You felt as though you had ridden with him in his car in bumper-to-bumper traffic. He didn't just tell you how the Scriptures speak to life. He *showed* you. He didn't just re-tell what happened. He relived it.

Illustrations always have been critical in speaking to people. It was a predominant teaching method used by Christ Himself. Matthew 13:3 reads, "then He [Jesus] spoke many things to them in parables." The *Nelson Study Bible* comments, "This teaching method, often used by the rabbis, utilized common sense from everyday life to teach new truths about the kingdom."[1]

William Carey, the "Father of Modern Missions," got off to a rough start. When he sought ordination from the Baptist Church in Olney, England, in 1785, he was rejected. After hearing him speak, the examining board felt he needed a period of probation. One member said, "You have no likes in your sermons. Christ taught that the kingdom of heaven was like to leaven hid in meal, like to a grain of mustard, etc. You tell us what things are, but never what they are like."[2] Those "likes" are even more critical in speaking to people of the twenty-first century.

Why are illustrations needed?

Examine your audience. You are talking to people whose minds are adapted to secular illustrations. A newspaper columnist observed, "People think with pictures in their heads." We are talking to a watching generation more so than a reading one. Television, movies, Internet, and video games have transformed us into an image-sensitive, story-shaped society. The modern man's mind has been called a picture gallery.[3] Roger Shank, in *Tell Me a Story,* makes the comment, "People think in terms of stories. They understand the world in terms of stories that they have already understood. New events or problems are understood by reference to old, previously understood stories and explained to others by the use of stories. We also understand just about everything this way."[4]

Therefore, when you skillfully use illustrations you meet listeners on their level. As Charles Haddon Spurgeon observed, "The sermon is the house; the illustrations are the windows that let in the light."[5] Thus the most effective speakers are those who turn an ear into an eye. Gary Smalley and John Trent, in *The Language of Love,* make the observation, "Take Cicero, the silver-tongued orator of the Roman Empire. He believed word pictures are 'lights' that illuminate truth. As he told his students, the more crucial the message, the brighter the lights must be."[6] Since an evangelistic speaker has the most crucial message—the message of the gospel— the lights must be the brightest they have ever been.

Preachers are often viewed as being detached from real life. A young boy sitting in church beside his mother asked, "Does the preacher live here or does he just come down from heaven every Sunday?" Some speakers cause you to wonder if they live on the same planet you do. Illustrations assist you in entering the listeners' daily life experiences. They demonstrate that we understand their struggles, entertain their thoughts, and have experienced some of the same discouragements. Our use of the Word should demonstrate that we understand the Bible. Our use of illustrations should prove that we understand life.

Another reason you need illustrations is that they make a message interesting. They get attention. Think of speakers you've heard who, in the midst of their messages, made comments such as:

"Let me illustrate."

"I will share something that happened at our house the other day."

"You will laugh at me, and with me, when I tell you a mistake I made two days ago."

"Were you as captured as I was by the story on the second page of yesterday's newspaper?"

Suddenly, heads raise and eyes focus on you. Nodding heads perk up. Illustrations enliven the audience and grab attention. Ralph Waldo Emerson once remarked, "I cannot hear a sermon without being struck by the fact that amid drowsy series of sentences what a sensation a historical fact, a biographical name, a sharply objective illustration makes!"[7] Spurgeon made the same observation in different words when he said, "Illustrations make a sermon pleasurable and interesting."[8] It doesn't matter where an evangelistic message is given, illustrations cause an audience to sit up and listen.

How do you gather them?

One week from today, you will stand before your audience. Where will you get the illustrations you need for your message? Some will come from your experiences, but it is unwise to take all of them from there. Hopefully, you can also pull them from your illustration file. But they cannot all be gathered that week. If you want illustrations available when you need them, you must collect them weeks, months, and even years in advance. How do you gather stories ahead of time so they are accessible when you need them?

The first suggestion is, always carry a recording device or have something to write on. It might be a palm pilot or an index card. Any piece of paper will do. I find a 3" x 5" card to be more durable. Plus, it fits easily into a pocket or purse. The point is, you need something to record on, either a piece of paper or something electronic.

The second suggestion is, set a goal. My goal is to collect ten illustrations each week. I may go over that goal, but I don't go under it. The comment is rather trite, but it is true: "Aim at nothing, hit nothing." The same is true with illustrations. If you do not have a goal of how many you want to find, you probably will not find any. Set a specific goal for the number of illustrations you wish to find, and you will hit it. As you practice this, you will establish a habit. Your goal doesn't have to be ten illustrations a week, but you do need to have a goal. A goal of a few illustrations each week will accomplish more than no illustrations a week.

With something to write on and a goal to aim for, you will discipline yourself to look for stories you can use. Jay Adams, in *Pulpit Speech,* correctly observes, "One way to begin to 'see' illustrations of truth wherever you turn is to discipline yourself to do so."[9] You will be amazed how many you've passed up on bumper stickers, billboards, magazines, newspapers, and conversations with friends.

Having a goal and a means to record illustrations makes it more likely that you will find them and use them. Otherwise, you will forget important details. As the old Chinese proverb says, "The faintest ink has a better memory than the sharpest brain."[10] It's the details that make the illustration come alive.

Ask other people to help. I've been approached by speakers who say, "I'm speaking on commitment." Then, after summarizing their message, they continue, "At this point, I need an illustration on apathy. Do you happen to have one?" One caution. Ask for a single specific illustration, not an illustration *file*. It is offensive to ask someone to do our work for us; it's not offensive to ask for assistance.

Become a person who uses illustrations well and others will help you find illustrations without being asked, particularly if your spirit demonstrates that you enjoy being helped. One person who can help may be your spouse. I've never asked my wife, Tammy, to help me find illustrations. She just began to do so. Because she's heard me speak more than anyone else, she knows the kind of illustrations I like. I'll often come home from speaking, and lying on my desk will be an illustration she's found for me. I have teased her that one of the reasons God instituted marriage was because He knew, "It is not good for a man to be without illustrations!"

Friends will hand them to you, e-mail, or mail them to you, and even call long distance to share one with you. If they know you use illustrations, they may read one and say, "I have to give this to him. He'll love this illustration." Weeks after speaking in an area, I've had people write or e-mail me to say, "I noticed how much you use illustrations. Would this one be helpful?" The ones I couldn't use have been the exception, not the norm.

We can also borrow from other speakers. Every speaker borrows illustrations from other sources—whether from books, conversations, or messages. You will not live long enough to be original about every illustration you use. Most illustrations are from other sources. Where necessary, give the source; where it is not required, don't.

Some ask, "What about illustrations from different stories in the Bible?" Don Sunukjian has expressed it well:

> Biblical illustrations are seldom as helpful or as effective as contemporary pictures from the everyday lives of your listeners and rarely should be used. This is true for a number of reasons.
>
> First, biblical events and situations are usually far removed from the experiences of our listens and tend to strike them as "from a foreign culture and from another age, when maybe God did such things." Few of your listeners, hearing of Joseph, for example, expect to be sold to Egyptian merchants, to be seduced by their boss's wife, to interpret dreams for convicts in prisons, or to become chief-of-staff to their country's leader. Such experiences are difficult for your listeners to identify with; they're not true in life today.[11]

What will be your single biggest source of illustrations?

Although you can find good stories through conversations, television, movies, radio, billboards, and bumper stickers, your single biggest source will be reading. This is simply because the more we read the more pages we turn. The more pages we turn, the more illustrations we collect. We will never watch enough television (and probably shouldn't), drive enough highways, or talk to enough people to gather all the illustrations we need.

Read everything—newspapers, magazines, books, devotionals. An advantage is that when much of what you read is current, you are able to keep your file updated. A report on a high school killing might contain a substitution illustration. A medical report on cancer gives a comment about the public's view of life and death. A public figure's prideful statement will offer an observation on the conceit with which we all wrestle. Read, read, read, and keep on reading. It is difficult to be a good illustrator without being a consistent reader.

Illustration books and Internet sources are helpful. However, one drawback to these sources is that everyone has access to them. Therefore, there is a much better chance of using an illustration that many have already heard. When I hear speakers say, "I pulled this illustration off the Internet," I've glanced around. Husbands smiled at wives and wives at husbands with that look of "I know what he's going to say." They had already read it or heard it from someone who also found it on the Internet. That's not necessarily bad, but it takes away from the freshness of the story.

Books by people who illustrate are more helpful than illustration books. A person who illustrates when he speaks will usually illustrate when he writes. Chuck Swindoll is a good example. I enjoy the way he relates to people through illustrations when he speaks. I have yet to read any book he's written without finding an abundance of illustrations. Speakers don't change who they are and how they communicate when they pick up a pen. Those who use illustrations behind a podium tend to use them when they write.

How do you file them?

Give each illustration a heading. Ask yourself, "What is the illustration's subject: sinfulness, substitution, trust, boldness, sacrifice, dedication, love, loneliness, happiness, Christlikeness?" The list of possibilities is endless. Then ask, "What is it saying about the subject?" Does the illustration show the characteristics of its subject? Or perhaps it highlights the need for its subject. Maybe it shows the benefits of a particular topic. To keep your file user-friendly, keep this part of the heading short—two to five words. Later, when you need an example of sacrifice, you look for an illustration with the heading "Sacrifice—example of." This way, you don't need to look through every illustration on sacrifice—just the ones that show an example of sacrifice.

If you find a good story in an illustration book, treat it as any other illustration. Reprint it and give it a heading and description that fits your thinking. For me to use an illustration, it has to be the way I think. Once they have been properly headed, file them alphabetically. Finally, always record the source, so you know where you obtained it.

Here are five examples.

Title: JESUS CHRIST
Subtitle: extraordinary
Illustration: Everything in Christ astonishes me. His Spirit overawes me, and his will confounds me. Between him and whoever else in the world, there is no possible term of comparison. He is truly a being by himself . . . I search in vain in history to find the similar to Jesus Christ, or anything which can approach the gospel. Neither history, nor humanity, nor the ages, nor nature, offer me anything with which I am able to compare it or to explain it. Here everything is extraordinary.—Napoleon

> **Source**: Vernon C. Grounds, *The Reason For Our Hope*
> (Chicago: Moody Press, 1945), 37

Title: GOD
Subtitle: perspective on
Illustration: Elie Wiesel said of the God described by Kushner, "If that's who God is why doesn't he resign and let someone more competent take his place?"

> **Source**: Philip Yancey, *Disappointment with God*
> (Grand Rapids: Zondervan,1992), 79

Title: SALVATION
Subtitle: can't buy
Illustration: There is a story that came from the life of Teddy Roosevelt. When some of his men were wounded and dying, he needed medical help. He went to the Red Cross and said, "I need to buy some medical supplies." She said, "Sorry, you can't." He said, "Look, money is no issue. Name the price. I'll pay it." She said, "You can't. But I can give them to you." He took the medical supplies that saved many of his men.

> **Source**: Rev. Ralph Marks,
> Hollywood, Florida

Title: STANDARDS
Subtitle: lack of
Illustration: Never in our culture has there been a time when more wrong has been called right and more right has been called wrong.

> **Source**: Dr. Mark Bailey

Title: FORGIVENESS
Subtitle: permanent attitude
Illustration: As Martin Luther King, Jr., said well, "Forgiveness is not an occasional act. It is a permanent attitude."

Source: Gary Inrig, *Forgiveness*
(Grand Rapids: Discovery House, 2005), 127

Computers have made filing illustrations easier. You can find any number of database programs to help you with this task. However, that still does not negate the fact that the illustration must have a proper heading to be user-friendly. The computer will be of little help if you give an illustration a heading of "boldness" when you should have listed it under "substitution." Computers are a great time-saver in browsing large illustration files. Also, should I remember a particular quote and know the person's name who said it, a quick search of that name will bring up the illustration. A good database will offer a number of different search possibilities.

How many do you need per message?

Three factors should influence the number of illustrations we use in a message: *Time*. Are you speaking for five, fifteen, or thirty minutes? *Audience*. Are they predominantly young? A younger audience often demands more illustrations. Regardless of age, though, people like stories. *Text*. Have you chosen a text that tells a story, such as the rich man and Lazarus in Luke 16, or are you speaking from a text that gives a series of declarations, such as a passage in the Pastoral Epistles? A biographical message often requires fewer illustrations than one from the epistles. The biblical story itself holds the listeners' attention.

One should normally think in terms of ten to fifteen illustrations per message. I'm now using the term illustrations in the widest sense of the word—an analogy, quote, statistic, story, poem, etc. Most are surprised at that number. Listen to some of the most effective communicators of our day, and you will discover they usually use that many illustrations per message. I attended a conference where there were a number of effective speakers. One was particularly praised for how well the audience related to his message. I assure you that his abundance of illustrations made his message pleasurable and interesting.

Another important aspect of choosing illustrations for expository evangelistic speaking is remembering that we are speaking to *unbelievers*. The importance of remembering our audience cannot be over stressed. This is because many of the illustrations we collect tend to be relevant to believers, which may not communicate well to a non-Christian audience. You need to develop a large collection of illustrations because you will have to pass over many that are addressed to Christians rather than unbelievers.

Within my message preparation for an audience of non-Christians, I ask several questions. *Is this relevant to non-Christians?* It should be something that comes out of their experience. *Is it interesting?* Unfortunately an illustration may be relevant but not that interesting. There can be a number of reasons it doesn't capture a listener's attention—too common of an occurrence, not enough details, etc. *Is it understandable and easy to explain?* Some illustrations are relevant and interesting, but too difficult to explain. The audience would have had to have been present to appreciate what happened. The illustration may be so difficult to explain that telling it takes more time than your message allows. *Can you tell it well?* Speakers are people. God uses our different personalities in different ways. One speaker may tell a particular story with ease; another just can't tell it effectively. One speaker friend of mine can take an inanimate object, such as a statue, and build a story around it that makes the cold, stationary object come to life. That kind of illustration is difficult for me to use and tell. Be yourself and use the stories that you can tell well.

We must be careful about how many personal illustrations we use, especially when speaking to non-Christians. Craig Larson gives a helpful word of caution: "Certainly well-crafted personal illustrations are some of our best illustrations, but they can never meet the majority of our needs. I must illustrate from a world bigger than my own. My listeners don't relate to everything in my life. They relate as well to the pervasive world of media and the experiences of other people."[12] Ken Davis agrees when he says to take care "that the word self doesn't become a huge part of our message."[13] More than once I have heard non-Christians criticize speakers who consistently refer to *their* families, *their* interests, *their* background. While a certain amount of that helps others get to know you, too much of it comes across to a non-Christian as being self-centered. When you use personal illustrations, avoid success stories. Unbelievers can handle hearing about your failures. You are one with them. But they can become annoyed when you appear to harp on your successes. Regardless of how humbly you attempt to come across, it borders on bragging.

How do you use them?

A scalpel is of no use to a doctor if he doesn't use it correctly. A hammer does a carpenter no good if he holds it incorrectly. Software is of little use on your computer if you don't know how to use it. Illustrations are the same. You must use them correctly if you want them to be effective.

How are you entering and exiting the illustration? You can help or hinder its effectiveness the way you come into it or leave it.

For example, the word "Christian" means different things to different people. The Bible defines a Christian as a person who has trusted Christ as his only way to heaven. Unbelievers, not understanding that, may define a

Christian as a person who goes to church, has been baptized, or takes the sacraments. I have a message where I answer the question, "What makes a person a Christian?" I begin by explaining a word that may mean one thing to someone but something different to another.

I speak of visiting one of the Caribbean islands. After engaging in conversation with the people, I said "Good night" and proceeded to walk away. Each time they looked at me rather strangely. My host, hearing and seeing what I did, took me aside. He explained, "On this island, Larry, we don't use good night to end a conversation; we use it to begin one. You walk up to the person, say good night, and begin talking. So the people here are trying to figure out why you say good-night when you're through speaking to them. Furthermore, as soon as you do so, you proceed to walk away." I discovered that a word as simple as "good night" can be used by some to close a conversation and by others to begin one. I then explain the same can be said of a word as simple as the word "Christian." Ask the average person, "What is a Christian?" and you will receive a variety of answers. I explain the different answers one receives.

How you walk into and out of an illustration is of critical importance. If you don't walk into it appropriately, the audience is unprepared for the illustration. If you don't walk out of it properly, you have hindered its effectiveness. If you haven't availed yourself of it, EvanTell's book entitled *How to Use Illustrations Effectively in Evangelistic Speaking* will be of help to you.

Illustrations are for communicating. Martin Lloyd Jones, in *Preaching and Preachers,* emphasizes, "Stories and illustrations are only meant to illustrate truth, not to call attention to themselves."[14] If the illustration does not support the point you are making, don't use it. Keith Wilhite and Scott Gibson, in *The Big Idea of Biblical Preaching,* make the excellent point: "The most important thing to remember about illustrations is that they must clearly focus on the point we are making. It is great to have a smashing story, but if it doesn't fit it will only serve to distract attention from the point we are trying to drive home."[15] I heard a speaker give an illustration that would have been effective in the proper message; however, in this one it did not fit and actually detracted from the message. By the same token, I heard another speaker give an illustration that so enhanced his idea, I thought about what he said for months to follow. The ultimate end of illustrations is not illustrating, but communicating. You have a point that you are trying to drive home. The purpose of the illustration is to help you do that. If it doesn't, it is of no use. Only use an illustration if it helps communicate or support your idea.

Conclusion

People like stories, and stories effectively used illustrate biblical and eternal truth. As we speak to people whose minds are picture galleries, we must use illustrations to communicate effectively. Once people hear the truth, a good illustration will help them see it. Effective speaking helps a listener say, "I hear what you're saying." Effectively used illustrations help the listener say, "I see what you mean."

REFLECTING...

1. Give two reasons illustrations are needed.

2. Why is it important in collecting illustrations to have a set a goal and a recording device?

3. What will be your single biggest source of illustrations?

4. What are the two questions you ask about each illustration as you prepare to file it?

5. How many illustrations should you normally use per message?

Chapter 21

What Part Does Humor Play?

THREE MEN ENJOYING COFFEE at Starbucks were talking about jobs, sports, children, and eventually their wives' pregnancies. "When my wife had twins," one man explained, "it really didn't surprise me. After all, I play for the Minnesota Twins." The second man added, "I know what you mean. When my wife had triplets that was no surprise either. I work for the 3M Company. The third man jumped from his chair and headed for the exit with the speed of an Olympic sprinter. His friends rushed after him. They caught up to him as he was unlocking his car. "What's wrong?" they asked. "I have to see my wife," he explained. "She's pregnant, and I work for 7–Up."

When a speaker uses humor, it does two things. It captures attention. And when tied to a basic truth, it sends a message. However, when used wrongly, it can do serious damage. Understanding what makes humor effective and how to use and not use it is essential in evangelistic speaking.

What makes humor effective?

Humor puts an anxious audience at ease. At an evangelistic event, unbelievers tend to be apprehensive, uncertain of what is to come, even a bit worried. One word sums up their mood: tense.

Humor has a way of saying, "Everything is okay. You are going to enjoy this." The shoulders relax. The closed heart opens up. A smile comes across the face. The mood changes. They think, "This might even be enjoyable."

Bill Hybels says of his own speaking:

I work hard at humor; it's one of the toughest parts of sermon preparation. As long as it's used appropriately, its importance when preaching can hardly be overemphasized. Some people come to church not expecting to find themselves enjoying the experience. If I can get them laughing, they relax and become more open to what I'm about to say."[1]

Humor also says something about the speaker. It says that he is an engaging person who knows how to laugh. This is absolutely critical if the speaker is a church leader. Non-Christians tend to connect the church and the preacher. What they think of the church, they think of the preacher and vice versa. They may be sitting there thinking the church, the service, and yes, even the preacher, will not be very enjoyable. A businessman told me that he assisted in helping his church take an informal survey of people in their community. They asked, "What is your opinion of the church?" (referring to the church in general, not their church). The three most frequent answers were as follows: The church is always talking about money. The church is always talking about death. The church is always sad.

Years ago, I walked through Amsterdam with some students. We asked a similar question. When you think of church, what do you think of? The four recurring answers were God, Jesus, buildings, and boring. Humor says, "This place might be different." This speaker isn't like the rest. He laughs and makes you laugh. The listener begins to think the speaker is someone he would like to know, maybe even talk with over a cup of coffee.

Humor doesn't stop there. It says that the speaker has found something to smile about, and it makes the audience wonder if the speaker knows something they don't. He's more positive than negative. He seems to feel there is a reason to get up in the morning. The speaker pulls the audience up, not down. He is not on the same page in life, but as they listen to a message spiced with humor, they may wish they *could* be on his page. The speaker's view of life, his mistakes, and the mistakes of others begin to interest them. A business friend of mine who speaks frequently has a great sense of humor. That humor has influenced non-Christians because they found something attractive about the life he was experiencing.

Humor talks. It communicates to non-Christians in a language they understand—laughter. When people are laughing, they are listening and you can tell them anything you want to tell them. That is universally true. If you speak in a reserved country such as Germany, the people may not laugh out loud when you use humor, but they will smile. Step into a third-world country such as India or a fourth-world country such as Haiti. There is little to smile about in these places. The government is a threat. Food is scarce. A bad economy only worsens. Disease is rampant. Crime abounds.

But innate in every person is a desire to laugh and to find something to laugh about. So even if we're speaking through an interpreter, when we use humor, we speak in a language everyone understands.

When humor talks, it's often convicting. It makes people admit something they'd otherwise rather not admit. If you tell me I'm conceited, I might get mad at you. But if you tell me in a way that forces me to laugh at myself, I'll probably admit, "You're right." A businessman's success had puffed him up. As he touted his successes to his wife, he compared himself with John D. Rockefeller and Bill Gates—the past and present greats. Finally he said to his wife, "Do you realize how many great businessmen there are in the world today?" She answered, "No. But there is one less than you think." That kind of illustration could be used of almost any occupation. It causes listeners to laugh with the speaker and at themselves. They may think, "I see how my conceit is similar to his." At this point, we have them laughing and listening.

Stuart Briscoe gives an illustration from his own speaking. He explains:

> A fellow once said to me, "I've been listening to you for quite a long time now and sometimes when I go home from church, I find a knife stuck in my ribs. I always wonder. How did he do that? So today I decided to watch you closely, and I found out how you did it. You got me laughing, and while I was laughing, you slipped the point home."[2]

Some speakers call this "tension management." Communicators must discover how much tension the audience can handle. Humor can be a pressure release that causes people to keep listening. The essential key is to know when to release and not to release the tension.

I love speaking to non-Christians. Their facial expressions apart from their words tell me how they feel. "I'd rather not be here." "You are probably going to be boring." "Don't think I'm going to respond to anything you say." "Please be as brief as possible." Humor meets those people where they are, communicates what they need to know, and causes them to give me a chance—a chance that may result in a change in their eternal destiny.

What do you avoid?

Humor has innate dangers. Used well, it communicates. Used poorly, it does nothing or, even worse, offends.

Don't try to be a stand-up comic. Make no attempt to enter the *Guinness World Book of Records* as the world's funniest speaker. Warren and David Weirsbe, in *The Elements of Preaching,* make the comment, "Preaching is serious business and the preacher must not stoop to become a comedian."[3] Evangelistic speaking is serious business. A thirty-minute message with proper humor does not devote twenty-five minutes to joke telling. Nor does a fifteen-minute message give ten minutes to funny stories. Humor ought to enhance our message, not *be* our message. We don't want the audience to leave saying "Wasn't he funny?" We want them to leave saying, "Wasn't that a good message? I liked the way he used humor."

Avoid humor that doesn't fit. Illustrations ought never call attention to themselves, but rather call attention to a truth you are attempting to communicate. The same principle applies to humor. That doesn't mean that you never use humor for humor's sake. There are times you do, such as when you first step up to speak. But if you are using humor to communicate a point, make sure it communicates the point. I once heard a speaker tell a hilarious story. I've used it myself. It will make the deadest audience laugh. As I listened to him I thought, *I don't understand what that has to do with his message. It's going to be interesting what connection he makes.* Keep in mind that the way he went into it, you were led to believe he was illustrating his point. After the laughter had subsided he said, "That doesn't fit anything I have said. I just throw it into every message." Never do that. Humor needs to accentuate the point you're making. Humor is more often misused in speaking than it is well used.

Avoid making your humor more prominent than your message. The audience ought to enjoy our humor but be influenced by our message. You might ask, "But if the humor is particularly good, how do you keep your audience from thinking about it?" The issue is not what they think about; the issue is what is *predominant* on their minds. If they thought about your humor, that's one thing. If that's *all* they thought about, that's another. They may forget our humor; they ought never to forget our message.

Avoid humor that might be insulting to a non-Christian. Insults don't communicate; they hurt, sting, and even offend. By using offensive humor, we have the opposite effect on our audience than we wanted. Instead of giving them a reason to listen and even enjoy us, we've given them a reason not to listen or even to disrespect us. This is one reason a speaker should avoid ethnic and culture-related jokes. The risk of offending is too great. Be careful of occupational jokes, too. If you use an occupational joke, begin with a joke about *your* occupation.

As I keep emphasizing, *always* remember that we are speaking to non-Christians. It's what *they* think that matters. I was the speaker at a friendship dinner for non-Christians. The master of ceremonies decided to use humor to relax the audience. Unfortunately, he chose humor surrounding a political figure about whom there were mixed opinions. Some admired him; others, particularly believers, abhorred him. I wanted to crawl underneath the table. I was embarrassed that non-Christians were hearing someone they admired being ripped apart. Political jokes are acceptable in many cultures. Jokes on political *figures* are not.

Good humor abounds. There is no need to use potentially offensive humor. Think about your audience. If I have a doubt, I ask someone who can be objective and honest. It is far better to discover the damage poor humor *could* do and not use it than to discover the damage poor humor *has done* and try to correct it.

What if using humor doesn't come easily?

For most speakers, humor doesn't come easily. It certainly didn't for me. It's a learned skill, developed through experience. A good way to learn how to use humor is to listen to speakers who have developed the art. Interact with them. What helped them in their development of a good sense of humor? What obstacles did they overcome? How did they become more comfortable in their use of humor? What mistakes did they make? Where have they obtained their humorous stories and anecdotes?

It also helps to relax around people when you're not speaking. Have fun. Laugh and enjoy life. Tease (properly) and accept teasing. You'll be surprised at how loosening up around people can affect you when you step into the pulpit.

I have several people whose friendship over the years has sustained me tremendously. We have cried together and shared one another's grief. But we've also laughed together—sometimes at each other's expense. They often tease me unmercifully. I'd be dishonest if I did not admit that I've deserved it, even encouraged it. But being able to relax in those relationships has helped me in speaking. I carry a bit of that relaxed attitude into the pulpit. So do my friends who are speakers. We try not to take ourselves too seriously.

Be yourself. Use humor that fits you. No two speakers have an identical sense of humor. If the humor you are trying to use doesn't fit you, you will know it—and so will your audience. While training a women's speaker, I said to her, "It is time to relax your audience. You are coming on quite strong, and necessarily so. But at this point in your message, so you don't lose them and also to help them digest the truth of what you're saying, a bit of humor would help." I immediately thought of humor I had used in similar situations. She answered, "I've seen you do that, and you do it well. I just can't do that." I said, "Great, let's use humor that fits you." We found humor that fit her style, and she used it well. Be the person God made you to be—yourself.

Where do you find humor?

You find humor in the same place you find other illustrations: bumper stickers, billboards, newspapers, magazines, conversations, advertisements, books, television, movie theater, other speakers, etc. Your single biggest source will always be reading. The more reading you do, the more humor you'll find.

If a speaker uses humor in speaking, read what he writes. He is likely to use humor there too. Are joke books helpful? Extremely few. First of all, it's difficult to find joke books filled with clean humor. It is not advantageous to your spiritual health to sort through unclean humor to find clean humor. Also, as mentioned concerning illustrations, the humor you find in a joke book often has been overused. Instead, read, read, read. By reading widely to find illustrations you will find humor as well. I set out to find illustrations, and in the course of finding illustrations I find humorous stories, too.

Once you find them, file them the same way you do all your illustrations. Ask the question, "What is it talking about?" Does it illustrate our struggle with conceit or our temptation to be selfish? Does it point to unnecessary fears or does it speak of our tendency to be gullible? Would it illustrate deceit or our proneness to make excuses? Then give the story a two- to five-word description. Conceit—example of. Selfishness—result of. Excuses—problem with.

Instead of having a section of your illustration file called humor, put humorous illustrations under subjects throughout your file. Only subjects where using humor would be inappropriate, such as the deity or substitutionary death of Christ, should be without humor.

Imagine how helpful it would be to have examples like the following in your illustration file. Keep in mind that the humor has to fit your personality. Some of these might not appeal to you. They do to me. Use humor that matches your personality, but use it.

Title: Tomorrow
Subtitle: lack of interest
Illustration: I was in a restaurant recently and saw a sign which said, "Due to lack of interest tomorrow will be postponed."

Source: R. Larry Moyer

Title: Retaliation
Subtitle: example of
Illustration: A six-year-old comes crying to his mother because his little sister pulled his hair. "Don't be angry," the mother says. "Your little sister doesn't realize that pulling hair hurts." A short while later, the mother hears more crying and goes to investigate. This time the sister is bawling, and her brother says, "Now she knows."

Source: Joseph E. James

Title: Death
Subtitle: reality of
Illustration: Two senior citizens were out for their usual morning walk. They passed a funeral home. One said, "Let's just go in and give ourselves up."

Source: *Preaching*, July/August 1998; 53

Title: Pride
Subtitle: rebuked
Illustration: A United Airlines gate agent in Denver, Colorado, was confronted with a passenger who probably deserved to fly as cargo. During the final days at Denver's old Stapleton airport, a crowded United flight was canceled. A single agent was rebooking a long line of inconvenienced travelers. Suddenly an angry passenger pushed his way to the desk. He slapped his ticket down on the counter and said, "I *have* to be on this flight and it has to be *first class*." The agent replied, "I'm sorry, sir. I'll be happy to try to help you, but I've got to help these folks first, and I'm sure we'll be able to work something out." The passenger was unimpressed. He asked loudly, so that the passengers behind him could hear, "Do you have any idea who I am?" Without hesitating, the gate agent smiled and grabbed her public address microphone. "May I have your attention please?" she began, her voice bellowing throughout the terminal. "We have a passenger here at the gate *who does not know who he is*. If anyone can help him find his identity, please come to gate 17." The folks behind him in line began laughing hysterically. Although people were late due to the canceled flight, they were no longer angry at United.

Source: Unknown

Title: Honesty
Subtitle: can be embarrassing
Illustration: When our son, David, was about six years old, we were invited to a friend's house for dinner. Part way through the meal David said to the hostess, "I'm sorry your squash didn't turn out very good." As Tammy and I were embarrassed to no end, he looked at the hostess and continued, "Are you sorry your squash didn't turn out very good?"

Source: R. Larry Moyer

What is important in using humor?

When using a humorous illustration, as with any illustration, watch how you enter it and how you exit it. You have to set up the audience for what you're about to say. Once they're laughing, they're listening. Then you have to drive home the point you're making as you exit. Otherwise, the audience will get the humor but may miss the message.

Suppose you make the point that when we examine our own sinfulness, we compare ourselves to one another. You then might say, "You and I are often like the boy who came home from school and had a most pathetic progress report. It appeared that the only thing he majored in was football and girls. The father asked the boy to explain his low marks. The boy responded, 'Well, at least I was the highest of all who failed.' That's what the Bible says we are like when we claim, 'I'm not as bad as most people.' But God is a holy God, and all sin must be punished. Whether we have sinned

159

once or one hundred times, we deserve punishment, and the punishment for sin is death."

To enter or exit humor improperly hinders its effectiveness. Prepare listeners for the humor you are about to use. Then while they're laughing, drive home the point. While laughing on the outside, they'll be convicted on the inside.

Seldom do I find humor that matches the main point of my message. I'm not trying to. Instead, I go down a particular trail to bring in humor and then get right back on track. Location of humor is critical. It's been said that the laws of humor are like the laws of real estate: location is everything. In discussing Nicodemus and his question about how an old man can be born a second time (John 3:4), you might find humor that depicts how we feel when people expect the impossible of us. In discussing the attitude of the Pharisee who thanked God he wasn't like other men (Luke 18:11), you might find humor that speaks to our struggle with pride. And in discussing the "whoever" of John 3:16, you might find humor that speaks of how we make offers that appear to be for everyone—until we read the fine print. Your humor fits a certain detail in your message. It is not always meant to coincide with the main idea. Each time you introduce humor, make your point and get back on track with your message.

Conclusion

Humor is a universal language. A speaker who does not use humor is missing a great opportunity. Non-Christians will find it hard to listen to him. But any old humor won't do. It must be chosen carefully and used effectively. One of the greatest compliments we could receive is, "You have a good sense of humor." Effectiveness in our use of humor increases our effectiveness as a communicator.

REFLECTING...

1. What makes humor effective with a non-Christian audience?

2. List at least three things to avoid in your use of humor in evangelistic speaking.

3. How can you improve your use of humor?

4. How does the way you enter and exit humor increase or decrease its effectiveness?

5. How does the effective use of humor increase your effectiveness as a communicator?

Chapter 22

How Important Is Repetition?

A MOTHER WAS ASKED, "Why do you tell your child the same thing twenty times?" She answered, "Nineteen just doesn't do it."

Repetition has been called "the mother of knowledge." It is critical in communicating our message.

Why is repetition important?

How important is repetition? On a scale of one to ten, with ten being the most important, repetition is closer to ten than you might imagine. Why?

People miss what we are saying.

To begin, non-Christians are people just like us. They are different from Christians, but only in the spiritual realm. They have not been born again. Otherwise, they are just people. Like others, they tend not to understand something the first time they hear it. The reasons could be many—not feeling well, tiredness, something else on their mind, a sudden distraction, anxiety about the illness of a loved one. Hearing information again and again enables them to catch what they missed. Haddon Robinson has said, "The ear is not a dependable instrument for getting things. That's why you have to say it, repeat it and state it again."

The reason people miss what we say may be due to their experience. If listeners are from a conservative religious background, a message from a liberal preacher may be an exercise in futility. The message may not make sense to them, and if it's not from a biblical worldview it will lack the power to change a life. If the speaker also was boring, the message became an opportunity to catch up on sleep. If our message is likewise irrelevant and boring, repetition isn't the cure. However, if our message is interesting, repetition helps people whose experience was more negative than positive. For those not trained to listen or, more accurately, having been trained *not* to listen, repetition helps people grasp what they ought not miss.

Repetition also helps those who hear but do not listen. Years ago I was speaking to teenagers. I stressed that any amount of goodness will not get us to heaven. Christ and Christ alone saves. A teenager approached me afterward. Teary-eyed, she explained, "I kept sitting there thinking, 'But how do you know when you're good enough?' Then it dawned on me. 'That's what he's been trying to tell you. Christ and Christ alone saves.' Sitting there in my seat, I trusted Christ alone as my only way to heaven."

Speakers sometimes face an audience that hears but doesn't listen. For example, we might emphasize that we are saved by grace, not works, but our audience is not listening. They continue to think even their activity of attending your speaking engagement is another good point toward their entrance into heaven. Although you emphasize Christ paid for *all* your sins, they keep thinking He paid for most of your sins. They think keeping the sacraments, being baptized, and keeping the commandments will help pay for the rest. The freeness of eternal life is completely surprising to them. They are putting what we said through their mental grid of works. When we say "free," they do not comprehend that what we mean is that eternal life is *free*. Repetition helps the inattentive audience hear as we explain something they so desperately need to understand. It is not Christ plus works that saves us, but Christ alone. I have often wondered if that is why, when God wrote the book of John to tell us how to receive eternal life, He mentioned the word "believe" ninety-eight times. Maybe He knew we wouldn't catch it the first time!

Does repetition guarantee people will not miss what we are saying? No. There have been times when I've repeated a point several times only to find out that a person in the audience *still* missed what I was saying. But the chances of people missing it are less. If they are not listening the first time we declare something, it's less likely they will miss it the second, third, or fourth time we say it. Repeated emphasis causes them to respond, "I get it." One who came to Christ in one of our outreaches said to me, "I heard it. I heard it. I heard it. I heard it. Then tonight I *heard* it."

Repetition adds simplicity to a message.

Repetition has another advantage. It adds simplicity to the message. Audiences vary in their educational level and ability to grasp truth. But one thing never changes: Even the sophisticated hearer loves to hear truth simply stated. A message has numerous thought-provoking ideas. But when a particular idea is stressed and repeated, it enhances the simplicity of the entire message.

If we say, "Christ died for sinners," over and over, we emphasize that *to those who deserve the opposite*. If we repeatedly say, "No one is promised tomorrow" we emphasize that *no one is promised tomorrow*. A woman who trusted Christ in one of our outreaches said to me, "I was so impacted by what you kept stressing, 'I don't care what you've done, God loves you.'" For an educated audience accustomed to studying and learning, the need to repeat is lessened. Even then, though, repetition properly done is helpful.

What are you repeating?

We certainly don't need to repeat every sentence. We repeat the main idea of our message. The main idea is the main thought that encompasses what we are saying. It's the specific thought that we want them to meditate on as they leave the service, drive to work the next morning, or mow their yard that week. It's the thought that captivated us as we studied and prepared the message. It's the thought that we want to so captivate the audience that their lives are never the same. It's the main thought of the biblical text that is now the main thought of our message. (I'll explain more about the "main idea" approach later.)

I have an evangelistic message on Luke 16:19–31, the story of Lazarus and the rich man. Lazarus, a beggar, being right with God, went from having nothing to having everything. The rich man, not being right with God, went from having everything to having nothing. The main idea that summarizes the text and my message is, "One of the biggest mistakes any person can make is to prepare for life but not prepare for death." That's the truth I want my audience to never forget. So I emphasize that one truth, saying it repeatedly the same way. Other ideas are involved in explaining the paragraph and delivering the message. But I want each person in the audience to leave asking one question of themselves, "Having prepared for life, have I prepared for death?" I want that same thought to come to their minds two days later. "Having prepared for life, have I prepared for death?"

For me, Philippians 3:4–9 has been a very effective passage from which to deliver an expositional evangelistic message. The main thought is this: When it comes to getting to heaven, everything you have done is as worthless as rubbish. Paul the apostle, as he reflected upon his own conversion, explained the worthlessness of his background and behavior in meriting God's favor. He said, "But what things were gain to me, these I have counted loss for Christ. Yet indeed I also count all things loss for the excellence of the knowledge of Christ Jesus my Lord, for whom I have suffered the loss of all things, and count them as rubbish, that I may gain Christ" (vv. 7–8).

I repeatedly drive home that idea. When it comes to getting to heaven, anything *you* have done is rubbish. I come at it from different angles. Having stated that idea, I amplify it by applying it. "When it comes to getting to heaven, having gone to church is rubbish. When it comes to getting to heaven, having lived a good life is rubbish. When it comes to getting to heaven, having been baptized is rubbish. When it comes to getting to heaven, having taken the sacraments is rubbish. When it comes to getting to heaven, *anything* you have done is rubbish." That repeated truth causes my audience, as the Holy Spirit works, to see that nothing about them merits His gift of salvation.

Ten years after speaking that message at a particular church, I was back in the area. Someone there said to me, "I still remember what you spoke on at our church: 'When it comes to getting to heaven, anything you have done is rubbish.'"

One more word. Make a distinction between restatement and repetition. Restatement is when you come at the main idea from different ways and say it in different words. That needs to be done, and there are ample opportunities to do it as you deliver your message. Repetition, though, is when you say the main idea several times in the same words—an idea you hope they never forget. I've chosen to address repetition because the need for that is often overlooked. But restatement and repetition both have their place.

Conclusion

Repetition is an instrument God uses in all of our lives to drive home eternal truth. Repetition is not merely important; it is essential. If you want the audience to grasp the particular truth of a passage, say it, repeat it, then say it again. If you want the audience to grasp the truth of a passage, say it, repeat it, then say it again. May I repeat…

REFLECTING...

1. Give two reasons why repetition is important.

2. Since the ear is not a dependable instrument, how does repetition assist in communication?

3. How does effective use of repetition add simplicity to a message?

4. What is the main thing you repeat in your message?

5. How does repetition add simplicity to a message?

Chapter 23

How Do You Aim for the Heart?

A COMMUNITY LEADER GAVE an evangelistic message at a Valentine's Day banquet. His point was clear. God loves us even though we are what we are—selfish, hateful, unkind, slanderous, wretched people. As he expounded on our sinful condition in undeniable ways, he presented Christ who is nonetheless the Friend of sinners. He gave abundant evidence of how people in the New Testament as well as people today have been overwhelmed that He loved them when they were so undeserving. The greatest proof was the cross. The message was personal and penetrating. A woman leaving the banquet said to him, "You sure stepped on my toes tonight." He responded, "Please forgive me. I was aiming for your heart."

An evangelistic speaker must be direct. We are aiming for the heart. Our goal is not to make the audience feel bad but to let the audience know they *are* bad. Although loved by God, they are sinners separated from Him. Without Christ, hell is their eternal destiny. At the same time, we want to win the audience, not turn them away. So how do we win the audience without jeopardizing truth?

Directness begins with appearance.

Directness doesn't start when we speak up. It begins when we stand up. It starts with our appearance.

"Wait a minute," you are tempted to exclaim. "Does the Bible not say, 'Man looks at the outward appearance, but God looks at the heart'?" You're right. You've quoted a portion of 1 Samuel 16:7 almost word for word. The verse reads, "But the LORD said to Samuel, 'Do not look at his appearance or at his physical stature, because I have refused him. For *the LORD does* not *see* as man sees; for man looks at the outward appearance, but the LORD looks at the heart.'"

God is instructing Samuel as to who among Jesse's sons He desires to make king over Israel. When Samuel sees the tall, handsome Eliab, he assumes the search for a king is over. But God informs Samuel that physical stature is not the issue. To use that verse to say physical appearance is not important is a stretch, to say the least. In fact, the verse supports the idea that our appearance before non-Christians is important. After all, the verse declares, "Man looks at the outward appearance."

Attitudes toward appearance vary with culture, setting, and even temperature. A speaker would annoy his audience if, in a sweltering auditorium, he refused to sensibly lay aside his coat. If no one has on a suit, the audience will identify better with a speaker who is casually dressed. In some cultures, regardless of the temperature or humidity, speakers, especially clergy, are expected to wear a tie. With other audiences, it's preferable that the speaker not wear one. An outdoor speaking event sometimes calls for different attire than an indoor one. A formal speaking situation by its very nature demands different clothing than an informal one. A luncheon outreach in the workplace might require different clothing than a Sunday morning worship service.

Here are three ideas to keep in mind. First, dress professionally, as defined by the particular setting. The audience needs to know you gave careful thought to your message; you can convey that by also giving careful thought to your dress. Ask yourself, "Am I well groomed? Does my clothing fit properly? Are the style and color choices appropriate?"

Second, wear what attracts not distracts. Are your shoes polished? Don't ask me why this is true, but marketing firms have confirmed that the first spot people often look at is your shoes. For male speakers, knee-length socks are important. If we sit on a platform prior to speaking and cross our legs, the audience will be more distracted than impressed by hairy legs. Also, if we're wearing a coat (and many times even if we're not) a long-sleeve shirt is more appropriate. If we lift our arm to make a gesture, a short-sleeve shirt makes our coat sleeve slide back to our elbow, calling attention to the fact that we have on a short-sleeve shirt. People are now thinking about our shirt instead of our Savior.

Women speakers are presented at their best in a modest suit (skirt or pants) or dress (if not wearing a jacket, wear a top with sleeves). Also refrain from wearing excessive jewelry. The best shoe to wear is a mid-heel pump or a sling-back style with closed toe. Sandals are inappropriate for speakers. The point is, wear what attracts rather than distracts.

Finally, keep this general principle in mind. A speaker needs to be one step above his or her audience. Underdressed is never appropriate, and overdressed can put a barrier between speaker and listeners. "One step above the audience" is the general rule. If the audience wears business casual, I'll probably wear a coat with a casual shirt. A full suit with coat and tie may be a bit much. If the audience is in jeans, I'll likely be dressed business casual or in khakis and a golf shirt. The "one step above the audience" principle should rule.

Keep the non-Christian foremost in mind. If I am speaking in a community where the clergy are expected to wear a suit, I'll dress accordingly. Even if the believer who brought them to the outreach is more casual, I want to identify with the unbelievers. I don't want to hinder my acceptance with the non-Christian through my dress. Consideration for the unbeliever must affect my clothing choices.

Clothing says to an audience, "What the speaker is about to say is important to him and needs to be important to you." I've never heard anyone sum up the subject better than Dr. Haddon Robinson, who said:

> Part of effective preaching is the ability to make the presentation match the internal conviction. The image we project will influence our credibility. Appearance in the pulpit will affect the way people respond. I'm convinced inwardly, for example, of the importance of discipline and order in the Christian life. How can I present myself in a way that matches the conviction? In the first thirty seconds, people are deciding whether they're going to listen. God looks on the heart, but people in our culture look on the outside. Am I disheveled? Do my shoes need to be shined? If I'm fifty pounds overweight, they may perceive that I'm not disciplined or that I'm careless about myself.[1]

Opening remarks matter.

Directness doesn't start with our message; it starts with the first words out of our mouth. What follows our remark, "I'm delighted and honored to be here"? Do we talk about the weather we came from or the weather we've come to? Do we ramble on about congestion at the airport we flew out of or the one we flew into? Our first words tell an audience how important this opportunity is to us. Our words will either increase or decrease its importance to them.

That doesn't mean that we step up to the podium and get directly into our message. It means we say something meaningful, not boring. If I'm in a farm community, I'll be quick to say how honored I am to be with them, having been born and raised on a dairy farm in Pennsylvania. If I'm in the city of the Super Bowl winners, I'll tell them how privileged I feel to be in the city whose team was number one. If I'm in a city hit by a major catastrophe that made people pull together, I'll tell them how impressed I've been with reports of their tenderness toward people and tenacity toward life. All of that takes less than a minute. Then, I'll move directly into my message.

Humor can also assist to relate to your listeners and then go directly into what you are going to say. I once stood before a secular audience and told them how honored I was to be there; then I admitted that being an after dinner speaker can be very intimidating. I confessed that no experience intimidated me like that one because I was frightened that what happened to one after-dinner speaker could happen to me. He was standing in the lobby with the Master of Ceremonies greeting the people who had attended. A six-year-old boy ran up to him and said, "Your speech stunk." The Master of Ceremonies, embarrassed, asked him to run along. But the boy ran right up to the speaker again and said, "We've heard all your jokes before. They're not even funny." The Master of Ceremonies again asked the boy to run along. But he ran right up to the speaker again and said, "I bet you they never invite you back." Just then the boy's mother, who was standing a short distance away, saw what was happening. She ran up to the speaker and said, "Please forgive my son. I don't know what in the world he said to you. But he's at the age where he repeats everything he hears." The audience exploded in laughter. I then added, "Now you know why this kind of opportunity intimidates me. I don't want that to happen to me." Then I got directly into what I was saying.

The point is, relate to your listeners, don't lose them. Say something quickly that will allow the audience to identify with you and then move directly into your message.

Count down to thirty seconds.

David Henderson, in *Culture Shift,* makes the observation, "People will decide in the first 30 seconds if you're going to be interesting or boring."[2] That's right! We don't have five minutes to get the attention of a non-Christian. We have thirty seconds. The people listening to us are accustomed to using a remote control. If what they hear doesn't interest them, their minds "click" to something else. Fred Smith observed, "I hear a lot of preachers, for instance, who are pretty sloppy in their opening comments. Perhaps it's because they haven't thought about them, but the mood they create right from the start makes it tough to benefit from the rest of the sermon."[3]

Speakers across the spectrum fall under that condemnation. If we are not careful, we get sloppy in our opening comments. The temptation every speaker faces is to think about his message but not enough about his first thirty seconds. That thirty-second rule is essential to directness in your message.

You might wonder how you can get the audience's attention in thirty seconds. That may even seem unrealistic. It all depends on how you start. Suppose you announce, "Let's talk about guilt." I may be struggling in that area but that doesn't arrest my attention. Why listen to someone talk about a problem I already know I have? Consider this introduction. "We've all struggled with it. We carry it from the bed to the breakfast table, from the breakfast table to work, work to home, and home to bed. It causes difficulties in marriage, and it distracts us at work. It makes us hesitant to make new friends because it burdens our relationships with old ones. We read all kinds of books and talk with a variety of people, but the problem remains. When we wake up at night, it keeps us from going back to sleep."

The audience begins to wonder, "What is he talking about? What problem is he addressing?" Then you continue: "The problem I'm addressing can be stated in four words: 'plagued by the past.' It can be reduced to one word: 'guilt.'"

I now have their attention, and I captured it in thirty seconds. This aspect of evangelistic speaking is rather simple—thirty seconds to get their attention, thirty minutes (or less) to keep it. Our opening words don't have to be sensational, but they must be interesting. Otherwise, directness is lost.

Here's another example. Suppose you decide to speak on the subject of death. To say, "Let's talk about death," is not very attention getting. It also indicates this is going to be a rather morbid message. But suppose instead you begin with something like this:

"We all know it will happen. The problem is we can't do a thing about it. Like it or not, it's a moment we have to face. It takes away from the excitement of living. It is the agony of dying. A former professional baseball umpire once made the comment, 'Life is a lot like a baseball game. It has its start and excitement, its rhubarb and dull moments, and its finish. Sometimes a game is called off unexpectedly because of an unexpected sudden storm; sometimes it runs to the normal nine innings and sometimes it runs a little extra, but every game comes to an end.'[4] All of us know that the umpire could not have been any more correct. Life *is* like a baseball game. It has its start and its excitement, its lively and its dull moments, and it has its finish."

Through the baseball game analogy, you captivate the attention of the audience in thirty seconds. You cause them to think about death in a different way than before. Your comments about tragedy and disease make you relevant and direct. In thirty seconds, you cause them to be interested in what you have to say.

That's why I cannot emphasize enough that the better we are in speaking to non-Christians, the better we are in speaking to anyone. If we give ourselves thirty seconds to get their attention it will become a way of life or, more accurately, a way of speaking to anyone, anywhere. We will not step before an audience without thinking carefully about the first thirty seconds of our message.

Don't make comments to believers.

In an evangelistic message, you are speaking to unbelievers; don't make comments to Christians. Don't err by saying, "I've been speaking to those who don't know the Lord. Let me pause here and say a word to any believers who are here." You've immediately lost your directness. Furthermore, if part of the audience is supposed to tune out while you speak to believers, how will they know when to tune back in? Neither do you say, "Now this is something that those of us who are Christians already know." How will unbelievers know if you are talking to the person beside them who might be a Christian or to them? There is a time and place for "double barrel" messages (those addressed to both believers and unbelievers). But *evangelistic* messages are more effective when we speak as though the entire audience is non-Christian.

Identify. Identify. Identify.

Meaningful opening remarks and getting attention in thirty seconds are not sufficient in being direct and aiming for the heart. We must also speak from their worldview so they sense that we have spent some time in their back yard, that we have walked in their shoes. The way we speak, the illustrations we use, the terminology we choose conveys that we understand life where they are living. We identify with them and their circumstances to the point that they may think we've spoken to their friends, hidden a surveillance camera in their home, or wiretapped their phone. As we speak, we come across on their team, not on their back.

I once helped a friend who had experienced major struggles. During the time I was helping him, he went to hear a Bible teacher who relates well to his audience. The next morning my friend asked me, in a kidding but serious fashion, "Did you talk to him about me? I felt like I was the only one he was speaking to." That's what an unbeliever ought to feel. You have identified with him and captured his attention. He senses you are speaking to him, not the person beside him. To that end, analogies, examples, illustrations, and terminology all become critical. I often go to my friends and ask them to evaluate the material I use to identify with my audience. If I'm not identifying, I want them to tell me, not the audience. That would be too late. Often they have given me ideas that improved the way I identified with the audience.

To identify with non-believers, as noted earlier, refrain from using church jargon. Use terminology familiar to them. The language used in the message should reflect the language used in the workplace. Instead of a pew, call it a seat. Instead of a hymn, call it a song. Use the phrase, "Let's read this paragraph" instead of "Let's read this passage of Scripture." Refer to the sanctuary as the auditorium. Use the word "Bible" when referring to the Scriptures instead of the Word of God, although we know it is

God's Word. Directness means using the terms unbelievers use. Speak their language.

Identify in such a way that from the start of your message to the end, unbelievers feel as if you've spoken to their friends, read their journals or their emails, and lived in their homes. Identify. Identify. Identify.

That's why the preparation of an evangelistic message starts on the sidewalk, not in the study. Unless we are around non-Christians, we won't know how to relate to their view of life.

Balance "all of us" and "you."

Balance is key in many areas of life. It is equally important in speaking to non-Christians. One way balance is seen in speaking to unbelievers is your use of "all of us" and "you."

The "all of us" is critical. The audience knows we are speaking to them, not down at them. We see ourselves as sinners. We are not just calling them sinners. We struggle with pride ourselves. We are annoyed about our own sin. We are not just pointing out their pride. We understand what it means to worry so we can identify with their anxieties. "All of us" conveys that I'm on your team, not on your back.

"You" is also critical. After all, I (the speaker) am not the one who needs Christ. I have already met Him. *They* are the ones who must come to the Savior. You are not the one who is resisting Him. *They* are. At certain points in your message "all of us" weakens its impact, "you" strengthens it. Suppose I'm lost in the woods and you're directing me out with a two-way radio. It's a bit senseless to say, "We must keep the sun to our back." It's essential to say, "You must keep the sun to your back."

This balance between "all of us" and "you" must be mastered. But it's mastered the hard way—through experience. You will develop both comfort and confidence the more you speak. Through experience you will learn which is necessary at a particular point of your message—"all of us" or "you."

As a general rule, "all of us" should be more prominent in the first part of the message, and "you" in the latter part. As you conclude your message, you are not calling on them to *consider* what you've said. You are calling on them to *act* upon it. As someone has said, "You can't give God a definite maybe. It must be a definite yes or a definite no." At that point what I, the speaker, have done with Christ is not the issue. It is what those in my audience have done that matters. The audience must sense that you are asking them to do what you have already done.

Examine Peter's sermon in Acts 2. He tells his audience, "Men of Israel, hear these words: Jesus of Nazareth, a Man attested by God to you by miracles, wonders, and signs which God did through Him in your midst, as you yourselves also know—Him, being delivered by the determined purpose and foreknowledge of God, you have taken by lawless hands, have crucified, and put to death" (Acts 2:22–23). Notice his use of "you" at that point, not "all of us." So affected were they by his directness that "when they heard this, they were cut to the heart, and said to Peter and the rest of the apostles, 'Men and brethren, what shall we do?'" (v. 37)

Conclusion

An evangelist speaking to non-Christians once said, "I'm not asking you to make a decision. You've already made one. I'm asking you to change it!" His directness was obvious. He was aiming for the heart. The audience knew that what he was saying was directed to them. It was of such eternal significance they could not remain neutral.

Directness is not merely helpful in evangelistic speaking; it's essential. That's why we must examine everything: our appearance, the first words out of our mouth, our identification with non-Christians, and even our use of "all of us" and "you." When directness is there, it moves your message from one that steps on their toes to one that through the Spirit of God changes their hearts.

REFLECTING...

1. Where does directness in your presentation begin?

2. How do your opening remarks and the first thirty seconds of your message impact your directness?

3. In what ways do you identify with your audience throughout your message?

4. How specifically do comments to believers hinder the directness of your message?

5. What is the general rule in achieving a balance between "all of us" and "you"?

Chapter 24

How Do You Put Together an Expository Evangelistic Message?

FASCINATING. I HAD NEVER been on the inside to see it happen. While speaking in Flint, Michigan, I had the opportunity to visit a General Motors assembly plant. The finished product was amazing. It rolled off the line new and clean. The paint glistened, the chrome sparkled, and the inside held that "new car" aroma. It was now able to take a driver from one destination to another. But that final product was possible only because those inside the plant knew how to put the vehicle together—one step at a time. With no procedure, there would have been no finished product.

A good message moves the listener from one spiritual point to another. Unless we know how to put the message together—the procedure—there will be no finished product.

What does that procedure involve?

The procedure for assembling a message requires work, thought, and time. The work can be strenuous. Some messages come together quite easily, but most do not. The person who wants to be not only a speaker but also an effective communicator must have a good work ethic. Time must be prioritized, diligence applied, and the proper tools acquired.

Preparing an expository evangelistic message takes thinking. As stated earlier, learning how to speak clearly means learning how to think clearly. In addition, you must know not only how to think as a speaker but also how to get your audience to think. If you are to be effective, the audience needs to be able to follow your thoughts and think along with you.

Finally, time is essential. Studying the Word in preparation for a message takes hours not minutes. You can wish it to come together quickly, but it usually doesn't. As you put your message together, you usually grab the time involved in several pockets of uninterrupted hours of focus.

Because of the work, thought, and time involved, we must delegate certain responsibilities to others. Consider what happened between the Grecian Jews and the Aramaic-speaking Jews in the infant church (Acts 6:1–4). The passage reads, "there arose a complaint against the Hebrews by the Hellenists because their widows were neglected in the daily distribution" (v. 1). The disciples of Jesus had multiplied, and many needed relief. The Grecian widows, having no one to represent them and being unable to speak Hebrew, were overlooked. Although this was an important issue, the twelve apostles recognized that their priorities had to focus on the study of the Word and prayer. Thus, they instructed the church leaders to carefully select seven men to "serve tables," in other words, to administer finances and care for the needy. The point to grasp in this passage is that those called upon to preach the Word recognized the importance of their time. They had to assign certain responsibilities to others so that they could devote necessary time to study the Word.

What are the steps to master in message preparation?

I am committed to the approach taught by Dr. Haddon Robinson in *Biblical Preaching*. Thinking through a message as he advises will equip the speaker to leave the audience with one central truth that can forever change their lives. His approach adapts quite well to expository evangelistic speaking.

You might ask, "Doesn't having a method take the Holy Spirit out of message preparation? Doesn't message preparation become mechanical?" I've found that you must work with a method of message preparation until you come to the point where it has mastered you. Then it no longer seems mechanical. The steps are no longer steps. They are as natural as breathing. Years ago I flew with a person whose hobby was building small planes. He gave me a ride in the smallest plane the FAA allows individuals to build and fly. As he spoke of how he built planes, I began to wonder if he ever consulted the manual. He had mastered plane construction to the point where it had mastered him. The same happens in message preparation. You master it, and then it masters you. I can sincerely say that despite having a system, I sense the presence of the Holy Spirit as much as I ever have as I step through my message preparation.

Choose your text.

An expository evangelistic speaker starts with the text. He does not prepare a message and then find a text that fits it. Instead, he selects a text and then develops a message from the text. The reason is obvious. An expositor has to say what the text says. Unless he starts with the text, he does not know what his message is. When the opposite approach is used, normally the text only *appears* to say what the message says. A study of the text often reveals it is saying something different from, and often not even close to, the speaker's message.

When you are developing your evangelistic speaking skills, start with simple passages. Expository evangelistic speaking is not easy. Choosing a text that does not have textual difficulties or phrases that can be interpreted in numerous ways will help make the job easier. I have found the following verses and passages to be some of the easier texts from which to develop an expository evangelistic message.

EASIER TEXTS FOR EVANGELISTIC MESSAGES	
Verses	**Passages**
John 3:16	Luke 19:1–10
John 3:36	John 3:1–15
John 5:24	John 14:1–6
Romans 4:5	Romans 3:10–18
2 Corinthians 5:21	Ephesians 2:1–10
Isaiah 53:6	1 John 5:11–13a

Keep in mind that the three truths every evangelistic message must contain are: 1) we are sinners; 2) Christ died for us and rose again; 3) we must trust Christ. Not one of these passages contains all three of those. The expositor needs to explain what the text does not at the most natural and appropriate place in the message.

What if we choose a text to speak from and, upon studying it, discover it doesn't say what we thought it said? Remember, God has promised to use *His* Word, not ours. If the text doesn't say what we want to tell a non-Christian audience, we need to choose a text that does. It's better to start over than misrepresent the truth of God's Word.

Study the text.

To know what the text says takes something that again involves time and work. Study. Study. Study. Cicero stated, "No man can be eloquent on a subject he does not understand."[1] Write down everything you see in a particular passage. Study the passage until you have observed everything you can find. Write down those observations in an orderly fashion. At this point, do not concern yourself with which observations you will use in your message. All you want to do is learn everything there is to learn from the passage. Don't stop studying until you are satisfied that you've exhausted what the paragraph is saying. Here are a few questions to ask as you study:

- What is the background of the passage?
- What is the setting of the passage?
- Is the setting outdoors or indoors?
- What verbs are used and what do they mean?
- What tense are the verbs?
- How many characters are involved?
- Who are the characters and what is significant about them?
- Are there any particular emotions in the passage?
- What descriptive words are used?
- What kind of flow is seen in the passage?
- What is the passage telling you?
- Are there any particular commands in the passage? Who are they addressed to?
- Is there a time of day mentioned?

At this point, there are two important things to remember. First, keep your notes organized. The more organized your notes, the more readily accessible the observations are as you put together the outline and the message.

Second, keep your notes. Don't discard them once the message is prepared. Later, if you need to know why you said something a particular way, your notes will be there for you to refer to. Furthermore, if you desire to give a different message on the same passage some time later, there is no need to re-do your homework. All you need to do is review your notes. Once the message is prepared, you can slide the notes into the folder that contains the message.

Determine your main idea.

Usually listeners will remember on;ly one truth in a talk. Give a person three truths, and he'll leave with one of them foremost in mind—often the one he least needs. How often have you heard someone say, "Something he said in his message really stuck with me"?

176

You will be a better communicator if you can condense your thoughts to a simple sentence. This demonstrates two things. First, it shows that you understand the passage so well that you can condense it into one sentence. Second, it demonstrates that you know how to express that truth in a way the audience can grasp and take home with them. The late, great preacher John Henry Jowett used to say that a minister doesn't deserve an hour to preach a sermon if he can't give it in one sentence. In *The Preacher: His Life and Work*, Jowett makes the comment, "I have a conviction that no sermon is ready for preaching . . . until we can express its theme in a short, pregnant sentence as clear as crystal."[2] People love truth that is simply stated. When he states his message simply, the speaker proves that he understands the passage and can help the audience understand.

This does not mean a passage contains on;y one thought or that an outline cannot have three points. What we are looking for is the *central* thought that encompasses the entire verse or passage. We determine that main thought by asking two questions:

- What is the text talking about?
- What is the text saying about what it is talking about?

To show how this method of message preparation comes together, I'll use Luke 19:1–10. (The resulting manuscript can be found in appendix I.)

Then *Jesus* entered and passed through Jericho. Now behold, *there was* a man named Zaccheus who was a chief tax collector, and he was rich. And he sought to see who Jesus was, but could not because of the crowd, for he was of short stature. So he ran ahead and climbed up into a sycamore tree to see Him, for He was going to pass that *way*. And when Jesus came to the place, He looked up and saw him, and said to him, "Zaccheus, make haste and come down, for today I must stay at your house." So he made haste and came down, and received Him joyfully. But when they saw *it*, they all complained, saying, "He has gone to be a guest with a man who is a sinner." Then Zaccheus stood and said to the Lord, "Look, Lord, I give half of my goods to the poor; and if I have taken anything from anyone by false accusation, I restore fourfold." And Jesus said to him, "Today salvation has come to this house, because he also is a son of Abraham; for the Son of Man has come to seek and to save that which was lost.

What is the text talking about? Christ's conversation with a sinful tax collector named Zaccheus. What is the text saying about what it is talking about? Zaccheus discovered that Christ came to save people like him. So what is the main idea? Zaccheus discovered that Christ saves lost people.

If you can't put the entire passage into one main idea, keep studying. If it is not clear in your mind, it won't be clear in the mind of the audience.

Now think through your main idea by asking yourself three questions:

- What does this mean? (Is this something the writer of Scripture is trying to *explain*?)
- Is that true? Do I really believe it? (Is this something the writer of Scripture is trying to *prove*?)
- So what? What difference does it make? (Is this something the writer of Scripture is trying to *apply*?)

These three questions determine the direction your message is going to go and the shape it is going to take. It will either have an explaining format, a proving format, or an application format.

One of the best ways to determine which question your idea answers is to imagine yourself stating your big idea to an audience. If someone were to stand up and respond, what would he likely say? Could you explain that? Would you prove that? Or what difference does that make to me?

Consider the main idea of Luke 19:1–10. Zaccheus discovered that Christ saves lost people like him. The question I could most see someone asking is, "What do you mean by that?" So the message takes on a "Let me explain" format. This is something I need to explain to the audience. Haddon Robinson, in *Biblical Preaching,* makes this helpful comment: "While a preacher may deal with all three questions in his sermon, usually one of the three predominates and determines the form his message will take."[3]

Suppose two speakers disagree on the question the audience most likely would ask. For example, suppose in response to Luke 19:1–10, a person says "So what? What difference does it make?" One speaker will be more closely aligned to what the text is doing than the other. But with either approach two things will happen: 1) the speaker's message will still be the message of the text; 2) the message will have a definite shape and direction. It will either have an explaining format, a proving format, or an application format.

You have determined the main idea and thought through the shape the message will take. Now you are prepared to simplify your main idea into a preaching idea—one the audience can easily remember.

This is critical because it's what people remember that matters most. We want to say one thing so effectively they will never forget it. Our idea should grab hold of us and then grab hold of them. They will think about it traveling to and from work, during conversations, when doing menial tasks around the house, surfing the Internet, and even while pumping gas at a local convenience store.

If possible, state the idea in a clever way. For example, I have a message on James 3:1–12, a thought-provoking paragraph about the tongue that addresses both its power and its poison. My main idea for the entire passage is captured in the statement: "The most dangerous animal in the world has his den behind your teeth." Many smile when they hear that, but their smile is followed by conviction. It's the kind of statement people find hard to forget. It can affect the way we talk to our children and the way we interact with our neighbor. An idea cleverly stated makes it more memorable. Years later you will still be reflecting on it.

At the same time, two things are more important than how cleverly the idea is stated. First, you must be true to the text and accurately represent what the text says. An idea that doesn't is just that—an idea. However, it's not an idea from the text. Second, keep the idea clear and simple. An idea that is clear and simple is memorable even if it isn't particularly clever.

To state the main idea of Luke 19:1–10, back up to the main idea first expressed: Zaccheus discovered that Christ saves lost people like him. How could that idea now be expressed to a non-Christian audience? One possibility: "God saves sinners." The truth you could then drive home in a powerful and personal way is this: "If you want to come to God, you have to come as a sinner. You cannot come to God as a good, moral, religious person. You have to come as a sinner."

Notice how that idea reflects the shape the message took, answering the question, "What do you mean by that?" My message will *explain* why and how if one wants to come to God he has to come as a sinner.

The audience should leave knowing details about the passage that they didn't know before. But the one central truth forever etched in their minds—a truth that brings the unbeliever to Christ—is the main idea, directly and succinctly stated. After speaking on Luke 19:1–10, I want my audience never to forget that God saves sinners.

Focus your message.

Focusing your message has two parts. First, answer the question, "What do you sense the Spirit of God desiring to accomplish through the message?" State your purpose in terms that are specific and clear. This helps to determine the *kind* of unbeliever you are attempting to reach. I do not try to reach every non-Christian in every message. Instead, I try to reach a particular *kind* of non-Christian. This is determined by the thrust of the text and, consequently, my message. One message might be directed to atheists and another one to religious people. One might be directed to those weighed down with guilt while another might be aimed at those overwhelmed by the fear of death. Ultimately, the Lord determines whom

He reaches. However, based on the text, I pursue a particular kind of non-Christian. That is why the focus of your message is heavily determined by the passage you are speaking from.

What would I sense the Spirit of God desiring to accomplish through Luke 19:1–10? My purpose statement is, "I want unbelievers to understand that they are never too bad for God to save, and I want them to trust Christ to save them." God could certainly use such a message to reach religiously proud people who trust their good works to save them. Again, whom God reaches is in His hands. But having a clearly stated purpose that reflects the text helps me to give a clear message.

Some aspects of evangelistic speaking are more difficult than other kinds of speaking. However, determining the purpose of evangelistic speaking is easier because ultimately your goal is to see your listeners trust Christ for their salvation. If I were using James 1 to speak to believers about trials, my purpose might vary as I sense what the Spirit of God wants to accomplish. It might be to cause them to stop being bitter against God for what He's allowed in their lives. It could be to develop godly character in recognizing the good lessons we learn through hard times. Or it could be to recognize the danger in going through trials without responding properly. But in evangelistic speaking, the purpose is very clear and similar in every message—to see unbelievers trust in Christ alone to save them.

The second aspect of focusing your message involves summarizing the development and flow into one paragraph.

Suppose you are going on vacation. If you cannot tell me in one paragraph how you are going to leave, where you are going, what you are going to do, and how you are going to get home, you'd better not leave your house. Likewise, if in one paragraph you cannot tell me how you are going to begin your message, walk through the text, apply the text, and conclude, you are not prepared to speak. What is unclear in your mind will be unclear in the mind of your audience.

Here is a summary of my message on Luke 19:1–10.

I begin by establishing a principle that everyone knows: there are certain offers that we do not qualify for. Many are convinced that the same thing is true in the spiritual realm—that God may offer everyone eternal life, but not everyone qualifies. After all, doesn't God help those who help themselves? We need to let God answer the question "What kind of person does God save?" He answers it in verse 10: "For the Son of Man has come to seek and to save that which was lost." Jesus said this to a man named Zaccheus. We know two things about him: He was short, and he was a sinner. After proving from the text that he was short, I'll explain the three things that prove he was a sinner—his job, the people, and his own confession. I'll then drive home the main idea. In answer to the question, "What kind of person does God save?" the Bible says that

God saves sinners. I'll then explain the gospel, telling how God saves them through His death and resurrection. And then I'll appeal to them to trust Christ.

The summarization of the development and flow of your message will be one of your greatest helps in becoming a clear communicator. You know how you are going to launch your message, the route you are going to travel in communicating it, and how you are going to return home. What is clear in your mind now becomes clear in the mind of the audience. It's been said that too many speakers are like Christopher Columbus. When they start out, they're not certain where they are going. When they get there, they're not certain where they are. When they come home, they're not certain where they've been. Summarizing your message into one paragraph makes you a communicator, not a Christopher Columbus.

In *Biblical Preaching*, Haddon Robinson comments, "There are three kinds of preachers: those to whom you cannot listen; those to whom you can listen; those to whom you must listen."[4]

You now know the text. You've torn the text apart, examining every detail of the passage. You're convinced of its central idea. Whether it is a message that you *can* listen to or *must* listen to depends on how you put it together. It must be put it together in a way that is relatable and life-changing. Your goal is to communicate. What is clear in your mind should become clear in your listeners' minds. You are not before your audience to give them your notes. You are before them to impart truth through a clear message. That is why the next six steps are as critical as the first four.

Outline your message.

With the message summarized into one paragraph, the outline follows.

Since we are talking about expository evangelistic speaking, the outline *must* reflect the text. The outline cannot be imposed on the text. It must be derived from the text. If Paul the apostle establishes a point and then gives one proof to support it, your outline has an "A" but not a "B." The writer of Scripture may be so excited as he writes under the inspiration of the Holy Spirit that he adds a "p.s." to his thoughts or heads down a side trail. Your message then has a "p.s." to it, as you explain the text.

Matthew 6:25–34 contains such a "p.s.," and it comes from the lips of Christ Himself. Speaking to the issue of anxiety, Christ laid out two principles. The first is, there is more to life than what you are worrying about. He established that by saying, "Therefore I say to you, do not worry about your life, what you will eat or what you will drink; nor about your body, what you will put on. Is not life more than food and the body more than clothing?" (v. 25). The second is, if God takes care of his creation, he'll also take care of His children. He used two lines of support as proof—the birds of the air (v. 26) and the lilies of the field (vv. 28–30). But after his first line of support (the birds) and prior to his second, he established a "p.s." That "p.s." is "What good would worrying do you anyway?" Or, as Scripture records, "Which of you by worrying can add one cubit to his stature?" (v. 27). This could be better translated, "Which of you by worrying can add one cubit to his life's span?" A cubit is a measure of length from the tip of the finger to the elbow. It was considered to be about eighteen inches. According to the book of Job, before we were ever born, God established the length of our days (14:5). Christ's point was that we, by worrying, cannot change the smallest amount, even the equivalent of eighteen inches. So what good is worrying?

The outline should also reflect the movement of the message. In walking through the outline, we establish the movement of the message from one part to another.

Two cautions. First, it is important that all the parts are related to one another. If they are disjointed in the outline, they will be disjointed in the message. Second, the outline needs to reflect the transition from one point to another. Here is one of many places where the outline helps—it makes certain that transitions are clear. Warren and David Wiersbe comment, "God is not the author of confusion, but some preachers are, and they do it in God's name."[5] Speakers often lose their audiences when they fail to transition clearly. A clear transition in the speaker's mind is not always a clear transition in the mind of the audience. The speaker has moved on. The problem is that he hasn't taken the audience with him. It often takes three statements to make a transition. For example, suppose we are speaking from a passage from one of the Pauline epistles. A suitable transition would be, "Having made one point, there is a second point that Paul, the apostle, makes. There is a second thing he wants to stress. The second thing he stresses is . . . " In this way, we make it clear to our audience that we are moving on to our second point so they can move on with us.

As established earlier, every expository evangelistic message must tell people three things: We are sinners; Christ died for us and rose again; we must trust Christ. No single passage, though, covers all three points. So in our message preparation, we need to decide where and how to bring in whichever of the three elements (sin, substitution, and faith) is not in the text. The reason is obvious. The outline must reflect the movement of the message. Since the presentation of those essential elements that cannot be brought out in the text are still part of the movement of the message, your outline should reflect where these items fit. For example, suppose the text speaks to the issue of substitution and faith, but does not discuss the issue of sin. The outline should reflect where in your message you are going to treat the issue of sin. For example, Luke 19:1–10 deals with the fact that we are sinners. I felt it was most appropriate at the end of the message to bring in 1) Christ died for us and rose again, and 2) we have to trust Christ.

Let's look at the message outline for Luke 19:1–10.

I.   Introduction
    A. We don't qualify for certain offers.
    B. We feel we don't qualify for eternal life.
    C. God tells us through one man what kind of person qualifies.
II. The text tells us two things about Zaccheus (vv. 1–8).
    A. He was short (vv. 1–4).
       1. The text says so (v. 3).
       2. His inability to see Christ says so (vv. 3–4).
    B. He was a sinner (vv. 1–8).
       1. His job tells you (vv. 1–2).
       2. The people tell you (vv. 5–7).
       3. He tells you (v. 8).
III. The text tells us that Christ said two things in response to who Zaccheus was (vv. 9–10).
    A. Salvation has come to this house (v. 9).
    B. The Son of Man seeks and saves the lost (v. 10).
IV. Conclusion
    A. Main idea: God saves sinners.
    B. This is how you come to Christ.
       1. Admit you are a sinner.
       2. Recognize Christ died for sinners and rose again.
       3. Trust Christ.
    C. Will *you* trust Christ?

Determine and develop your support material.

You have your main idea. The flow of your message is established. The outline is in place. Now it is time to choose the supporting material.

Note that I used the phrase "supporting material." This includes illustrations but is not limited to that. Supporting material can include factual information, illustrations, quotes, analogies, statistics, contrasts, etc. It includes anything that supports particular points made in the message. Some of the supporting material will be serious; some of it needs to be humorous. We cannot lose sight of the fact that we are speaking to unbelievers. Therefore, whatever we use needs to fit a non-Christian audience.

Be certain you have enough supporting material. The temptation is to have too little, not too much. Also be sure to have variety. Avoid using two airplane stories in the same message or quoting only athletes (unless of course you are speaking to a sports-only crowd). The supporting material should represent a wide variety of places, people, and situations so as to identify with the different people in your audience.

The supporting material needs to be properly placed in the outline. Let's look at the supporting material for Luke 19:1–10.

I. Introduction
   A. We don't qualify for certain offers.
      Illus.—Firm in New York City looking for exceptional employee
      Illus.—Offer of flying a plane
   B. We feel we don't qualify for eternal life.
      Illus.—Businessmen in Longmont, Colorado
      Illus.—Statements we've heard
   C. God tells us through one man what kind of person qualifies.
      Illus.—Phrases in the Bible we don't understand

II. The text tells us two things about Zaccheus (vv. 1–8).
   A. He was short (vv. 1–4).
      1. The text says so (v. 3).
         Illus.—President visiting our city
      2. His inability to see Christ says so (vv. 3–4).
         Illus.—Friend's first date
   B. He was a sinner (vv. 1–8).
      1. His job tells you (vv. 1–2).
         Illus.—Man who cheated on income tax
      2. The people tell you (vv. 5–7).
         Illus.—Family tree
         Illus.—Presidential primary
         Illus.—Woman who tried to kill her husband
      3. He tells you (v. 8).
         Illus.—The White House being in Washington, D.C.

III. The text tells us that Christ said two things in response to who Zaccheus was (vv. 9–10).
   A. Salvation has come to this house (v. 9).
      Illus.—Good news is sometimes bad news
   B. The Son of Man seeks and saves the lost (10).

IV. Conclusion
   A. Main idea: God saves sinners.
      Illus.—Lost, least, last
   B. This is how you come to Christ.
      1. Admit you are a sinner.
         Illus.—76-year-old woman in Kansas
      2. Recognize Christ died for sinners.
         Illus.—Baby left in burning apartment
      3. Trust Christ.
         Illus.—George Whitefield
   C. Will *you* trust Christ?

Develop your conclusion.

During the Civil War, President Lincoln reportedly attended a church not far from the White House on Wednesday nights. The preacher allowed the president and his Secret Service agent to sit in the pastor's study with the door open and within hearing distance of the pulpit so they wouldn't be a distraction to the people. One Wednesday, Lincoln and the Secret Service agent were walking back to the White House. The agent asked, "What did you think of tonight's sermon?" Lincoln reportedly answered, "Well, it was brilliantly conceived, biblical, relevant, and well presented." The agent asked, "So, it was a great sermon?" Lincoln answered, "No, it failed. It failed because he didn't ask us to do something great."[6]

That's what a good conclusion to a message does. It calls upon people to do something.

A conclusion reviews what has been stated. A primary organizing principle of speechmaking is, "Tell them what you're going to tell them, then tell them, then tell them what you already told them."

Once we review, we then appeal for action. In evangelistic speaking, the "action" is one thing. We ask them to admit they are sinners, to recognize that Christ died for them and arose, and to *trust* in Christ alone to save them. Notice I used the term "trust." As discussed previously, we must use clear terminology. We are not inviting unbelievers to "invite Jesus into their hearts" or "give their lives to God." We are inviting them to do what the New Testament asks them to do—believe—which means to trust in Christ alone to save them.

The conclusion to the message on Luke 19:1–10 is quite simple. I review what I've told them, "When the Bible explains what it means by lost, it points to a man who is a sinner. So if you want to come to God you have to come as a sinner. You cannot come to God as a good, moral, religious person. You have to come the way Zaccheus came—as a sinner who needs Christ."

I then appeal for action. Using the gospel to explain what Christ did for sinners through His death and resurrection, I appeal to them to trust in Christ alone to save them.

As mentioned earlier, certain aspects of evangelistic speaking are more difficult than other kinds of speaking. The conclusion is one of the easier aspects. Regardless of our audience, the situation, or the passage we've chosen to speak from, we are asking each person to trust Christ.

This is one of the most humbling aspects of evangelistic speaking because only the Holy Spirit can cause them to see their need and come to Christ. We do our best to explain the text as carefully as we can. We endeavor to put it in words they can understand. We make the gospel as clear as we can. The results are now in God's hands. Jesus said, "No one can come to Me unless the Father who sent Me draws him" (John 6:44). Our appeal invites them to come to Christ. Only the convicting power of the Holy Spirit can bring them.

Develop your introduction.

"What?" you might exclaim. "*Now* I develop the introduction?" That's correct. The introduction is not the first thing you do; it is the last. Only *after* discovering what the paragraph is saying will you know how to introduce it. There are three things an introduction needs to do.

First, it needs to arouse attention. If we don't get their attention, they will not hear what we have to say. It needs to make them sit up and listen. Consider the Sunday school teacher who asked her children as they were entering the church service, "And why is it necessary to be quiet in church?" One bright little girl replied, "Because people are sleeping." Our introduction should cause people to say, "This is *one* message I can't sleep through. I need to hear what he's going to say."

Second, it needs to strike a need. Even if our introduction gets the audience's attention, their attention span will be limited if we fail to address a need. What questions are they asking that you are answering? What struggle do they have that you are going to help them with? What weakness or temptation are they facing that you will tell them how to overcome?

Third, it needs to introduce the text. Since this particular message is an *expository* evangelistic message, we are not explaining what we have to say. We're explaining what God has *already* said. Therefore our introduction must direct them to the text we're explaining. An introduction that arouses attention and strikes a need but does not take them to the text falls short.

An introduction normally takes three to five minutes. It takes *time* to accomplish the preceding goals and draw the entire audience into your message. But those three to five minutes will determine how well they listen—or even *if* they listen—to the remainder of the message. Don't confuse a message "start" with a message introduction. A speaker who begins a message by saying "I want us to look at (text) and then begins discussing it has no introduction. He is simply starting his message. Only when an introduction does the three things just mentioned is it an introduction.

Perhaps now you understand why the introduction is the last thing you work on. Until we know the text and its main idea, we do not know how to introduce it. The context of the message gives rise to ideas that will help us figure out how to gain our hearers' attention. And our study of the passage will reveal what real life needs are being addressed. Suppose a class of thirty speakers were asked to develop a message on Isaiah 53:6: "All we like sheep have gone astray; we have turned, every one, to his own way; and the Lord has laid on Him the iniquity of us all." Although the thirty speakers would express the meaning of the verse in different words, they'd basically say the same thing. There would be, however, thirty different introductions. No two would be the same. But each introduction should strive to do what every introduction must do—arouse attention, strike a need, and introduce the text.

In my message on Luke 19:1–10, I tell a humorous story about a firm in New York City that was looking for an exceptional employee. It ends with the explanation of an elderly man who, knowing he didn't qualify, traveled from the back hills of Kentucky to New York City to tell them, "Don't count on me." I continue by establishing the point that we are all aware there are certain offers for which we just don't qualify. I then explain something humorous that happened to me when a peer misunderstood my comment about how much flying I do. Owning a small airplane company and assuming I was a pilot, he offered to let me fly one of his small planes and he'd go along for the ride. I could have given him a ride! The hilarity behind the story captures the audience's attention. I then reestablish my point. We are all aware that there are certain offers for which we don't qualify. I explain we are convinced the same thing is true with the Lord. We may not qualify for His free offer of eternal life. Doesn't God help those who help themselves? That raises the question, "What kind of person do you have to be in order for God to accept you?" What kind of person does God save?" Their need to listen to what I have to say has now been addressed. I then proceed to explain that God answers that question in verse 10, "For the Son of Man has come to seek and to save that which was lost." Christ saves lost people and this passage explains what He means by lost.

Keep in mind two things. First, it is best to read the entire passage you are speaking from prior to speaking. That way your listeners have the text open before them. You can then give the introduction and go directly to the text and begin unfolding its meaning to the people. Taking time to read the text after the introduction sometimes disconnects your introduction from your message.

A second thing to note is that you need an effective title for your message. Good titles are helpful. When used properly, they can cause a non-Christian to come and hear what you have to say.

The title of my message on Luke 19:1–10 is "What kind of person do you have to be in order for God to accept you?" Think "non-Christian" when choosing a title. Titles such as "The conversion of Zaccheus," "The man most hated but Christ-loved," "The way to meet your greatest Friend," may interest you. However, they are not likely to interest a non-Christian. The title has to capture both the ear and the interest of a non-Christian.

Write your message.

Now it's time to write out your entire message—start to finish—the way you plan to say it. Write every word, analogy, contrast, illustration, all humor, every point and every sub point. Why? Your goal is not to speak. Your goal is to communicate.

Don't forget, speaking is when the words of my mouth enter the openings of your ears. Communication is when what is understood in my mind is understood in yours as well. Writing out our message aids our communication. It allows us to look at every word we plan to say and ask, "Do those words convey what I want to communicate?" Would a different word choice help to drive home the point?

It enables us to look at transitions. As I move from one point to the next, am I taking the audience with me? Are my transitions smooth and easy to follow?

It allows us to look at the length of our message. Based on the speed I normally talk and the pauses I take, I know that when I have forty-five hundred words I have a thirty-minute message. Since I won't speak more than thirty minutes to a non-Christian audience, anything over that has to be cut. The manuscript allows me to look at every point of my message and determine where to delete material. If I do not have enough material, the manuscript helps me determine where to add.

Torrey Robinson summarized the benefits of a manuscript:

> Once the sermon is structured, you are ready to write a sermon manuscript. A manuscript strengthens a sermon in three ways. First, a sermon manuscript helps to polish wording. Words are powerful. Choosing words well can make a good sermon great. Second, writing the sermon helps make sure that important details in the story are included. Finally, the process of writing forces you to think through the sermon. When you stand up to tell the story, you already know where you're going.[7]

If it's worth saying once, it is worth saying again. By having the message written out, all that work and study is reserved for future use. Questions like, "Now how did I say that?" "What illustration was so helpful?" "What was the question I asked at the end of the message that seemed so effective?" don't have to be asked. Your work and study are preserved for future use.

Whether writing or typing, use only one side of the paper. If you are writing your manuscript by hand, write on one side only, and if you are typing or printing from a computer, double space. By having the message written on one side only, you can add thoughts or reword thoughts that come to you as you drive down the highway, watch television, dine out, or carry out your household chores.

You don't need to memorize the message, nor do you want to. Personally, I could not quote any of my messages. But prior to speaking I read through the message a minimum of ten times, often twenty times. By that time the message is so well fixed in my mind, I can look at my audience, not my notes. This is essential in communication. Speakers look at paper; communicators look at people. Should someone's facial expression reveal they did not catch something I said, I say it again. Should the audience suffer an unavoidable distraction, I know where to go back and begin again. Scripting the message allows you to master it. Mastering it allows you to communicate it. Your focus is on the people. The manuscript of my message on Luke 19:1–10 can be found in Appendix II.

Go speak it.

Here's the reward. A car comes off the assembly line ready to take a person from one point to another. Your message, empowered by the Holy Spirit, is now ready to take a person from one destination to another. It is an instrument used of God to take a person from the kingdom of darkness into the kingdom of light.

Conclusion

Evangelistic speaking, like other aspects of evangelism, involves a partnership with God. We do our part. God does His. Our part is the prayer, study of the text, and preparation of the message. His part is to take what He through His Spirit has helped us prepare and use it to convert unbelievers. When God changes a sinner's eternal destination, He makes all of our hard work worthwhile. Our message, carefully prepared, effectively communicated, and prayerfully supported, has more than an earthly impact. It has an eternal one. Our message brings Christ to them. His Spirit brings them to Christ.

REFLECTING...

1. What are the ten steps in putting together an expository evangelistic message?

2. What are the two questions you ask to formulate your main idea?

3. What does Focusing your message involve?

4. What should every conclusion do?

5. Where in message preparation do you develop your introduction and what three things should an effective introduction do?

Chapter 25

What About the Invitation?

WHAT DO THE FOLLOWING three have in common? A drowning swimmer. A man with prostate cancer. Someone trapped beneath an overturned car. Answer? They all need someone who can save them. Second question: What will keep that someone from saving them? Answer? If the person in need will not accept the savior.

The gospel demands a response. The unbeliever must trust the Savior. As the good news is heard, the hearer must either receive the gift of eternal life or reject it. Evangelism, biblically defined, is information and invitation. Once the gospel is presented—Christ died for your sins and arose—non-Christians must be invited to trust Christ as their personal Savior. How does one handle the invitation?

Clarifiy three concepts.

The first clarification is this: When we talk about the invitation in this chapter, we are talking about the public way we find out who is interested in trusting Christ. We are not talking about the invitation contained within the message. As noted earlier, every evangelistic message must explain three things: 1) we are sinners; 2) Christ died for us and rose again; 3) we must trust Christ. The moment a person places his trust in Christ alone, he is forever His. A public invitation of any kind is simply a way of finding out who is interested and ready. The public invitation is usually done after a speaker says, "Let's close in prayer," while heads are bowed and eyes are closed.

The second clarification builds on the first. A public invitation of any kind does not save. Trusting Christ is what saves. A public invitation of any kind is a way of finding out who is interested and ready.

Some might ask, "Can one be saved if he does not publicly confess Christ?" The answer is "Yes." One can trust Christ in the privacy of his seat. Nowhere in Scripture is a public confession of Christ essential to salvation. John 3:16 does not say, "Whoever believes and confesses," it says, "Whoever believes."

Examine John 12:42: "Nevertheless even among the rulers many believed in Him, but because of the Pharisees they did not confess Him, lest they should be put out of the synagogue." Many of the Jewish people refused to believe in Christ despite the miracles He performed. At the same time, there were those leaders who "believed in Him." "Believed in Him" is the Johannine expression used throughout the Gospel of John to refer to eternal salvation. John testified that they had trusted Christ and thus were eternally His but were fearful of making a public confession. The reason is that they concentrated too much on what people might think. They loved the praise of men more than the praise of God (v. 43). Once more, nowhere in Scripture is a public confession of Christ a requirement for salvation.

To teach that confession is a requirement of salvation, some have used Romans 10:9–10: "That if you confess with your mouth the Lord Jesus and believe in your heart that God has raised Him from the dead, you will be saved. For with the heart one believes unto righteousness, and with the mouth confession is made unto salvation."

That, though, is not the meaning of the passage. Examine the context. Paul is addressing the question of how a Jew could be saved from God's wrath and experience the sanctification in which He wants all believers to live. (Note the transitional verses of Romans 5:9–10.) They first must be justified by His blood. There is no other way they could be forever justified in His sight. Paul even warned them about seeking their own righteousness instead of submitting to His. He says, "For I bear them witness that they have a zeal for God, but not according to knowledge. For they being ignorant of God's righteousness, and seeking to establish their own righteousness, have not submitted to the righteousness of God. For Christ is the end of the law for righteousness to everyone who believes" (vv. 2–4). Paul then elaborates on that righteousness by faith, explaining that it centers on the Messiah—the One the Jews had rejected. A righteousness by faith does not ask, "Who will ascend into heaven to bring Christ down?" because He has already come (v. 6). Nor does it ask, "Who will descend into the abyss to bring Christ up?" because He has already risen" (v. 7). Instead, the righteousness that is by faith concerns a word from God, which they knew well but now only had to believe. So Paul says, "That if you confess with your mouth the Lord Jesus and believe in your heart that God has raised Him from the dead, you will be saved" (v. 9).

To be saved from God's wrath they needed to openly confess Him. However, we first have to know Him. Justification must precede any amount of sanctification or confession. Thus Paul continued, "For with the heart one believes unto righteousness, and with the mouth confession is made unto salvation" (v. 10). The word translated "righteousness" is the noun form of the verb "justifies" found in Romans 4:5: "But to him who does not work but believes on Him who justifies the ungodly, his faith is accounted for righteousness."

Trusting Christ as our only way of salvation justifies us before God. God places His Son's righteousness on our account—"with the heart one believes unto righteousness." But in order to avoid the wrath of God on present day sin, we must be willing to openly confess Christ. We can experience eternal life without confessing Him publicly as evidenced in John 12:42. But we cannot experience a *victorious* Christian life without being willing to openly confess our faith in Christ. A public confession of Christ is critical to a walk of sanctification before God, but not to receiving eternal life.

Romans 10:9–10 is not saying that we can be saved only if we publicly confess Christ. Paul is arguing that just as we are justified by faith from the heart, a confession from the mouth saves us from the wrath of God on present day sin. (For a fuller description of this passage and others used to support confession as a requirement for salvation, see "If I don't confess Him, do I possess Him?" which is chapter 8 of my book *Free and Clear*.)

A third clarification is that there will be times when we cannot give a public invitation of any kind. At such times we can tell unbelievers only of their need to trust Christ. We must trust God with the results. We must also trust Him to send someone to follow up one on one. Many times the gospel seed is sown at such an event and later the person trusts Christ and tells others about it.

When we *can* give a public invitation, what should characterize it?

What characterizes an effective public invitation?

Start with the same thing that characterized the message—directness. This is not a time to say, "If you're here tonight and don't know you're going to heaven." Instead say, "Some of you are here and you don't know you're going to heaven." Don't say, "Perhaps tonight is the night you need to come to Christ." Say, "Tonight is the night you need to come to Christ."

The invitation, just like the message, needs to be direct. It needs to be said warmly and lovingly but it needs to be direct.

It makes the issue trusting Christ.

Make it clear to the audience that you are trying to find out who is interested in trusting Christ. They need to understand that if they are interested, you want to talk with them one on one and give them information on how to grow in their new faith. That way, they know they are responding to Christ, not to you. It is His offer they are rejecting or receiving, not yours.

It must be clear in its details.

Put yourself in the shoes of a non-Christian and ask yourself, "Would I understand what the speaker is asking me to do?" If we invite them to come forward, do they know what's going to happen when they get there? Might they think they will be asked to give a speech or have we told them they will be taken aside and spoken to privately? If we ask them to raise their hands, do they know the reason, and what is going to happen if they do? The invitation is no place for confusion. As we give the invitation, we need to carefully explain what we are asking them to do and what's going to happen once they've done it.

An essential that cannot be stressed enough is that it must be warm and personal. When I give an invitation, I imagine myself sitting in the seat alongside the non-Christian. My arm is around his shoulder and I'm focused on him. That's why I make statements such as, "Some of you are sitting here thinking, 'Larry, I've never understood this before. No one has ever explained it the way you did tonight.'" I want them to know that since I've just presented *the* friend of sinners, I'm now talking as their friend. The message has to reflect our love for them. The invitation needs to reflect that as well. Remember, we are God's messengers. To feel wanted and loved by God they must feel wanted and loved by us.

It must be positive and expect results.

When you give an invitation, be positive and expect results. Every time I give an evangelistic message, not every unbeliever in the audience is going to come to Christ. At the same time, I speak optimistically, as though I expect them all to respond. That expectation has to be there. A speaker once said to me, "I don't like giving an invitation because I'm afraid there won't be a response." We cannot be controlled by that fear. We have to expect God to work. A student of Charles Spurgeon once came to him complaining that he wasn't seeing conversions as a result of his preaching. Spurgeon asked, "Surely you don't expect conversions every time you preach, do you?" The young man answered, "Well, I suppose not." Spurgeon then said, "That's precisely why you're not having them."[1] An evangelist who is committed to Scripture must recognize that the results are in God's hands: "No one can come to Me unless the Father who sent Me draws him" (John 6:44). God ultimately determines how many respond. The speaker brings Christ to the non-Christian; God brings the non-Christian to Christ.

The invitation must be characterized by integrity. For the sake of Christ and for the sake of the non-Christian, we cannot say, "All I'm going to ask you to do is raise your hand." Then, once hands are raised, say, "Now I'm going to ask you to step into the aisle and come forward." We have just lied before God and before the non-Christian. We said we were only asking one thing, but instead we asked two. We cannot say, "We're going to sing two more stanzas of 'Just As I Am' and then close our service" and then proceed to sing five more stanzas. The book of James says, "But let your 'Yes' be 'Yes,' and your 'No,' 'No,' lest you fall into judgment" (5:12). James was saying, "Say what you mean and mean what you say." Your invitation has to be characterized by that kind of integrity. Don't say one thing and do another.

What are different ways of extending an invitation?

When it comes to evangelism, there is one message, many methods. The message never changes. Methods do change. There is not just one way to reach non-Christians. There are many.

The same thing can be said of the invitation. The need to trust Christ never changes. He and He alone is the only way to salvation. However, methods for finding out those who are interested and ready vary. What proves helpful in one situation may not prove helpful in another. Flexibility and variety are key words.

The invitation can be given in different ways. I have used all of these and know the pros and cons of each.

Altar call

This is the type of invitation most people are probably familiar with. While the audience is standing and singing a hymn, those interested in trusting Christ are encouraged to walk forward. A counselor meets them at the front and talks with them. Commonly referred to as the "altar call," this was introduced by Charles Finney in the 1820s and then popularized under the ministry of D. L. Moody. There is no record of it being used prior to the first part of the nineteenth century. When Finney and Moody first used it, many criticized the altar call for being too manipulative—just a manmade and emotional way of securing a response to the gospel. Since then, largely due to the ministry of Billy Graham, it's been widely used and accepted.

The advantage of an altar call is that it's the easiest way we can speak with a person one on one. Altar calls also have their disadvantages. For one, it can be misunderstood if it's mishandled. The more common and prominent something is, the greater the chance of it being misunderstood. This form of invitation is probably best known throughout the world. Its familiarity has encouraged its misuse and even an unbiblical application. I once heard an evangelistic speaker say, "There are two conditions of salvation. One is to come to Christ. The other is to come forward." That statement is false and unbiblical. It's also interesting that I've never heard that said of any kind of invitation other than the altar call. I can't help but think its familiarity has encouraged mishandling.

A second problem is that altar calls can be difficult for people to respond to, perhaps due to the physical facility where we are meeting or shyness on the part of the person responding. I once led a person to Christ who said to me, "I would have gone to hell before I would have gone forward." Because I gave a different kind of invitation, he responded. Since then he has led others to Christ. One can argue that if the Holy Spirit is working, they won't let that bother them. I disagree. One can be sincerely led by the Holy Spirit to trust Christ and yet be shy. How many people do you know who are terrified to get up in front of people? Let's not call those people "ashamed of Christ." Instead, just call them what they are—people afraid to get up before others in a public setting.

A final disadvantage is the day in which we are living. Non-Christians and Christians alike make sincere and serious decisions in the privacy of their own homes. They can bank by phone or on-line. A businessman told me he had just taken on his largest debt ever, and he did it over the phone with his banker. Purchases small and large are made over the Internet. A signed statement, sent through a fax machine, solidifies an agreement between two people. My point is, people are used to making decisions in the privacy of their home or office. Non-Christians may not identify with the concept of an altar call. "Are you accusing me of not being sincere if I don't come forward? Are you afraid I don't mean what I'm doing and somehow walking forward will verify my integrity?" As one who has spoken all over the world, I have found that the altar call has been more helpful in less developed countries than in more developed ones. I credit a lot of that to the development of technology and the way people make serious decisions right where they are, in homes, offices, or even the privacy of their cars.

Come to the side room

In this invitation, those interested in trusting Christ are encouraged to meet in a room beside the auditorium where you or a counselor will talk with them. Instead of coming to the front, as in an altar call, they are directed to a room to the side.

This approach has two advantages. First, although they can come forward during the program, they also have the opportunity to respond when the service is dismissed. This allows others to leave. Second, it helps those who are shy. Unbelievers wanting to trust Christ come forward as everyone else is leaving. They no longer fear they will be asked to speak in front of a group of people. They simply go to a room where they can talk to someone who can spiritually help them.

The side room's disadvantage is obvious. Not all facilities have such a room. If we direct a non-Christian to a side room, it has to be on the same level as the auditorium and it has to be within view. That way, when we refer to that room and point to it, the unbeliever can see it. Once they are there, the side room has to be large enough that several, along with their counselors, can be dealt with at the same time. Few churches or auditoriums have that kind of facility. Most that do are newly built and were constructed with that need in mind. If the room is not on the same floor or within view, it will be too difficult for the person to locate.

"Raise your hand if you trusted Christ tonight and want to talk about how to grow"

In this invitation, non-Christians are encouraged to trust Christ where they are and given the time and opportunity to do so. The speaker leads them in prayer phrase by phrase as they tell God they are trusting His Son to save them. When doing this, keep in mind two things. First, saying a prayer does not save. Trusting Christ saves. Prayer is how they tell God what they are doing. I tell people that. Second, if you lead them in prayer phrase by phrase, give them time to follow you. In other words, when you encourage them to repeat after you, "Dear God, I'm a sinner," give them time in the quietness of their heart to say, "Dear God, I'm a sinner." Pause long enough for them to say the words you've encouraged them to say before going on to your next phrase, "Nothing I do makes me deserving of heaven." Then again, pause and give them time to tell God what you are encouraging them to say.

After they've trusted Christ, while heads are still lowered, explain, "If you are here tonight and have trusted Christ, we would like to talk with you about how to grow as a Christian. But we need to know who you are." You then encourage them to raise their hand to indicate two things: 1) that they've trusted Christ; 2) that they'd like to talk with someone about how to grow as a Christian. The speaker, and perhaps a few others, watch carefully to see who raises their hands. After the service is dismissed, someone walks up to them, noting they raised their hands, and arranges a time to meet with them.

The advantage to such an invitation is that it is very easy for people to respond. We don't ask them to come before a crowd of people but simply acknowledge that they have just trusted Christ. Also, for those who have the mentality that coming forward is what saves, this method makes it clear that they can trust Christ right where they are.

The disadvantage of the "raise your hand" invitation is that it can be difficult to do with a large crowd. It is helpful when the crowd numbers one hundred or less. However, if numerous people raise their hands in a crowd of several hundred, it is difficult to spot them.

The second difficulty of this approach is bigger than the first. Even though we recognize the hands of those who respond and make a point of approaching them afterward, the crowd can make it difficult to get to them. After the service dismisses, many people may be standing between the new convert and us. Getting to them without being inconsiderate to others is often difficult. This emphasizes the need for variety in the way we give the invitation. Whereas this could be effective with a small group of people, it may not be nearly as effective with a large group. I decided to use this invitation after one evangelistic message because I had found it helpful. At that time, though, I did not take into account the size of the crowd—close to five hundred people. When I gave the invitation, it was obvious that God was working. After I gave them a chance to trust Christ in their seats and encouraged them to raise their hands if they had done so, twenty to twenty-five people responded. Our desire was to approach them afterward and arrange a time to talk further. Since they all raised their hands at the same time there was no way that I and the others watching them could see each one. When the service was dismissed, we could not get to them fast enough. I learned through experience to keep the size of the audience in mind.

"If you trusted Christ tonight, come forward afterward for information on how to grow as a Christian"

This is one of my favorites. With this invitation, non-Christians are encouraged to trust Christ right where they are. If you have them pray in their seats to tell God they are trusting Christ, make sure you emphasize that saying a prayer does not save. It's trusting Christ that saves. Make sure that you also give them time to verbalize phrase by phrase the prayer from their hearts as you say it aloud. Then encourage those who trusted Christ in their seats to meet you in the front where you will give them a booklet that will help them grow as a Christian. It helps to even give the name of the booklet and show it to them to encourage their interest. Many have used EvanTell's *Welcome to the Family* and *31 Days to Living as a New Believer*. With such an invitation, people no longer feel as if they are on stage. They are meeting us in the front of the room, as would be true of the altar call, but they are doing it *after the program*. If people are shy, walking to the front is not what bothers them. It's walking to the front *before a group of people*. Another advantage of this invitation is that it makes a distinction between trusting Christ and growing. In evangelism, it's important not to confuse entering the Christian life with living it. First, we enter it and then we live it. We enter it by trusting Christ. We live it by growing as a Christian. Such an invitation makes clear that since they have trusted Christ, we now want to encourage them in their spiritual growth.

This type of invitation has two disadvantages, but they do not impede its use. One, if we mention something that will help them grow, those who have been Christians for some time might want a copy of it. When using such an invitation, I've had people say, "I've been a Christian for a while, but could I have one of those booklets?" I'm delighted to give them one. Regardless of how long they've been a Christian, they've expressed a need to grow, and I want to encourage that. However, our time is primarily for new converts. This disadvantage is not serious enough to keep us from using it.

A second problem is similar. When you invite those who have just trusted Christ to come forward after the program, others who have been believers for some time will also come forward for other reasons. Those reasons may include an appointment with you they need to change, a matter of interest between the two of you that happened during the week, or even a question related to a point in your message. If you use this invitation frequently, there is a way to solve that problem. Simply educate the people beforehand. Christians do not mean to be insensitive, but sometimes they can unintentionally hinder what you are attempting to do. You explain that from time to time you will give such an invitation, and you encourage those who have been believers for some time to see you at another time. That way you will be free to talk with the new believers. They will be most happy to oblige and assist.

"Please fill out a communication card"

Another type of invitation is the communication card. Here's what it looks like.

COMMUNICATION CARD			
Date			
Mr. Mrs. Miss Ms.			
Address			
Phone			
Age	____ Elementary	____ 26–35	
	____ Middle School	____ 36–49	
	____ High School	____ 50–59	
	____ 18–25	____ 60 and over	
I was invited by			

As people enter the room, or after the program, give each one a communication card. Whoever is leading the program informs the people not to do *anything* with them, not even fill them out. He tells them that the speaker will explain what to do with them at the end of the program. At the end of the message, the non-Christians are encouraged to trust

Christ right where they are, in the privacy of their seats. Once more, give them the time and opportunity to tell God in prayer what they are doing. Then close in prayer yourself. Each person is then given a communication card (if they weren't distributed before the program) and asked to complete it. Those who trusted Christ that night are asked to put a check in the upper right hand corner. In doing so, they are saying two things: 1) I have trusted Christ; 2) I would like to receive information about how to grow as a Christian. The cards are then passed upside down to the aisle, and the ushers collect them.

This invitation has several advantages. For one, *everyone* fills one out, not just those who trusted Christ. Those who trusted Christ check the upper right hand corner. In so doing, you have a record of everyone who attended. It is good not only to follow up those who have trusted Christ but even to follow up non-Christian visitors. Many times a non-Christian who did not respond at the outreach will do so in his home. A second advantage is that this is probably the most non-threatening of all the invitations. Like several of the others, this method allows people to trust Christ in the privacy of their seats. At the same time, they can tell us in a way that is not intimidating to them. People fill out cards for all kinds of reasons, so they won't mind completing a card that tells you they have just received the gift of eternal life and want to grow as a Christian. Another plus is that this approach can be used in a wide variety of settings—a normal church service as well as gatherings of any nature, and virtually anywhere.

The disadvantage is the expense of producing enough cards for each person. These need to be neatly printed on card stock, not paper. They can, however, be generic so that cards not used on one occasion can be used on another. It's important not to ask for any information other than what is asked for above. If you put the name of the church on the card, it appears as if you are signing up for church membership, which they are not prepared to do. If you ask for additional information, it becomes a bit cumbersome to fill out. The simpler the card, the better.

I have preferred to use this approach many times and have been asked to put into print exactly what I say at the end when I use this invitation. After inviting people to trust Christ and leading them in doing so, I close in prayer. Then, looking at the audience, I say:

> May I ask all of you to do something today that will be a tremendous help to those who have made this special event possible? When you came in, you should have received a card that says, *Communication Card*. Those who made this day possible would like to know how many were here, where they were from, and what ages they represent. Would each of you be so kind right now to take a moment and fill out that card? We're going to give you a

moment to do so. Just take a moment right now, if you would, and fill out that card—not one per couple but one per person. If you did not get one of these cards, please hold up your hand, and someone will bring one to you. Also, if you need a pen or pencil, someone alongside you will be happy to lend you theirs. (You may want to have pencils available with the cards.) Just take a moment, if you would, to fill out that card.

Please listen carefully. If you trusted Christ tonight, if you've never understood this before and trusted Christ tonight for the first time, would you put a check mark in the upper right hand corner. That way we can see that you get some helpful information on how to grow as a Christian and live a life that says "thank you." Take a moment right now and fill out that card, if you would. Again, not one per couple, but one per person.

Once you've completed the card, turn it over and pass it to the nearest aisle. In a moment, an individual will come and collect them, but we'll give you a moment. And don't forget, if you trusted Christ tonight put a check mark in the upper right hand corner so we can make sure you get some helpful information on how to grow as a Christian. Then, turn your cards over and pass them to the aisle. Thank you for allowing us to help you in that way.

Notice that three times I've said, "If you trusted Christ *tonight*," "If you trusted Christ *tonight*," "If you trusted Christ *tonight*." If you do not stress "*tonight*" those who have previously trusted Christ will check the card. Those are not the ones you need to hear from with the appropriate check. Instead, it's the ones who trusted Christ *that* night.

Which method do you use?

Two things help determine the preferred method. One is to be sinner sensitive. Years ago I spoke at a community in North Dakota. A cold wave had come down from Alaska putting the chill factor at seventy degrees below zero (a chill goes up my spine just thinking about it). That night, the place was packed for the outreach. People left their cars running the entire program knowing their radiators would freeze if they didn't. After my message, a man came up to me and complimented my ministry. He then explained, "There's one thing that bothers me. You did not give an altar call." I asked, "Did I invite people to trust Christ?" He said, "Yes, you did." I then asked, "Did people respond?" He said, "Yes, and it's been exciting." So I said, "Then the only thing that bothers you about what I did is that I didn't give an altar call? Is that correct?" He said, "That is correct." I then explained, "Here's why I didn't. In this community, almost everyone is from a denominational background known for having members who are scared by altar calls. I was from that same background, so I understand. The altar call used to scare me too. If word had gotten out that I would give an altar call, I promise you we wouldn't have had this placed packed by closing night. The altar call itself would have kept them away." I did not realize that another believer was overhearing our conversation. He walked up and said, "Let me verify what Larry said. I brought a non-Christian to hear his message. He not only came, he came back. He is very close to coming to Christ. But the first question he asked me was, 'Is he going to give an altar call, because if he is, I'm not coming.'" I then looked at the person who approached me and said, "That's the reason I did not give one. I will not let an altar call stand in the way of people coming to Christ."

Do things that encourage people to come to Christ, not hinder them from doing so.

You must not only be sinner sensitive, you must also be situation sensitive. Examine your situation. What are the limitations? What would be the most natural thing to do. How can you make the best use of the facilities in which the outreach is being held? These factors should influence your decision about what kind of invitation to use.

Conclusion

There is one message: Christ died for our sins and arose. There is one way to heaven. Trust Christ as your only way there. There is more than one way to find out who is interested and ready. Use variety. Be sensitive to your audience. Be sensitive to your situation. Then do the right thing

REFLECTING...

1. How does our understanding of the clarity of the gospel affect our approach to a public invitation?

2. What are six things that should characterize a public invitation of any kind?

3. What are five different ways a public invitation might be extended depending on the situation?

4. What are two things to keep foremost in mind when determining which method of public invitation to use?

5. Why is "sinner sensitivity" so critical in the way we approach a public invitation?

Chapter 26

How Do You Talk to God as You're Talking to Men?

WHICH OF THE FOLLOWING brings people to Christ?

- A clear message
- A well-structured sermon outline
- Good and relatable illustrations
- Convincing rhetoric
- Biblically based truth spoken in love
- Well-used humor

None! All of them may be used of God to enlighten a person's understanding. All are important for effective communication. But ultimately none are *the* reason people come to Christ.

An unbeliever walked into one of our evangelistic outreaches as a convinced atheist. He walked out a believer. What convinced him? My message was not designed to prove there is a God. Its thrust was, assuming there is a God, how can you know Him? He trusted Christ, the Son of God, whom thirty minutes earlier he was not convinced existed. The comment I often hear from people like that is "I cannot explain what happened. But something convinced me God is real. I want to trust Christ."

The Great Converter is the Holy Spirit. Rest assured, God expects us to do our part in message preparation. Our faithfulness in that area God uses greatly. Without His supernatural work, conversion cannot occur.

That's why prayer is essential. When we speak evangelistically it is not our work through Christ that brings people to Him; it is His work through us. E. M. Bounds, the great Methodist preacher, once said, "The character of our praying will determine the character of our preaching. Light praying makes light preaching. . . . Talking to men for God is a great thing, but talking to God for men is greater still."[1]

Our dependency must not be on ourselves. It must be on Him. Humble dependence on God is essential. *Mastering Contemporary Preaching* contains a helpful illustration as well as a warning to all speakers. "A young preacher went to preach his first sermon. He'd done so much work on this masterpiece that he was full of his own importance. He entered the pulpit with tremendous confidence, but once up there, he blacked out and couldn't think of a thing. Finally he came down from the pulpit utterly humiliated. As he slumped down the steps, an old preacher said to him, 'If you'd gone up the way you came down, you'd have come down the way you went up.'"[2]

As you prepare to speak evangelistically, how specifically should you pray and encourage others to pray?

Opportunity

Begin by praying for opportunities to invite non-Christians. You bring them to the outreach. God brings them to Christ. But even your bringing them to the outreach requires the work of the Holy Spirit. Paul the apostle spoke of *God* opening doors to evangelize and to approach people with the gospel:

> "Now I will come to you when I pass through Macedonia (for I am passing through Macedonia). And it may be that I will remain, or even spend the winter with you, that you may send me on my journey, wherever I go. For I do not wish to see you now on the way; but I hope to stay a while with you, if the Lord permits. But I will tarry in Ephesus until Pentecost. For a great and effective door has opened to me, and there are many adversaries." (1 Cor. 16:5–9)

After speaking of the offering for the poor and his approaching visit to Corinth, Paul spells out his plans. He apparently planned to leave Ephesus at an early date and sail directly westward to Corinth. Now he desires to prolong his stay in Ephesus and come to Corinth by way of Macedonia. The reason Paul gives for his delay in Ephesus, a major city in Asia Minor, is because "a great and effective door has opened to me." "Great" indicates the occasions are numerous. "Effective" refers to the power of the gospel in the midst of these opportunities. Opposition is indicated by his words "there are many adversaries." That opposition consisted of both superstitious beliefs and persecution. In the midst of obstacles, *God* provided opportunities for the gospel.

Sometimes Paul could not take advantage of open doors: "Furthermore, when I came to Troas to preach Christ's gospel, and a door was opened to me by the Lord, I had no rest in my spirit, because I did not find Titus my brother; but taking my leave of them, I departed for Macedonia" (2 Cor. 2:12–13). Titus had planned to meet Paul at Troas with tidings from Corinth. Paul had written a difficult but necessary letter to them and needed to know how it was received. So much was at stake that, not finding Titus, he could not endure the suspense and took leave of them and passed overnight to Macedonia. Unfortunately, that prevented him from taking advantage of the opportunity to preach the gospel in Troas, a favored Roman colony. The words "a door was opened to me by the Lord" means it was a door the Lord provided.

Examine Colossians 4:2–4: "Continue earnestly in prayer, being vigilant in it with thanksgiving; meanwhile praying also for us, that God would open to us a door for the word, to speak the mystery of Christ, for which I am also in chains, that I may make it manifest, as I ought to speak." Paul wrote that passage as a prisoner of the Roman Empire. He was probably handcuffed to a Roman soldier twenty-four hours a day. Paul took advantage of his opportunities in prison. But he did not want to be limited by the walls of a prison. He wanted to make it "manifest" to all that Christ's death on the cross was the only basis for a right standing with God. Therefore thinking of himself and his associates, he requested prayer that God might "open to us a door for the Word." He knew God had to open doors for the gospel.

God gave Paul presence before non-Christians. The open door for us may be an opportunity to preach the gospel in a city-wide outreach. It may be the opportunity to present the gospel through a message given at a luncheon for business men and women. The opportunity may be something as simple as a businessperson being asked to give his testimony at a recognition banquet or retirement party in his honor. It may be an open door given at some kind of training seminar in character development in the workplace. The opportunity could be a special Sunday morning evangelistic service. Or it may be an opportunity to present the gospel to unbelievers invited to the outreach. God opens doors. We pray for opportunities.

Understanding

The opportunity can be there, and the gospel may be presented clearly, but still it may make no sense to a non-Christian. The things of God are not understood the way we understand the things of math and science. Spiritual things are spiritually understood.

Paul testified: "But the natural man does not receive the things of the Spirit of God, for they are foolishness to him; nor can he know them, because they are spiritually discerned" (1 Cor. 2:14). The gospel pertains to truths that belong to the realm of the Spirit. Since an unregenerate man is without the Holy Spirit, he cannot understand. Spiritual truths are "fool-ishness to him"; he cannot "know them." Unless the Holy Spirit illumines his mind there can be no understanding. Lowery comments, "Like a deaf critic of Bach or a blind critic of Raphael is the unregenerate critic of God's Word."[3] We must pray for understanding.

Conviction

Understanding is not enough. The unbeliever must come to a point of being convinced that "I'm lost. Christ saves. I need Him."

As noted earlier, the three things the Holy Spirit convicts unbelievers about are sin, righteousness, and judgment: "And when He has come, He will convict the world of sin, and of righteousness, and of judgment: of sin, because they do not believe in Me; of righteousness, because I go to My Father and you see Me no more; of judgment, because the ruler of this world is judged" (John 16:8–11).

The Holy Spirit wants a non-Christian to agree with God that 1) he, the unbeliever, is a sinner, who has not believed on Christ; 2) Christ is who He said He is, the perfect Son of God who became our substitute; and 3) with Christ there is salvation; without Him, the judgment that awaits Satan awaits himself. A non-Christian must not only understand these truths, he must agree with God about them.

A Christian camp uses Evantell's popular *Bad News/Good News* tract for evangelism. A few years ago, we received the following e-mail:

> There was a camper named Adam here at camp. Adam was a high school student at the time and it was obvious when he arrived that he was different than most campers. He wore a tough exterior and due to his words and actions, it was obvious that Adam was not a believer. Adam arrived on Sunday and by Tuesday, he was so angry that it was affecting the other campers in his cabin. The camp director confronted Adam, who began to lash out verbally at the director and threatened to hurt the people around him. At that moment, the director told Adam he was going home. The director called Adam's father that night and asked him to pick up his son immediately as he realized that nothing he said was going to change Adam's attitude. Before Adam left camp that night, the director decided to put one of your *Bad News/ Good News* tracts in Adam's medicine bag. He was hoping that as Adam reflected on the love shown to him that week that God would use the *Bad News/Good News* to change Adam's life for eternity. The next night, Adam left a message with the director and told him how he had trusted Christ and become a believer the day after he was sent home from camp. When the director called Adam back, he asked

Adam what had happened. Adam said that when he got home, he looked in his medicine bag and saw a tract. He read through it and believed the truths laid out in the little tract. Adam came back to camp later that summer and it was obvious that God had radically changed Adam's life.

Knowing a bit of the situation, I have no doubt that Adam heard the truths of the *Bad News/Good News* tract at camp. Then, when he got home and recalled them, he agreed with God about them. Conviction occurred that allowed salvation to take place.

As we present the gospel through evangelistic speaking, the unbeliever must not only understand, but also agree with God, "You're right. I'm lost. You died for me and rose again. I need to trust Christ now and receive His gift of eternal life." That conviction, accomplished through the working of the Holy Spirit, is essential to salvation.

Salvation

The emphasis of Scripture, as it relates to evangelism, is not praying for non-Christians but praying for believers doing the evangelism. However, there *are* a few passages that encourage us to pray for unbelievers. The clearest is 1 Timothy 2:1–4:

> Therefore I exhort first of all that supplications, prayers, intercessions, and giving of thanks be made for all men, for kings and all who are in authority, that we may lead a quiet and peaceable life in all godliness and reverence. For this is good and acceptable in the sight of God our Savior, who desires all men to be saved and to come to the knowledge of the truth.

The clear teaching of 1 Timothy 2:1–4 is to pray for all men. Since no one is outside of His love, no one should be outside of our prayers. As we pray for all men, what is foremost on God's mind ought to be first on ours—their salvation. He "desires all men to be saved and to come to the knowledge of the truth" (v. 4).

Even with understanding and convicting, the non-Christian can turn from God instead of to God. Understanding and agreeing with God is not enough. The gift of eternal life must be received by trusting Christ. Therefore we must pray for salvation—that the non-Christians will place their trust in Christ to save them.

As we pray, we must recognize that salvation might not occur the night the gospel is spoken. I spoke at an evangelistic outreach in Illinois. A couple considering marriage attended the opening friendship dinner. She was saved; he wasn't. When I gave the invitation, he did not respond.

A week later, the pastor visited them. They were interested in premarital counseling. The pastor explained that he could not marry them unless they both were believers. He also told the man he could not trust Christ in order to get his fiancée. It had to be because he sincerely understood his lost condition and need of Christ. He once again explained the gospel. The pastor found fruit that was ripe. The man assured the pastor that he understood and desired to trust Christ because of his personal need. The pastor was struck by the man's humility and sincerity. He trusted Christ and immediately committed himself to being discipled. Fruit can come a day, week, month, or even years later. Always pray for salvation to occur.

Conclusion

Evangelism is filled with privileges. There is the privilege of coming before men on behalf of Christ. There is also the privilege of coming before Christ on behalf of men. We come before a prayer-answering God on behalf of the people for whom He died. Since no one is outside of His reach, no one needs to be outside of our prayers. Praying for opportunity, understanding, conviction, and salvation is one of the greatest favors we can do for the unbeliever—a favor they may only appreciate after they come to the Savior.

REFLECTING...

1. What does the Holy Spirit as the Great Converter want to convict people about?

2. What are four things to ask God for on behalf of non-Christians?

3. According to John 16, what are three things the Holy Spirit wants to convict non-Christians about?

4. Why can prayer not be used as an excuse for not doing our part in message preparation? Be specific.

5. How does depending on the Holy Spirit to bring the unbeliever to Christ affect our attitude and demeanor when we speak before a non-Christian audience?

Chapter 27

What About Follow-Up?

THE SON OF A performance-driven dad, Bryan felt love and acceptance only from his peers. Little did he know how conditional their acceptance was. They loved and accepted him as long as he participated in their gang activities or drug trafficking. Five years in a state penitentiary sobered him up. But it did not teach him how to handle life and relationships. A live-in girlfriend, a two-year marriage that ended in divorce, and job termination due to poor performance brought him to the end of himself. The speaker's message appealed to him. He knew he needed Christ—the One who makes miracles out of messes. He trusted Christ for forgiveness and eternal life.

But what happened? He came through the front door of the church. Everyone was delighted to see him. Eventually he walked out the back door. Nobody saw him again.

How do we help believers become disciples? How do we take a person who sincerely recognizes his sinfulness before God and need for a Savior and help him or her "grow in the grace and knowledge of our Lord and Savior Jesus Christ" (2 Pet. 3:18)?

Is there a possibility the person did not trust Christ? Certainly. If the gospel was not made clear, he may know the language but not the Lord. Some have responded to an invitation to come to Christ, but because they did not trust Christ, nothing happened spiritually. It's difficult to live for Christ if you don't know Him. But for many, the decision was very real. So why didn't they move past the point of conversion? In other words, how do we get new converts to be eager about growing spiritually and excited about church?

Observe two cautions

Two things must be noted. First, follow-up is not the job of the evangelistic speaker. Although we should have a concern that those who respond to the Holy Spirit's pleading are properly discipled, the ultimate responsibility is not ours. It is the responsibility of the local church. Paul's letter to the Ephesians explains why God has given gifted people to the church:

> For the equipping of the saints for the work of ministry, for the edifying of the body of Christ, till we all come to the unity of the faith and of the knowledge of the Son of God, to a perfect man, to the measure of the stature of the fullness of Christ; that we should no longer be children, tossed to and fro and carried about with every wind of doctrine, by the trickery of men, in the cunning craftiness of deceitful plotting, but, speaking the truth in love, may grow up in all things into Him who is the head—Christ. (Eph. 4:12–15)

Should a large number of people come to Christ, practically speaking, the evangelistic speaker cannot follow up each one. Time alone will not allow it. In Paul the apostle's ministry there were nearly forty people who worked with him in missions of follow-up. Furthermore, we as evangelistic speakers may not be the best at doing follow-up. Someone with gifts in teaching or encouragement may make a better discipler.

Second, the New Testament does not answer the question, "How do you assimilate new believers into the life and activity of the local church?" Instead, it answers the question, "How do you get close to a new believer?" If we get close to a new believer, we most likely will get him into our church. As we'll see in a moment, Paul the apostle spoke of caring for new converts the way a "nursing mother cherishes her own children" (1 Thess. 2:7) and "as a father does his own children" (v. 11). That relationship makes one open to an invitation to attend the given church you attend. This is particularly significant since one of the most effective means of getting an unchurched person to attend church is a personal invitation from a friend.

How does the New Testament advise us to follow up new believers?

Prayer is critical.

The role of prayer in follow-up often is underemphasized. In Paul the apostle's writing, prayer appeared to be an essential part of follow-up. Consider two examples.

One is his prayer for the new converts of Ephesus:

> Therefore I also, after I heard of your faith in the Lord Jesus and your love for all the saints, do not cease to give thanks for

you, making mention of you in my prayers: that the God of our Lord Jesus Christ, the Father of glory, may give to you the spirit of wisdom and revelation in the knowledge of Him, the eyes of your understanding being enlightened; that you may know what is the hope of His calling, what are the riches of the glory of His inheritance in the saints, and what *is* the exceeding greatness of His power toward us who believe, according to the working of His mighty power which He worked in Christ when He raised Him from the dead and seated *Him* at His right hand in the heavenly *places,* far above all principality and power and might and dominion, and every name that is named, not only in this age but also in that which is to come. And He put all *things* under His feet, and gave Him *to be* head over all *things* to the church, which is His body, the fullness of Him who fills all in all. (Eph. 1:15–23)

Paul the apostle understood their past state by nature and their present standing by grace. Before, they were without Christ; now they are in Christ. Before, they were far from God; now they are near. Before, they were strangers; now they are sons. But the thing that moved him to prayer was the encouraging report he received of their present spiritual condition. His prayer was that they might continue to pursue the course they had begun and grow in their knowledge of Christ. He says, "That the God of our Lord Jesus Christ, the Father of glory, may give to you the spirit of wisdom and revelation in the knowledge of Him" (v. 17).

Now examine Paul's prayer for the new converts at Colossae:

For this reason we also, since the day we heard it, do not cease to pray for you, and to ask that you may be filled with the knowledge of His will in all wisdom and spiritual understanding; that you may walk worthy of the Lord, fully pleasing *Him,* being fruitful in every good work and increasing in the knowledge of God; strengthened with all might, according to His glorious power, for all patience and longsuffering with joy; giving thanks to the Father who has qualified us to be partakers of the inheritance of the saints in the light. He has delivered us from the power of darkness and conveyed *us* into the kingdom of the Son of His love, in whom we have redemption through His blood, the forgiveness of sins. (Col. 1:9–14)

He prayed that these new converts would have wisdom and understanding, both spiritually given, that would allow them to comprehend God's desire for their lives. With that wisdom and direction, they would be less likely to accept the appeal and false teaching of the Gnostics.

For Paul, prayer was a means of follow-up. No matter how many times he revisited the new believers, or how many fellow-workers he sent to labor among them, or how much communication he maintained, their spiritual growth could only be accomplished through the Holy Spirit. His letters to the new converts of Ephesus and Colossae were both written while he was imprisoned in Rome. Even while imprisoned, Paul engaged in follow-up through prayer.

Flexibility is essential.

Paul's approach to follow-up was quite simple. New converts received whatever assistance they needed. Flexibility is seen in his "I'll do what it takes" attitude. Paul's first letter to the Thessalonians tells how he cared for new converts. His words are particularly interesting in light of the fact that he was with them about three months at the most. He got a lot accomplished in a short time. He explained, "As you know how we *exhorted*, and *comforted*, and *charged* every one of you, as a father does his own children" (1 Thess. 2:11, italics added). There is not a sharp distinction between those three words. Basically, though, "exhort" includes the idea of laying a particular course of conduct before a person and urging him to pursue it. "Comfort" represents the need to cheer him on in the midst of trying circumstances. "Charged" means to bear witness, confirm, or testify. It depicts a solemnity and earnestness—an urgency—behind the encouragement.

Paul practiced those three things with the Thessalonians. He exhorted them when he said, "Finally then, brethren, we urge and exhort in the Lord Jesus that you should abound more and more, just as you received from us how you ought to walk and to please God; for you know what commandments we gave you through the Lord Jesus" (1 Thess. 4:1–2). He comforted them by sending Timothy to them. He explained that "[we] sent Timothy, our brother and minister of God, and our fellow laborer in this gospel of Christ, to establish you and encourage you concerning your faith, that no one should be shaken by these afflictions; for you yourselves know that we are appointed to this" (1 Thess. 3:2–3). The urgency behind everything Paul tells new converts demonstrates his "charging." He makes comments such as "we urge you, brethren..." (1 Thess. 5:12).

God saves people, not machines. He saves human beings who are different and varied in their needs. One comes to Christ from a background of drug addiction. He accepted what he should have refused. Another comes to Christ as a Pharisee, extremely religious but trying to merit entrance into heaven. Another comes to Christ from a background of parental abuse. It was difficult to accept the love of a heavenly Father because he had never experienced the love of a human father. Need-oriented flexibility in follow-up is essential.

Children born into the same physical family often differ. One has a hearing ailment, another suffers from a weak eye muscle. One has a problem with coordination while another suffers from a weak heart valve. One is extremely outgoing, while another is bashful. One loves books, the other sports. A parent's "I'll do what it takes" attitude can make a difference in their physical growth. The same kind of attitude makes a difference in the spiritual growth of new converts.

Parental attention is required.

When people came to Christ, Paul considered them not just God's children,but his as well. He cared for them the way a parent cares for a child. Examine the following references and the words I've italicized:

1 Corinthians 4:15—Even though you might have ten thousand instructors in Christ, yet *you do not have many fathers;* for in Christ Jesus I have begotten you through the gospel.

Galatians 4:19—*My little children,* for when I labor in birth again until Christ is formed in you.

1 Thessalonians 2:7—But we were gentle among you, just as *a nursing mother cherishes her own children.*

1 Thessalonians 2:8—So, affectionately longing for you, we were well pleased to impart to you not only the gospel of God, but also *our own lives, because you had become dear to us.*

1 Thessalonians 2:11—As you know how we exhorted, and comforted, and charged every one of you, *as a father does his own children.*

"Father," "my little children," "nursing mother," "dear to us," all depict an attitude of parental attention. Even the "every one of you" of 1 Thessalonians 2:11 stresses the individual approach Paul used with new converts. Dawson Trotman, founder of the Navigators, wrote, "Is the answer merely materials to distribute to those who come to Christ? No, it is always from the experience of successful follow-up programs, both in the New Testament and out of it, that follow-up is done by someone, not by something."[1]

Parental attention provided a basis for effective follow-up by focusing on the needs of the new convert to whatever degree necessary. With an "I'll do what it takes" attitude, parental attention reveals how best to help a new believer.

Time and hard work are needed.

Each missionary journey the apostle Paul took increased in length by at least one year because of visits he made to places he had previously ministered. Paul went back to visit the people and confirm churches in at least nine of the places he evangelized.

"Follow-up made easy" doesn't exist. Proper follow-up requires time and hard work. Paul speaks of the hard work often involved: "Him we preach, warning every man and teaching every man in all wisdom, that we may present every man perfect in Christ Jesus. To this end I also labor, striving according to His working which works in me mightily" (Col. 1:28–29). "Labor" depicts work that can be exhausting—work that sometimes causes weariness. "Striving" conveys the idea of agonizing. As a general rule, follow-up is more difficult than evangelism. Dawson Trotman said, "You can lead a soul to Christ in from twenty minutes to a couple of hours. But it takes from twenty weeks to a couple of years to get him on the road to maturity."[2]

The times of hard work are worth it. Paul testified, "For what is our hope, or joy, or crown of rejoicing? Is it not even you in the presence of our Lord Jesus Christ at His coming? For you are our glory and joy" (1 Thess. 2:19–20). A person who leads another to Christ or assists in his growth will rejoice when the new convert stands before the Lord. The discipler lived his life for people, not for things.

The goal is maturity.

The first thing we often suggest to new converts is their need to find a church to attend or a Bible study to begin. Those are the means to the end. They are not the end. The goal is maturity.

Paul says, "Him we preach, warning every man and teaching every man in all wisdom, that we may present every man perfect in Christ Jesus. To this end I also labor, striving according to His working which works in me mightily" (Col. 1:28–29). "Perfect" conveys the idea of maturity and completion. Only when a person was mature in Christ did Paul feel his labors and the labors of others had been completed.

There is an extent to which that growth to maturity is a lifelong process. Although it can be said of someone, "She is a mature believer," no one can look back and say, "I've arrived." The most we can say is, "I'm consistently moving along on the path to maturity." Everything that enhances that growth is the means, not the end.

It is important to convey the proper goal of spiritual growth to new converts. Otherwise, they may do one of two things. First, they may settle on an activity, such as going to church, without examining the "why" behind what they are doing. Second, they may settle for less than they should in terms of the degree of spiritual maturity.

To assist a new convert in spiritual growth, several steps should be taken.

Meet with him quickly.

As soon as possible (the sooner the better) disciplers should meet personally and privately with new converts. Three things are important to do during that time.

Make sure they understand the gospel. We cannot assume that just because they responded to our evangelistic message, they understand it. Go through the plan of salvation as though they had never heard the gospel. Ask questions such as the following to determine how well they understand.

- If you were to die right now, where would you go?
- If you stood before God right now and He were to ask you, "Why should I let you into heaven, what would you say?"
- "Where would you go if you were to die five years from now?"
- "Suppose tomorrow you explode in a fit of anger because of an unexpected criticism and died of a heart attack, where would you go?"

Give assurance of salvation. One of the best verses to use is John 5:24: "Most assuredly, I say to you, he who hears My word and believes in Him who sent Me has everlasting life, and shall not come into judgment, but has passed from death into life."

Have the person interact with that verse by asking the following questions:

- "He who *hears* My word"—Did you do that?
- "and believes in Him who sent Me."—Did you *believe* what God said and trust Christ as your Savior?
- "Has everlasting life"—Does that mean later or right now?
- "And *shall not* come unto judgment"—Does that say "shall not" or "might not?"
- "But has *passed from* death into life."—Does that say "shall pass" or "has passed?"

Encourage new converts to memorize that verse within twenty-four hours. Explain that Satan may make them doubt their salvation, and there may be days they do not necessarily feel saved. Eternal life is based on fact, not feelings. God said it; that settles it.

Talk with them about spiritual growth. Give them a follow-up booklet written on a new believer's level that is biblically based. As noted earlier, many have been helped by Evantell's two booklets *Welcome to the Family* and *31 Days to Living as a New Believer*.

Meet one-on-one for eight weeks.

Assure new converts that growth doesn't happen overnight. It takes time and effort. Ask them to meet once a week for eight weeks to get started. This kind of intimacy can sometimes be threatening to a new believer. If it is, ask them to take one week at a time. Then each week look at the possibility of meeting the next week. Patience and sensitivity are essential with anyone, but particularly with new believers.

Group meetings with new converts can be helpful, but you shouldn't neglect individual attention. Although the circumstances and problems of new converts may be similar, no two are alike. Meeting with them one-on-one allows for personal attention to their situation and provides a basis for the required flexibility.

Who should serve as disciplers? To avoid temptation and even the appearance of evil, disciplers should work with a believer of the same gender (1 Thess. 5:22). Disciplers should also be growing believers. Spiritually, the issue is not where we are but the direction we are headed. A stagnated believer will have difficulty helping a new convert. The new convert may be hindered instead of helped by someone who is spiritually at a standstill. (From a spiritual perspective, I believe it is impossible to be at a standstill. You are either going forward or backward spiritually.) It is important to place the right believer in front of the new convert.

Disciplers need to be patient—not easily frustrated. New converts proceed at varying speeds of growth. Some believers expect new converts to be in one month at a point they did not reach for two years. Patience is critical.

Disciplers should be willing to commit time. Meeting with the new convert once a week for eight weeks is time consuming. The discipler cannot say, "I think I can do that." He must say, "I *will* do that."

During that eight-week series, cover at least five topics:

1. SALVATION

Assuming he understands salvation, review the greatest thing he has ever heard: the gospel of Jesus Christ and what it means to believe (trust) in Christ alone for salvation. Firmly implant in his mind and heart that salvation is not a matter of what he has done for Christ but what Christ did for him on a cross. Although you reviewed this on your initial visit, review it again so he is certain to understand the freeness and certainty of his salvation.

Be sensitive to the fact that some only *thought* they understood the gospel when they responded to your invitation. They may come to grips with the freeness of salvation and actually trust Christ in the process of follow-up.

2. SPIRITUAL GROWTH THROUGH BIBLE STUDY AND PRAYER

Remind him that spiritual growth comes through communication. God desires to talk to him through the Bible. He needs to talk to God through prayer. Encourage him to start with the book of Philippians and read one chapter a day, staying in that book for a month. The repetition allows him to learn truths he missed earlier. Each day ask him to concentrate on one thing he's learned that he can meditate on throughout the day. Philippians is the best book to begin with because it talks about daily Christian living and is the easiest book of the entire Bible for a new Christian to understand.

3. BAPTISM

Explain that in the New Testament those who believed were baptized. A helpful verse is one such as Acts 2:41: "Then those who gladly received his word were baptized…" It is important to stress that baptism has no saving value. It is the first step of discipleship and the way to publicly tell others, "I belong to Christ and desire to follow Him." Assist him in arranging a time when he can be baptized.

4. FELLOWSHIP WITH OTHER BELIEVERS

Explain that church is important because of his need to be encouraged by other believers who also desire to spiritually grow. "And let us consider one another in order to stir up love and good works, not forsaking the assembly of ourselves together" (Heb. 10:24–25). Also explain that other believers need him. He needs to go to give, not merely to get. Even though his knowledge of the Word is limited, he can pray with other believers, study with them, and encourage them.

It's best to take the new convert with you to church. New believers often feel awkward walking into a crowd of people they've never been with before. If that is not possible, ask another believer to take the new believer and introduce him to others. If there is no way you can take him or even find someone else to do so, explain what a Bible-teaching church is and encourage him to find one. Explain that a Bible-teaching church is one where each Sunday the pastor takes a different passage of the Bible and explains it to the audience.

5. EVANGELISM

Teach the basic elements of the gospel: Christ died for our sins and rose from the dead. Teach a method you've found effective in sharing the gospel with others. Every person consistent in evangelism uses a basic method. Let him observe you evangelizing non-Christians. Evangelism cannot be mastered apart from actually speaking with unbelievers.

Organize a band of people to pray for new converts.

As seen in Paul the apostle's ministry, prayer is an important part of follow-up. Organize a band of people who pray *by name* for new converts.

This is a great place to involve widows or shut-ins of a church—those who can pray at home and are deeply committed to prayer. First Timothy 5:5 speaks of the ministry widows have in prayer: "Now she who is really a widow, and left alone, trusts in God and continues in supplications and prayers night and day." These are believers for whom prayer is not an off -and-on activity but something they continue day and night. The ministry they can have in praying for new converts is tremendous.

As they pray, they need to pray specifically. Note the specific requests Paul gave to God on behalf of the Colossians: "For this reason we also, since the day we heard it, do not cease to pray for you, and to ask that you may be filled with the knowledge of His will in all wisdom and spiritual understanding" (1:9). His specific request was that they might have wisdom in and understanding of all things spiritual. Why? "That you may walk worthy of the Lord, fully pleasing Him, being fruitful in every good work and increasing in the knowledge of God; strengthened with all might, according to His glorious power, for all patience and longsuffering with joy" (vv. 10–11). A person who has wisdom and understanding of all things spiritual tries to please the Lord in all things, bears fruit in all kinds of good deeds, and responds properly to difficult situations and people.

They should talk to God on behalf of new converts in five specific areas:

- That they will grow in their knowledge of Him
- That God will help them adjust to their new life
- That they will have wisdom and understanding in how to live for Christ
- That God will help them take out of their lives what shouldn't be there and put in what should be there
- That God will use them to reach unbelieving friends, family, and acquaintances

You don't need a lot of people praying. A few praying fervently and expectantly will make the difference.

Involve them.

As you meet with new believers, disciple them, and pray for them, don't forget to involve them. Look at "handle-able" tasks that help further the work of God's kingdom. Help them feel a part of what's happening.

Consider the new believer's strengths, abilities, and skills. A new convert who is a carpenter may be honored when you ask for his advice and help on a building project the church has undertaken to assist a community struck by disaster. He realizes at this early stage in his Christian growth that there is a place where he can contribute. You might give new converts with acting abilities parts in a drama outreach to non-Christians. A new convert with ability in decorating might be encouraged when you ask for her assistance in decorating tables for a friendship dinner. She begins to see how her talent can be used to touch others. The ways new converts can be used is almost endless.

One caution: the new convert needs to be a helper, not a leader. When Paul spoke to Timothy about the qualifications for leaders, he gave this warning about new converts: "not a novice, lest being puffed up with pride he fall into the same condemnation as the devil" (1 Tim. 3:6). Choosing a new convert to be a leader can have disastrous results. Rapid advancement to leadership can fill him with conceit, the same sin that caused Satan himself to suffer severely (Ezek. 28:11–19).

Conclusion

Where does the responsibility for follow-up lie? The new convert needs a desire to grow. We cannot do for her what she has no interest in doing. But responsibility also rests upon the believer doing the discipling. Follow-up is done by someone, not some *thing*. The discipler must understand the biblical directives and be characterized by love, time, and patience. Everything you need to do can be done when those three are in place. When we follow the New Testament teaching for follow-up there will be many new converts characterized by Paul's words: "For what *is* our hope, or joy, or crown of rejoicing? *Is it* not even you in the presence of our Lord Jesus Christ at His coming? For you are our glory and joy" (1 Thess. 2:19–20).

REFLECTING...

1. Finish the following sentence by Dawson Trotman: "Follow-up is done by_____, not by_____."

2. What are five things the New Testament emphasizes are critical in following-up new believers?

3. What is the one thing you should not assume when beginning to disciple a new believer?

4. Why is flexibility essential in disciplining new believers?

5. Why is it important to not immediately make a new convert a leader?

Appendix 1

An Expository Evangelistic Message on John 3:16

THE ADVANTAGE OF A message like this is that it could be given in a church setting but also in other settings. The verse is simple and so well known among some people that the audience does not need the text in front of them.

MESSAGE ON JOHN 3:16	
Title	Three Things God Cannot Do
Verse	John 3:16
Main Idea	There are three things God cannot do.

Every one of us has limitations. There are things we cannot do. It may be something to do with time or it may be something to do with talent. It may be in the realm of our job as a mechanic or it may be in the realm of our position as a medical doctor. It may be a matter as serious as science or as simple as sightseeing. But every single one of us has limitations. We may feel relieved or we may feel resentful, but we all have things we cannot do.

My wife and I are excellent illustrations. To witness the greatest show on earth, listen to me in the area of music and look at my wife when it comes to anything mechanical. When it comes to music she has been told that she sounds like a nightingale. I've been told I sound like a nightmare. It is so bad that when I sing in the shower she leaves the bathroom. When our son was just a baby she said to me, "Now I know why God brought us together. When it's time for him to sleep, I'll sing. When it's time for him to wake up, you sing." I said to her one time, "What do you think my problem is? Do you suppose I'm not putting enough fire into my songs?" She said, "No, honey, I think the problem is that you are not putting enough of your songs into the fire." I had a man who sat alongside of me on a platform one time say to me, I was listening to you as you were singing and I'm convinced that you are a tenor." I didn't have the foggiest idea what a tenor was, but I told him afterward, "That's the first compliment that I've ever received about my singing." He said, "Larry, I didn't mean it as a compliment. When I said that you were a 'ten-or' I meant that your singing was 'ten or twelve' times worse than anything I've ever heard."

But by the same token, when it comes to anything mechanical, it's my wife who has the limitations, and if she were here tonight she'd admit it. She can look at something and not be able to figure out the first from the last and the front from the back. My son probably saved her life one time when she went to play with his slingshot. She took the strap of the slingshot and had it pointed at her own face. She finds it easy to identify with the woman whose husband said to her, "There is a short circuit in the house. Call the electrician." So the wife called the electrician and said, "There is a short circuit in our house. Could you send someone out to lengthen it?" Part of her problem is a difficulty she's had that I've never had. That is, she is very intelligent. In fact, she graduated as valedictorian in her high school class of more than seven hundred students. That's one reason I married her. I felt someone that intelligent needed a humbling experience. But when it comes to certain things mechanical, my wife has limitations.

Every one of us has limitations. Sometimes they are agonizing and sometimes they are amusing. But every one of us has our limitations. There are things we cannot do.

But some people believe that there is one Person who has no limitations. There is nothing He cannot do, and that one person is God.

And yet, contrary to popular opinion, the Bible makes it clear there are three things God cannot do. There are three things that God has never, and God will never, be able to do. I guarantee that if you understand these three things, you will leave here with a better understanding of yourself, a better understanding of God, and a better understanding of what God is asking you to do.

All of them are brought out for us in one of the best known sentences in the entire Bible: John 3:16.

The first thing John 3:16 tells us that God cannot do is that God cannot love you any more than He has loved you. Notice that the first phrase of John 3:16 says, "For God so loved the world."

Quite honestly, if there is one thing we do not know how to do it is love; we do not know how to love. In fact, if most of us were honest with each other we would confess we know a lot more about matters such as revenge than we know about love.

One time a young woman was bitten by a dog, and she got rabies. As soon as the doctor informed her that she had rabies, knowing how deadly rabies can be, she sat down and started making out a whole list of people she knew. The doctor, assuming she was making out her will, said, "Now wait a minute. Rabies are serious, but you do not need to make out a will yet." She answered him, "Oh, this isn't my will. It's a list of people I plan to bite."

If there is one thing we do not know how to do, it's to love. It's a word we can pronounce, but we don't know how to practice.

And notice that the verse is not saying, "God knows how to love." It is saying something about five hundred times greater. God cannot love you any more than He has loved you.

Look again at verse 16: "For God *so* loved the world."

To understand the love of God, take the word "so" and let the S stand for *something* and let the O stand for *other* because His love is *something other* than you have ever known. He doesn't love you with the love of a two-year-old who says, "I'll love you as long as you do things my way." He does not love you with the love of a twelve-year-old who says, "I'll love you for what I can get out of you." He doesn't love you with the love of a twenty-two-year old who says, "I'll love you as long as you love me in return." Instead, He loves you with the kind of love that says I'll love you. Period.

It is a deep love. It is an unselfish love. There is no greater love. It is not based on who you are. It is not based on what you do. It doesn't matter if you are a great athlete, president of the United States, or a person who pushes a broom in an office where everybody else pushes a pencil. He knows where you live, He knows what you are like, and He says "I love you!"

You have lied, yet He loves you. You have been unfaithful to your mate, yet He loves you. You have spent a lot of time entertaining thoughts you shouldn't have, yet He loves you. You take His name and use it as a curse word, yet He loves you. You have engaged in pornography, yet He loves you.

I would challenge every one of you to think of your personal friends. Some of them will love you as long as you are on your good behavior, but God will love you even if you're at your worst. Some of them will love you if you speak well of them. God will love you even if you curse His name. Some of them will love you as long as you take what you have and give it to them, but God will love you even if you take everything He has given you and never give Him a thank you. As someone remarked, "The true measure of God's love is that He loves without measure."

Years ago there was a man who, after his father died, seemed to go from bad to worse until one day he was arrested for murder. When the day of his trial came it was discovered that he had not murdered just one individual; he had murdered five. From one end of that city to the other there was an angry cry against him. The anger of the people in the town was so great that during the trial guards had to stand at the doors of the courtroom to keep out the angry mob. But during that trial his mother sat as close to her son as she could possibly sit and anything said about her son seemed to hurt her more than it could possibly hurt him. When the judge sentenced him to be hung on the gallows, she embraced her son, and it took several grown men to separate the two of them. Then she went outside the courtroom and walked up one sidewalk and down the other trying to get people to sign a petition requesting that he be pardoned. She found no one who was interested in that petition. Sometime later when he was hung, she stood at the foot of the gallows with tears streaming down her face. She even went to the judge and pled that he give her the body of her son so that she could bury it where she pleased. But they refused to give it to her. Only a few months later she died. On her deathbed, the one thing that she requested was that her body be placed next to the body of her son. There was a mother who so loved her son that she was not afraid to identify herself with one of the worst criminals of that time.

That is the kind of love God has for us. For that reason, although we are sinners who deserve His anger and not His love, instead of turning His back toward us, He turned His face to us.

John 3:16 says there is a second thing God cannot do. Not only can He not love you any more than He already has loved you, the second thing God cannot do is give you any more than He has already given you. Notice that John 3:16 says, "For God so loved the world that He *gave* His only begotten Son."

Now I assure you, and I am certain you will agree, just as we do not know how to love, neither do we know how to give. We are far better at taking than we are at giving.

A young mother heard her son crying to no end. She went outside and, sure enough, there he stood sobbing uncontrollably. So she said to his older brother who was standing alongside of him, "What's your brother crying about?" He said, "I don't know. I'm just eating my dessert, and I won't give him any." So his mother asked, "Is his own finished?" And he answered, "Yes, and he cried when I ate that too."

Even in our best moments, when we do give, we give with ourselves in mind. We have our best interests at heart. A Hollywood star was quoted in a national magazine as saying, "I want my children to have all the things I could never afford. Then I want to move in with them."

The fact is, it doesn't matter if we are young people or adults, we give with our own best interests at heart.

But when God gave, He didn't have Himself in mind. He had you in mind. Look at the end of verse 16: "that whoever believes in Him should not *perish*." The word "perish" does not simply mean "die," because for many that would be a relief. Instead, it has the idea of separation. Because we are sinners, we are facing eternal separation from God. And all the good works we have done, or all the good behavior we have practiced, will not change our condition.

But the Bible is saying that there is hope. Our hope comes because God gave His only begotten Son, so that, instead of you dying on a cross for your sin, Christ died in your place. Instead of you paying by your death for what you have done, Christ paid by His death for what you have done.

A newspaper in Chattanooga, Tennessee, told about a man and his eleven-year-old son who were working on a storage building in their front yard. They were jacking up the building that was part metal and part wood so they could put a trailer with an axle under it to move it. The boy was under the trailer helping his dad prop up the building when the father noticed one of the concrete blocks was starting to crumble, causing the trailer to shift to one side. The father immediately placed himself between the trailer and the boy, holding up the building long enough for the son to escape. Seconds later the weight of the building crushed the father. The father was killed, and the son escaped with only minor cuts and scratches. The father died in his place. The Bible says that Jesus Christ gave His life in your place. God gave His only begotten Son.

The thing you must know is that God's Son was like you and like your son. He breathed the way you breathe. He had feelings the way you have feelings. But He never sinned. He never told a lie, and He never stole. He never had a wrong thought, and He never said a harsh word. He was God's perfect Son. And not only was He God's perfect Son, He was God's *only* Son. That is what those words "only begotten" are telling us. At a particular time in history, God took the only Son He ever had, and He allowed Him to take the punishment for our sins.

The first home my wife and I owned was a very small house where the kitchen, living room, and garage were basically the same room. Not quite, but almost. To this day I remember when we paid off that house. We got the mortgage papers back, and there, stamped across them on every page, were the words "Paid in Full." That is what Christ did with our debt of sins. On a cross, He died as our substitute and marked our debt of sins "Paid in Full." And God cannot give you any more than He's given you.

For that reason, God will not bring someone from the grave to convince you of your need to come to Christ. With His Son came an entire book of revelation about Him that everyone can read. And after His death and resurrection on the third day came an empty grave that no one can deny. And God cannot give you any more than He's already given you because He gave you His only Son.

In fact, that is the reason God gave His Son. God is not a policeman looking for people to punish; He's a Person looking for people to save.

One time a teenager ran away from home because his parents were trying to break up his relationship with his girlfriend. But what he did not know is that after he ran away from home, the disease he had been seeing the doctor about was diagnosed to be cancer. So the police were trying to find him lest he lose his life, and the boy was running from them afraid of losing his love. In a similar fashion, God is not a policeman looking for people He can punish. He is a Person looking for people He can save.

This brings me to a third thing that God cannot do. Not only does John 3:16 tell me that God cannot love you anymore than He's loved you. Not only does it tell me that God cannot give you any more than He's already given you. The third thing it tells me is that God cannot make it any simpler than He's made it. Look again at verse 16. The end of that verse says, "whoever believes in Him should not perish, but have everlasting life."

As difficult as it is for us to love, and as delinquent as we are in giving, we are a disaster when it comes to keeping things simple. A politician known for being difficult to follow when he spoke said to his campaign manager, "As I was shaving this morning I was thinking of my speech and cut my face." The manager answered, "Well the next time, think of your face and cut your speech." We make our lives complicated and confusing. For example, if you ask someone from China for some tea, within five minutes, he'll bring you a simple cup of hot tea. But if you ask an American for some tea, he'll ask you five different questions. Do you want hot tea or cold tea? Do you want it sweetened or unsweetened? Do you want sugar or Sweet 'n' Low®? Do you want one teaspoon or two? Do you want it with lemon or without? A person from China said, "Those Americans are so confusing. They first boil their tea to make it hot. Then they put ice in it to make it cold. Then they put sugar in it to make it sweet. Then they put lemon in it to make it sour." We take simple things and make them complicated.

But God is a genius when it comes to keeping things simple. And all John 3:16 is trying to tell us is that God cannot make it any simpler than He made it. Look again. That whoever—any Joe, any Tom, any Barry, any David, any Frank, any Beverly, any Carol, any Rebecca, any Debbie, anyone in Texas, anyone in Georgia, anyone in Florida, anyone in Pennsylvania, anyone in Ohio, anyone in North Dakota, anyone in Montana, anyone in California, anyone in New Mexico, anyone in France, and anyone in Italy. Anyone in Central America, anyone in South America, anyone with brown hair, anyone with red hair, anyone with black hair, anyone with no hair—anyone—whoever believes in Him should not perish but have everlasting life.

The word "believe" means to trust.

Close to the brink of Niagara Falls there is an old flat-bottom boat that has been there since August 6, 1918, when it broke lose from a tugboat. Two men who were on that boat were rescued by a man named William Red Hill, a famous Niagara River daredevil. They recognized that they could not save themselves and trusted him to save them. God has asked you to come to Him as a sinner, recognize Christ died for you and arose, and put your trust in Christ alone to save you.

You might think of it this way. On the one hand, God is a righteous judge who commands a man to die by lethal injection. On the other hand, He is a loving God who allows His Son to take that lethal injection. So you are faced with the greatest decision of your life. Will you accept what He has done in your place? If you will, God can pardon you and give you eternal life. If you won't, God has no choice but to punish you for your own sin in eternal separation from Him. God cannot make it any simpler than that.

The text does not say, "Whoever is a committed Catholic" or "Whoever is a behaving Baptist." That is not what the text says. The text says, "Whoever believes in Him." That means, whoever trusts Christ alone as his only way to heaven, that man shall never perish but have eternal life.

For that reason, I am not asking you, "Have you led a good life?" Because that text does not say, "Whoever lives a good life shall never perish." I am not asking, "Have you been baptized?" The text does not say, "Whoever has been baptized shall never perish." I am not asking you, "Have you ever taken the sacraments offered by your church?" The text does not say, "Whoever takes the sacraments shall not perish." I'm not asking, "Do you believe there is a God?" The text does not say, "Whoever believes there is a God shall not perish." Instead, all I'm asking is, "Have you trusted Jesus Christ as your only way to heaven?" Not Christ *and* your good life or Christ *and* your baptism or Christ *and* your church attendance, but Christ *alone* as your only way to heaven. Because the text says "Whoever believes in Him should not perish but have eternal life." God cannot make it any simpler than that.

Contrary to popular opinion, there are three things God cannot do. God cannot love you any more than He has loved you because God so loved the world. God cannot give you any more than He has given you because He gave His only Son. God cannot make it any simpler than He has made it because whoever believes in Him will not perish but have eternal life. For God so loved the world that He gave His only begotten Son, that whoever believes in Him should not perish but have everlasting life.

This is why, when we stand before God, we will stand there without the smallest excuse. We cannot say, "But I never felt like God loved me" because God could not love you more than He loves you. We cannot say, "There was no way to be forgiven. I've done too many things wrong." That's what the cross was all about. God gave His Son to take your punishment. We cannot say, "But I didn't understand it. I always thought that as long as I went to church and kept the commandments and did what was right and stayed out of jail and loved my neighbor, I'd get to heaven." Because God could not make it any simpler than He made it. That whoever believes in Him shall never perish, but have everlasting life.

A young woman made the statement, "For years I sat in church and could not believe all that I was hearing. And then I came to the point that I had to either trust Christ or reject Him in His entirety." That is the decision every one of us faces—the decision to either trust Christ or reject Him in His entirety.

If God should ever give me a microphone that reaches the entire world and tells me I have one minute to say anything I wish to everyone listening, I assure you I am going to take that microphone and I am going to say, "There are three things God cannot do. God cannot love you any more than He loves you because God so loved the world. God cannot give you any more than He has given you because He gave you His only Son. God cannot make it any simpler than He's made it because He said that everyone who believes in Him will not perish but have eternal life."

Years ago when steamers went up and down the Mississippi River, they had an interesting practice. The people from one steamer would come up on deck and wave to the people on the other steamer. One day two steamers were passing and a fireman from below came up on deck and stood alongside a well-dressed gentleman. All of a sudden, the fireman started to wave frantically and yell at the top of his voice, "Look, there's the captain, there's the captain!" The distinguished gentleman was upset by the man's boisterous voice and lack of manners. "So what?" he said. "Every ship has a captain. I thought you were intelligent enough to know that but obviously I was mistaken." Then the fireman said, "Oh, yes, I knew that, but that one's different. The other day I was on his ship and there was a storm at sea and I was standing too close to the edge. Suddenly I was thrown overboard and I cannot swim! That captain kicked off his shoes, pulled off his shirt, and threw off his hat. He jumped in the water and saved my life. Every time I get the opportunity I just love to point him out."*

The reason I came this morning is to tell you that I was headed to hell but God saved my life and whenever I have the opportunity I just love to point Him out. And I want you to know: He cannot love you any more than He has loved you. He cannot give you any more than He has given you. He cannot make it any simpler than He's made it.

And one more thing. The sentence makes it obvious that He can save you. It also makes it obvious that He wants to save you. The question is, will you let Him?

Appendix 2

An Expository Evangelistic Message on Luke 19:1–10

THIS IS AN EXPOSITORY evangelistic message based on the story of Zaccheus. It shows how to appeal to unbelievers and keep their interest as you explain the passage.

MESSAGE ON LUKE 19:1–10	
Title	What kind of person do you have to be in order for God to accept you?
Verse	Luke 19:1–10
Main Idea	God saves sinners.

An exclusive firm in New York City was looking for an exceptional employee, so they placed this ad in the paper: "Wanted: very exceptional employee. Must be good looking, must have a graduate degree, must have credit references, and must have published ten books, five in a foreign language." An elderly man who lived in the hills of Kentucky saw the ad. In his tattered shirt and torn jeans, he made his way to New York City. When he got to the Manhattan skyscraper, where the firm was located, he rode the elevator to the ninth floor and walked into the office. A young receptionist was seated behind the desk. He looked at her and said, "Are you the guys looking for an employee?" She said, "Yes, sir, we are." He said, "Are you the guys who say he must be good looking?" She said, "Yes, sir, we are." He said,

"Are you the guys who say he must have credit references?" She said, "Yes, sir, we are." He said, "Are you the guys who say he must have a graduate degree?" She said, "Yes, sir, we are." He said, "Are you the guys who say he must have published ten books, five in a foreign language?" She said, "Yes, sir, we are." Then, with sarcasm on her face and in her voice, she looked at him and said, "If you don't mind me asking, what in the world are you doing here?" He leaned over her granite-top desk, stared her in the eye, and said, "Well, I just came the whole way up here to tell you, don't count on me."

The first time I read that, I laughed just like you. But the more I thought about it, I realized: behind that humorous story is a very honest point. That is, we're all very aware that when it comes to certain offers, we just don't qualify.

Some time ago I was scheduled to have lunch with a man who owns a small airplane company that sells planes and gives flying lessons. When I arrived he was busy with a customer, so he asked an employee, "Would you take Larry out and show him the planes?" Remember, this was a company that both sold planes and gave flying lessons. The employee didn't know me, and I didn't know what was going through his mind. So things got a little mixed up. His first question was, "Do you fly a lot?" I said, "Yes, I do; but usually I fly commercially." I meant that when I want to go to Chicago I take American Airlines. He assumed that I was a commercial airline pilot. His second question was, "What kind of plane do you usually fly?" I said, "Oh, I've flown all kinds, but the bigger they are, the better I like them." You can imagine how he misunderstood that. But the situation reached its greatest hilarity when he led me to a plane, motioned toward the controls, and said, "Here, why don't you take this one up for a while. And if you don't mind, I'll go along for the ride." Well, I assure you, I could have given him a ride. Had I flown that plane, we would have been the closest we've ever been to seeing the Maker face to face. Because nobody knows better than I do that when it comes to the offer of flying a plane, I just don't qualify for it.

When it comes to certain offers, we know we don't qualify. And there are those who are convinced that the same thing is true with the Lord. All we have to do is read the Bible to find out that God offers everyone the gift of eternal life completely free. He is offering everyone the opportunity to live forever. But many are convinced that they just don't qualify for what He wants to give them.

When I spoke in Longmont, Colorado, I expressed the desire to talk to anyone who did not know they were going to heaven. A businessman said, "I want to talk." The next day we met. He admitted that he did not know he was going to heaven, but said, "I'd like to, but one thing is standing in my way." So I asked, "What's that?" He said, "I've broken every law in the book. I am too big a sinner for God to save." He's not the first person to say that to me. Some are convinced that because of everything from their record to their reputation, even if they were interested in Him, there is no way He would ever be interested in them. They have heard, "God helps those who help themselves." So, if you don't have some decency or self-respect, you might as well forget it. They have heard, "God helps those who help others." So, if you have not been a giving person, don't put in your application. That raises the important question, "What kind of person do you have to be for God to accept you? What kind of person does God save?"

Don't ask a preacher. There is no need to ask someone else what God Himself tells you. Jesus answered that question when He said, "For the Son of Man has come to seek and to save that which was lost." In other words, the kind of person God saves is the person who is lost. The term "lost" confuses some of us just like other terms in the Bible confuse others.

One time a Sunday school class was studying the paragraph in the early part of the Bible that says, "God took a rib from Adam and made Eve, his helper." A young boy in the class could not figure out what it meant that God took a rib from a man and made a woman. He was running home after Sunday school thinking about this story. All of a sudden, he felt a sharp pain in his side. His first thought was, "Oh, my word! I'm going to have a wife!"

The term "lost" confuses some people. If you want to know what the Bible means by "lost," the man you have to understand is Zaccheus. He is the one the Bible calls lost. If you understand Zaccheus, you will know what the Bible means by lost. The paragraph tells us two main things about Zaccheus. Not two hundred. Only two.

Not everyone will be able to identify with the first thing it says about him. One of the first thing we learn is that he was a short man. Look at verse 1. "Then Jesus entered and passed through Jericho. Now behold there was a man named Zaccheus who was a chief tax collector, and he was rich. And he sought to see who Jesus was but could not because of the crowd for he was of short stature." In that day, when a man and his disciples came through town, people responded the way they do today when someone important visits. They line up along the road to get a chance to see them. But Zaccheus had a problem. He was only knee high to a grasshopper. When he was in a crowd, he was so short that he could not see between people, and he could not see over them. But Zaccheus knew that where there is a will there is a way.

A man in Pennsylvania told me what he had to go through in order to have his first date with his future wife. He'd fought with his dad that week, so he was fortunate to get the car. He knew he couldn't ask him for money, too, and he did not have a dime for the date. When his dog walked by, he got an idea. He said to his sister, "You and I own the dog together. I'll sell you my half for ten dollars." She said, "No, thank you. I don't care to buy it."

So the brother said, "Well, then, I'm going to go out back and shoot my half because I don't want him anymore." The sister got so upset she gave him the ten dollars. Where there is a will, there is a way.

Zaccheus operated on the principle, "Where there is a will, there is a way." Although he was short, he wasn't going let that prevent him from seeing Christ. Look in your Bible at verse 4. "So he ran ahead and climbed up into a sycamore tree to see Him, for he was going to pass that way." Another name for the sycamore tree was a fig mulberry tree—fruit like a fig and a leaf like a mulberry. It produced poor fruit eaten only by poverty-stricken people. But since its branches were spread out and low to the ground, climbing it was as simple as walking up a stepladder. He had a balcony seat from which he could see the Lord.

Obviously, that's not what the Bible means by lost. It is no sin to be short. For some it might be a disadvantage, but it is most certainly no sin.

But notice a second thing the Bible tells us. Not only does it say the man was short; it says he was a sinner. Three things tell us that. First, his job tells you. Look at verse 2: "Now behold, there was a man named Zaccheus who was a chief tax collector, and he was rich." I don't know most of you here today. Some of you might be in some kind of government-related job. You might feel like stopping me and saying, "Larry, don't you dare say it's a sin to collect taxes." Others in non-governmental jobs are tempted to say, "Oh, yes it is!"

Regardless, it was a sin to collect taxes the way Zaccheus did it. In our day, at least our system is organized. If we don't pay what you should, at least we know what we should have paid.

Some time ago a man cheated on his income tax. Afterward it really bothered him, so he wrote to the Internal Revenue Service and said, "I cheated on my income tax last year. It has bothered me ever since. Enclosed, find a check." Then he wrote, "P.S. If it continues to bother me, I'll send you the rest later." In our day, the system is so organized that if you don't pay what you should, you know what you should have paid.

In the days of Zaccheus, the system was not organized; it was arbitrary. Tax collectors stood by the city gates. As people came by with their boxes and bundles, tax collectors would rip them open. Then, on the basis of the contents, charge a tax. If they wanted to be kind to their in-laws and hard on their outlaws, they could. If they wanted to treat the Jews one way and the Romans another, they could. The Roman government even allowed them to overtax people and keep the remainder for themselves. People learned that first thing to do is pay up and the second thing is hush up. If you didn't, when you came by the next time, you would be charged double what you were the first time. Apparently, Zaccheus was hard on everyone. He stole as many pennies as he could from as many people as he knew—so much so that, as the end of verse 2 says, "he was rich." There was no better city to be a tax collector in than Jericho. That was like being told, "Go sell snowmobiles," then being sent to Alberta, Canada. It was the place to be a tax collector because people would come from the east and the west. It was the trading center—the number one hot spot for a tax collector. So the first thing that tells you that he was a sinner is his job.

But notice a second thing that tells you he is a sinner. Not only does his job tell you, the people tell you. Look at verse 5. "And when Jesus came to the place, he looked up and saw him and said to him, 'Zaccheus make haste and come down, for today I must stay at your house.' So he made haste and came down and received Him joyfully. But when they saw it, they all complained saying, 'He has gone to be a guest with a man who is a sinner.'"

It is never popular to be a tax collector. I doubt that most IRS workers could make *People* magazine's "Ten Most Popular People" list. But tax collectors were particularly unpopular in that day. It was a disgrace to have a tax collector as part of your family tree.

I read of a family diagramming their family tree. They discovered that years earlier one of their relatives had gone to the electric chair for murder. If they put that in the family tree, it would disgrace everybody. So when they came to his name, they wrote alongside of it, "Uncle Charles occupied a chair in one of our leading institutions. His death came as a true shock."

In the days of Zaccheus, if you had a tax collector in your family, you would try to cover it up. The thing that was most despised about them is the way they would use their occupation to rob and to cheat. So much so that Christ said to one of them, "Take only what belongs to you and no more." So the people were furious when Jesus went with Zaccheus. They were not upset. They were *mad*! And you would have had no problem determining how they felt. Look at verse seven: "But when they saw it, they all complained." The word "complain" means to grumble and murmur out loud.

Years ago, I was in a speaking engagement. After speaking, I went to the place where I was staying, and before going to bed I watched the evening news. It was during the presidential primaries. A candidate was about to give an address. But just as he stepped on the platform, someone said something and the whole place erupted. You could not distinguish one word being said. All you heard was grumbling and complaining.

Had you been a TV reporter on the streets during Jesus' day, the situation would have been similar. You would have had trouble distinguishing anything being said. All you would have heard was grumbling and complaining. But there was one thing these people did not understand. And a lot of us don't either. That is, God does not love you based on what you have done. God loves you in spite of what you have done.

Time magazine told of a thirty-seven-year-old owner of a pizza place in Allentown, Pennsylvania, who bailed his wife out of jail, and in doing so shocked the entire state. Why? She had tried to kill him on several occasions. First, she had her daughter's boyfriend come into his bedroom, take the pistol under his pillow, and fire it into his head. When that did not kill him, she stuffed barbiturates into his mouth. Those actually saved his life because they slowed the bleeding. Two days later, when he still wasn't dead, she paid two men five hundred dollars each to finish the job. One fired a bullet that entered one inch from his heart. Two days later, the police received a tip and went to his house. They found him unconscious but alive. Paramedics rushed him to the hospital, where his life was saved. When he gained consciousness, he vowed to stand by his wife during the murder-for-hire trial and bailed her out of jail with fifty thousand dollars. When the *Time* reporter asked the officer in charge, "How could he do such a thing?" he threw his arms up and said, "The only thing he will tell us is that he loves her." That husband was saying, "I don't love her based on what she has done. I love her in spite of what she has done." If there is one thing God is saying to everyone here it's this: "I don't love you based on what you've done. I love you in spite of what you've done."

But there is a third thing that tells you he was a sinner. Not only does his job tell you. Not only do the people tell you. But he tells you. Look at what happened after he came to know the Lord. Verse 8 says, "Then Zaccheus stood and said to the Lord, 'Look, Lord. I give half of my goods to the poor, and if I have taken anything from anyone by false accusation, I restore four-fold.'" Asking the question, "Was Zaccheus a sinner?" would be like asking the question, "Is the White House in Washington, D.C.?" Who doesn't know that? Who didn't know that Zaccheus was a sinner, including Zaccheus himself?

In the Old Testament, if you stole one item you were expected to return four times what you took. Steal one sheep, you had to return four. For that reason, he said, "If I have taken anything from anyone by false accusation, I will restore four times that amount." There is no better way he could have said, "I am a sinner." For that reason, the next words out of Jesus' mouth was the best news Zaccheus had heard in a long time: "And Jesus said to him, 'Today salvation has come to this house, because he also is a son of Abraham'" (v. 9).

Sometimes you expect good news and get bad news. A husband walked into a Dillard's Department Store and bought a bottle of Chanel perfume for his wife. As the clerk wrapped it up, she said, "I take it you are going to surprise her." He said, "Am I ever! She's expecting a new car!"

Sometimes you are expecting good news and you get bad news. Other times, you expect bad news and get good news. Zaccheus had a right to expect bad news. Instead, he got good news.

Look again at verse 9: "And Jesus said to him, 'Today salvation has come to this house, because he also is a son of Abraham.'" God's blessings were given to Abraham. In the Old Testament we read, "I'll make of him a great nation." Anyone who received blessings was called a son of Abraham. The way to become a son of Abraham is to place your trust in Christ as your only way to heaven. That day Zaccheus placed his trust in Christ and became a son of Abraham.

So when the Bible explains what it means by lost it points to a man who is a sinner. The Bible is saying, "If you want to come to God, you have to come as a sinner." If you want to come to God and talk about what a good life you have lived, you cannot get to heaven. God does not save people who live good lives. God saves sinners. If you want to come to God and talk about how often you've been to church, you cannot get to heaven. God does not save people who go to church. God saves sinners. If you want to come to God and talk about the time you were baptized, you cannot get to heaven. God does not save people who have been baptized. God saves sinners. If you want to come to God and talk about the commandments you've kept and the sacraments you've taken, you cannot get to heaven. God does not save people who have kept the commandments and taken the sacraments. God saves sinners.

That is why those from a rough or impoverished background often find it easier to come to Christ than those who spent time at elite country clubs. You are never too bad for God to save. But you just might be too good.

It's been said that God saves the lost, the least, and the last. If you want to come to God, you have to come admitting that you are part of the "lost, the least, and the last." Please do not misunderstand what I am about to say. I detest murder. And I detest the idea of someone breaking into your house, stealing what is yours, not theirs. But there have been times I have said to people, "I wish you were a murderer. I wish you were a thief. Because you'd find it easier to come to Christ if you were."

That means, in order to be saved, there are only two things you can do. The first is: Admit you are a sinner.

I once talked to a seventy-six-year-old woman in Kansas about the good news that Christ died for her. Then I said, "In order to get to heaven, you have to admit that you are a sinner. Do you admit that?" She said, "I'm not half as bad as a lot of folks I know." We talked some more, and I said, "Now, in order to get to heaven, you have to admit you are a sinner. Do you admit that?" She said, "You ought to know what so and so down the street has done!" We talked some more and then I said, "Now, in order to get to heaven, you have to admit you are a sinner. Do you admit that?" She said, "The Lord knows I'm trying to do what is right." We talked some more and then I said, "Now, in order to get to heaven, you have to admit you are a sinner. Do you admit that?" She said, "I've done a lot of things right in my time." We talked some more and then I said, "In order to get to heaven, you have to admit you are a sinner. Do you admit that?" All of a sudden, tears flowed down her cheeks. Trembling, she said, "Yes, I'm a sinner."

The first thing you have to do is admit you are a sinner. The second thing you have to do is put your trust in Christ alone, nothing else, as your only way to heaven because He paid for all your sins by dying for you. He died in your place. He was your substitute. He saved you by dying for you.

Years ago, a young mother left a baby unattended in an apartment in Brooklyn. After she left, fire spread through the complex. One fireman risked his life to go into the building and save the baby. But when he got in, he could not get out. So as the flames licked at his feet, he stepped through them, picked up the baby, and clutched the baby to his chest. He rushed to a window and dropped the baby to the firemen below. He fell back into the flames, dying an agonizing death. Twenty years later, the woman who had been that baby was seen kneeling at the man's grave. When asked, "Whose grave is this?" she answered, "This man died for me."

The Bible is saying, "Jesus Christ died for you." On a cross two thousand years ago, He took the punishment you deserved, placed it upon Himself, and died in your place. He was your substitute. The third day He arose. Therefore, you have to come to God admitting you are a sinner, recognizing that Christ died for you and rose again, and putting your trust in Christ alone, nothing else, as your only way to heaven. Not Christ *and* your good life, not Christ *and* your baptism, not Christ *and* your church attendance, but Christ alone as your only way to heaven. The moment you do, God gives you completely free His gift of eternal life because God saves sinners.

What kind of person do you have to be in order for God to accept you? God answers that with six words: *God saves those who are lost.* God saves sinners. If you want to come to God, there are not five conditions, there are not four, there are not three, there are not two. There is only one. You have to come as a sinner. And if you can come as a sinner, there is no question God can save you.

George Whitefield, a prominent preacher from the past, often spoke to his brother about spiritual things, but the brother never seemed interested. One day he was more despondent than usual and more open. A woman who took care of his house and understood this paragraph was once again talking to him about the good news that Christ died for him. All of a sudden, George Whitefield's brother said, "It's no use, it's no use! I'm lost! I'm lost!" The woman said, "Well, praise God for that." He asked, "What do you mean?" She said, "If you can say, 'I'm lost,' then you are the person Christ came to save."

If you can say, "I'm lost. I deserve to go to hell," I extend to you my deepest congratulations. You are the one Christ came to save. If you let Him, He'll do it right now, because God saves sinners.

Appendix 3
May I Ask You a Question?

ON THE FOLLOWING PAGES is a small booklet from EvanTell that asked an important question: Has anyone ever taken a Bible and shown you how you can know for sure that you're going to heaven? The booklet shows how you can be sure. There is information at the end about how to contact EvanTell.

may I ask you a question

The Bible contains both bad news and good news.
The *bad news* is something about YOU.
The *good news* is something about GOD.

Let's look at the bad news first...

The Bible contains
both bad news and
good news.
The *bad news* is
something about
YOU.
The *good news* is
something about
GOD.

Let's look at the bad news first...

Bad News 1

We are all sinners.
Romans 3:23 says, *"For all have sinned and fall short of the glory of God."*

"Sinned" means that we have missed the mark. When we lie, hate, lust, or gossip, we have missed the standard God has set.

Suppose you and I were each to throw a rock and try to hit the North Pole. You might throw farther than I, but neither of us would hit it.

When the Bible says "All have sinned and fall short," it means that we have all come short of God's standard of perfection.

In thoughts, words, and deeds, we have not been perfect.

But the bad news gets worse...

Bad News 2

The penalty for sin is death.
Romans 6:23 says, "For the wages of sin is death."

Suppose you worked for me and I paid you $50. That $50 was your wages. That's what you earned.

The Bible says that by sinning we have earned death. That means we deserve to die and be separated from God forever.

Since there was no way we could come to God, the Bible says that *God came to us!*

Good News 1

Christ died for you.
Romans 5:8 says, *"But God demonstrates His own love toward us, in that while we were still sinners, Christ died for us."*

Suppose you are in a hospital dying of cancer. I come to you and say, "Let's take the cancer cells from **your** body and put them into **my** body."

If that were possible,
What would happen to me?
What would happen to you?

*I would die and
you would live.*

*I would die in
your place.*

The Bible says Christ took the penalty
that we deserved for sin, placed it upon
Himself, and *died in our place.*
Three days later Christ came back to life
to prove that sin and death had been
conquered and that His claims to be God
were true.

Just as the bad news got worse,
the good news gets better!

Good News 2

You can be saved through faith in Christ.

Ephesians 2:8-9 says, *"For by grace
[undeserved favor] you have been saved
[delivered from sin's penalty] through faith,
and that not of yourselves; it is the gift of God,
not of works, lest anyone should boast."*

Faith means *trust.*

Q. What must you trust Christ for?
A. You must depend on Him alone to
forgive you and to give you eternal life.

Just as you trust a chair to hold you through no effort of your own, *so you must trust Jesus Christ to get you to heaven* through no effort of your own.

But you may say,

"I'm religious."

"I go to church."

"I'm a good person."

"I help the poor."

"I don't do anything that's really bad."

These are all good, but good living, going to church, helping the poor, or any other good thing you might do cannot get you to heaven. You must trust in Jesus Christ alone, and God will give you eternal life as a gift.

Is there anything keeping you from trusting Christ right now?

1. _____

2. _____

3. _____

4. _____

Think carefully. There is nothing more important than your need to trust Christ.

Would you like to tell God you are trusting Jesus Christ as your Savior? If you would, why not pray right now and tell God you are trusting His Son?

243

Remember!
It is not a prayer that saves you. It is trusting Jesus Christ that saves you. Prayer is simply how you tell God what you are doing.

Dear God, I know I'm a sinner. I know my sin deserves to be punished. I believe Christ died for me and rose from the grave. I trust Jesus Christ alone as my Savior. Thank You for the forgiveness and everlasting life I now have. In Jesus' name, amen.

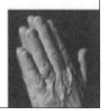

What just happened?

John 5:24 explains, "*He who hears My word and believes in Him who sent Me has everlasting life, and shall not come into judgment, but has passed from death into life.*"

» Did you "hear" God's word?
» Did you "believe" what God said and trust Christ as your Savior?
» Does "has everlasting life" mean later or right now?
» Does it say "shall not come into judgment" or might not?
» Does it say "has passed from death" or shall pass?

Eternal life is based on fact, not feeling.

Memorize John 5:24 today.

What do you do now?

Having trusted Christ as your only way to heaven, here's how to grow in your relationship with Him.

» Tell God what's on your mind through prayer (Philippians 4:6,7).

» Read the Bible daily, to learn more about Him and learn from Him (2 Timothy 3:16,17). Start in the book of Philippians.

» Worship with God's people in a local church (Hebrews 10:24,25).

» Tell others about Jesus Christ (Matthew 4:19).

If you have found this booklet helpful, please share it with someone else. If you have further questions about what is contained in this booklet, contact:

The Gospel Clear and Simple.

p.o. box 741417 | dallas, tx 75374
www.evantell.org | 800.947.7359
© 2007 evantell, inc.

TRMEN004

Notes

Chapter 2: Evangelistic Speaking—*You* Can Do It!
1. Bill Bright, *Red Sky in the Morning* (Orlando: New Life Publications, 1998), 239.
2. Sterling W. Huston, *Crusade Evangelism and the Local Church* (Minneapolis: World Wide, 1983), 85.
3. Luis Palau, February 16, 1986.

Chapter 3: What Exactly Is Expository Evangelistic Preaching?
1. Haddon Robinson, *Biblical Preaching: The Development and Delivery of Expository Messages* (Grand Rapids: Baker, 1980), 20.
2. Scott Gibson, ed., *Preaching to a Shifting Culture: Twelve Perspectives on Communicating that Connects* (Grand Rapids: Baker, 2004), 82.
3. Haddon Robinson and Craig Brian Larson, eds., *The Art and Craft of Biblical Preaching: A Comprehensive Resource for Today's Communicators* (Grand Rapids: Zondervan, 2005), 237.
4. Jokes Mailing List Archive, "Joke Number 322," FunWorld, Oct. 1999, http://www.hehe.at/funworld/archive/fun4you.php?joke=322, (accessed August 30, 2008).
5. Robinson and Larson, eds., *The Art and Craft of Biblical Preaching*, 27.
6. Peter Teague, *President's Perspective* (Lancaster, PA: Lancaster Bible College, Spring 2006), 10.
7. John Stott, *Between Two Worlds* (Grand Rapids: Wm. B. Eerdmans, 2006), 10.

Chapter 4: Why Is There So Little Expository Evangelistic Speaking?
1. Haddon Robinson and Craig Brian Larson, eds., *The Art and Craft of Biblical Preaching: A Comprehensive Resource for Today's Communicators* (Grand Rapids: Zondervan, 2005), 572.
2. Don Sunukjian, *Invitation to Biblical Preaching: Proclaiming Truth with Clarity and Relevance* (Grand Rapids: Kregel Publications, 2007), 15.

Chapter 5: Why Is Expository Evangelistic Preaching Needed and What Are Its Benefits?

1. Tullian Tchividjian, "Biblical Authority & Today's Preacher," *Leadership* 29, no. 1 (Winter 2008), 33.
2. Zane C. Hodges, "Hebrews," *Bible Knowledge Commentary: An Exposition of the Scriptures,* eds. John F. Walvoord and Roy B. Zuck (Wheaton, IL: Victor Books, 1983), 790.
3. B. F. Westcott, *The Gospel According to St. John* (Grand Rapids: Eerdmans, 1973), 228.
4. Merrill C. Tenney, *John: The Gospel of Belief* (Grand Rapids: Eerdmans, 1976), 236.

Chapter 6: What Challenges Face an Expository Evangelistic Speaker?

1. Jay E. Adams, "*Theology of Powerful Preaching,*" Christianity Today International, copyright 1994–2006, http://www.preachingtodaysermons.com/thofpopr.html, (accessed August 31, 2008).

Chapter 7: How Do You Develop Your Evangelistic Speaking Skills?

1. Richard DeHaan, "Do Your Best," *Our Daily Bread* 35, no. 7 (July 7, 2002),
2. A. W. Tozer, *The Root of the Righteous* (Harrisburg, PA: Christian Publications, 1955), 137.

Chapter 8: Where Does Evangelistic Speaking Start and Why?

1. Warren W. Wiersbe and David W. Wiersbe, *Ten Power Principles for Christian Service: Ministry Dynamics for a New Century* (Grand Rapids: Baker, 1997), 19.
2. Robert Emerson Coleman, *The Master Plan of Salvation* (Westwood, NJ: Fleming H. Revell, 1964), 92.

Chapter 10: What Are False Assumptions to Be Avoided?

1. Haddon W. Robinson, *Biblical Sermons* (Grand Rapids: Baker Academic, 1989).
2. Warren Wiersbe and David Wiersbe, *The Elements of Preaching* (Wheaton, IL: Tyndale House, 1986), 95.

Chapter 14: What Is This Thing Called Sin and How Do You Explain It to an Unbeliever?

1. E. C. McKenzie, *14,000 Quips & Quotes for Writers and Speakers* (New York: Crown Publishers, 1983), 419.
2. Quoted in *Our Daily Bread* (November/December 1984).
3. As told in *Reader's Digest* (July 1996), 26.

Chapter 15: What Is Our Message for Non-Christians?

1. *Pulpit Helps* (Chattanooga: AMG International), March 1998.
2. Warren Wiersbe and David Wiersbe, *The Elements of Preaching* (Wheaton, IL: Tyndale House, 1986), 78.
3. Paul C. Pritchard, "The Best Idea America Ever Had," *National Geographic: Official Journal of the National Geographic Society* 180, no. 2 (August 1991): 45.
4. Wilbur M. Smith, *Therefore Stand: Christian Apologetics* (Grand Rapids: Baker, 1972), 425.
5. Ewan Huffman, "The Empty Tomb: What Does it Mean?" Outreach, Inc., 2005–2008, http://www.sermoncentral.com/sermon.asp?SermonID=45057, (accessed March 2002).
6. Henry M. Morris, "The Resurrection of Christ—The Best-Proved Fact in History," Institute for Creation Research, http://www.icr.org/ChristResurrection/ (accessed May 15, 2010).

Chapter 16: What Do We Mean by "Believe"?

1. Don Ziadle, "Killer Cougars," *Outdoor Life* (Feb 2001): 46–47.

Chapter 17: Where Does Repentance Fit?

1. Lewis Sperry Chafer, *Systematic Theology* (Dallas: Dallas Seminary Press, 1948), 3:376.
2. William Evans, *Great Doctrines of the Bible* (Chicago: The Bible Institute Colportage Association, 1912), 40.

Chapter 19: How Short Is Short?

1. Haddon Robinson and Craig Brian Larson, eds., *The Art and Craft of Biblical Preaching: A Comprehensive Resource for Today's Communicators* (Grand Rapids: Zondervan, 2005), 585.
2. James S. Stewart, *Heralds of God* (New York: Charles Scribner's Sons, 1946), 136.
3. Michael Green, ed., *Illustrations for Biblical Preaching* (Grand Rapids: Baker, 1989), 7.
4. Robert Andrews, ed., *The Routledge Dictionary of Quotations* (London: Routledge & Kegan Paul, 1987), 208.

Chapter 20: How Do Illustrations Help?

1. Earl D. Radmacher, Ronald B. Allen, H. W. House, eds., *The Nelson Study Bible—New King James Version* (Nashville: Thomas Nelson, 1997), 1597.
2. Robert J. Morgan, Stories, Illustrations, Quotes (Nashville: Thomas Nelson, 2000), vii.
3. Warren Wiersbe, *Why Us? When Bad Things Happen to God's People* (Grand Rapids: Baker, 1985), 53.

4. Roger C. Shank, *Tell Me a Story: Narrative and Intelligence* (Evanston, IL: Northwestern University Press, 1995), 214.

5. Dr. Robert T. Henry, *Golden Age of Preaching: Men Who Moved the Masses* (New York: iUniverse, Inc., 2005), 244.

6. Gary Smalley and John Trent, *Language of Love* (Colorado Springs: Focus on the Family, 1991), 21.

7. Michael J. Hostetler, *Illustrating the Sermon* (Grand Rapids: Zondervan, 1989), 19.

8. C. H. Spurgeon, *Third Series of Lectures to My Students* (Whitefish, MT: Kessinger Publishing, 2007), 2.

9. Jay Edward Adams, *Pulpit Speech* (Grand Rapids: Baker, 1971), 17.

10. Ken Davis, *Secrets of Dynamic Communication: Preparing and Delivering Powerful Speeches* (Grand Rapids: Zondervan, 1991), 66.

11. Donald Sunukjian, *Invitation to Biblical Preaching: Proclaiming Truth with Clarity and Relevance* (Grand Rapids: Kregel Publications, 2007), 133.

12. Haddon Robinson and Craig Brian Larson, eds., *The Art and Craft of Biblical Preaching: A Comprehensive Resource for Today's Communicators* (Grand Rapids: Zondervan, 2005), 527.

13. Robinson and Larson, eds., *The Art and Craft of Biblical Preaching,* 137.

14. Martyn Lloyd-Jones, *Preaching and Preachers* (Grand Rapids: Zondervan, 1972), 232.

15. Keith Wilhite and Scott Gibson, *The Big Idea of Biblical Preaching: Connecting the Bible to People* (Grand Rapids: Baker, 2003), 142.

Chapter 21: What Part Does Humor Play?

1. Haddon Robinson and Craig Brian Larson, eds., *The Art and Craft of Biblical Preaching: A Comprehensive Resource for Today's Communicators* (Grand Rapids: Zondervan, 2005), 669.

2. Robinson and Larson, eds., *The Art and Craft of Biblical Preaching,* 387.

3. Warren Wiersbe and David Wiersbe, *Elements of Preaching* (Wheaton, IL: Tyndale House, 1986), 100.

Chapter 23 How Do You Aim for the Heart?

1. Haddon Robinson and Craig Brian Larson, eds., *The Art and Craft of Biblical Preaching: A Comprehensive Resource for Today's Communicators* (Grand Rapids: Zondervan, 2005), 215.

2. David W. Henderson, *Culture Shift: Communicating God's Truth to Our Changing World* (Grand Rapids: Baker, 1998), 80.

3. Haddon Robinson and Craig Brian Larson, eds., *The Art and Craft of Biblical Preaching: A Comprehensive Resource for Today's Communicators* (Grand Rapids: Zondervan, 2005), 145.

4. Ted Springer, "Former Baseball Professional Umpire," Athletes in Action, 1970.

Chapter 24: How Do You Put Together an Expository Evangelistic Message?

1. Haddon Robinson and Craig Brian Larson, eds., *The Art and Craft of Biblical Preaching: A Comprehensive Resource for Today's Communicators* (Grand Rapids: Zondervan, 2005), 602.
2. John Henry Jowett, *The Preacher: His Life and Work* (Rahway, NJ: George H. Doran Company, 1912), 133.
3. Haddon Robinson, *Biblical Preaching: The Development and Delivery of Expository Messages* (Grand Rapids: Baker Books, 1980), 96.
4. Robinson, *Biblical Preaching,* 167.
5. Warren Wiersbe and David Wiersbe, *The Elements of Preaching* (Wheaton, IL: Tyndale House, 1986), 29.
6. Bruce Larson et al., "What Can We Promise That God Will Deliver?" *Leadership* 15 (Winter 1994), 19.
7. Robinson and Larson, eds., *The Art and Craft of Biblical Preaching,* 450.

Chapter 25 What About the Invitation?

1. Roy J. Fish, *Giving a Good Invitation* (Nashville: Broadman Press, 1974), 221.

Chapter 26: How Do You Talk to God as You're Talking to Men?

1. Haddon Robinson and Craig Brian Larson, *The Art and Craft of Biblical Preaching: A Comprehensive Resource for Today's Communicator's* (Grand Rapids: Zondervan, 2005), 541.
2. Bill Hybels, Stuart Briscoe, and Haddon Robinson, *Mastering Contemporary Preaching* (Colorado Springs: Multnomah, 1990), 149.
3. David K. Lowery, "1 Corinthians," *The Bible Knowledge Commentary: An Exposition of the Scriptures by Dallas Theological Seminary Faculty,* John F. Walvoord and Roy B. Zuck, eds., (Wheaton, IL: Victor Books, 1987), 510.

Chapter 27: What About Follow-up?

1. Robert D. Foster, *The Navigator* (Colorado Springs: NavPress, 1983) 123.
2. Foster, *The Navigator,* 124.